The Complete Keto Diet

Cookbook 2023

Super Easy and Delicious Ketogenic Recipes with Step-by-Step Instructions for Beginners and Advancers. Include 30 Days Meal Plan

Rebecca L. Dodson

Table of Contents

Chapter 3 Beef, Pork, and Lamb

Chapter 4 Fish and Seafood

Chapter 5 Vegetarian Mains

Chapter 6 Salads
51

Chapter 7 Stews and Soups
58

INTRODUCTION

Welcome to the world of the keto diet, where bacon and butter are celebrated, and avocados are the reigning royalty of the produce kingdom. Imagine a diet where you can indulge in rich, savory foods while still shedding those extra pounds. Intrigued? Let's dive into the fascinating world of the ketogenic diet!

Imagine a culinary adventure where you bid farewell to carbs and embrace healthy fats as your new best friends. The ketogenic diet, or keto for short, is a low-carb, high-fat diet that takes your taste buds on a thrilling ride. It's like a food lover's dream come true, where you get to indulge in luscious cuts of steak, creamy cheeses, and velvety avocados, all while burning fat for fuel.

Say goodbye to the sugar roller coaster and hello to stable energy levels that keep you feeling sharp and focused. With the keto diet, you'll experience a metabolic shift that turns your body into a fat-burning machine, helping you shed those extra pounds and achieve your weight loss goals.

Eat Healthy in a New Way

Picture this: you're savoring a mouthwatering dish of crispy bacon-wrapped asparagus drizzled with garlic-infused butter, or perhaps you're relishing a generous slice of creamy cheesecake made with almond flour crust. Yes, you read that right - bacon and cheesecake can be part of a healthy diet on keto! With a wide array of delicious and satisfying foods to choose from, you'll never feel deprived on this unique culinary journey.

But it's not just about the food. The keto diet has been associated with numerous health benefits, such as improved insulin sensitivity, reduced inflammation, and increased mental clarity. It's a powerful tool that can transform your body and mind, helping you become the best version of yourself. Take a look at the advantages of the keto diet:

◊ Weight Loss: One of the primary reasons people turn to the keto diet is for weight loss. By significantly reducing carbohydrate intake and increasing healthy fats, the body enters a state of ketosis, where it burns fat for fuel instead of glucose. This can lead to effective weight loss as the body taps into its fat stores for energy.

◊ Improved Insulin Sensitivity: The keto diet has been shown to improve insulin sensitivity, which is beneficial for those with insulin resistance, metabolic syndrome, or type 2 diabetes. By reducing carbohydrate intake, the keto diet can help regulate blood sugar levels and improve insulin sensitivity, potentially leading to better blood sugar control.

◊ Increased Energy Levels: On a keto diet, the body becomes efficient at burning fat for fuel, which can result in more stable energy levels throughout the day. Many people report increased mental clarity, focus, and sustained energy levels while following a ketogenic eating plan.

◊ Reduced Inflammation: Chronic inflammation has been linked to various health issues, including heart disease, diabetes, and certain cancers. The keto diet has been shown to reduce inflammation markers in the body, potentially leading to improved overall health and a reduced risk of inflammatory diseases.

◊ Appetite Control: The high-fat, moderate-protein, and low-carb nature of the keto diet can help with appetite control. Healthy fats and proteins tend to be more satiating, helping you feel fuller for longer, which can aid in weight loss efforts by reducing overall caloric intake.

◊ Improved Blood Lipid Profile: Contrary to popular belief, a well-formulated keto diet can actually improve blood lipid profiles. Studies have shown that the keto diet can increase levels of "good" HDL cholesterol while reducing levels of "bad" LDL cholesterol, which can lead to improved heart health.

So, whether you're a foodie looking to expand your culinary horizons or someone seeking a science-backed approach to weight loss and overall well-being, the keto diet is your passport to a fascinating and flavorful adventure. Get ready to tantalize your taste buds, rev up your metabolism, and discover a whole new world of delicious possibilities with the keto diet! Bon appétit!

30 Days Keto Diet Meal Plan

DAYS	BREAKFAST	LUNCH	DINNER	SNACK/DESSERT
1	Coffee Smoothie	Bacon Lovers' Stuffed Chicken	Caprese Salad	Caponata Dip
2	Herbed Buttery Breakfast Steak	Eggplant and Zucchini Bites	Creamy Haddock	Parmesan Crisps
3	Heart-Healthy Hazelnut-Collagen Shake	Vegetable Burgers	Tuscan Kale Salad with Anchovies	Savory Mackerel & Goat'S Cheese "Paradox" Balls
4	Rosti with Bacon, Mushrooms, and Green Onions	Tandoori Chicken	Mixed Green Salad with BLT Deviled Eggs and Bacon Vinaigrette	Garlic Meatballs
5	Bacon Cheese Egg with Avocado	Italian Baked Egg and Veggies	Crab Cakes	Hangover Bacon-Wrapped Pickles
6	Mocha Protein Keto Coffee	Zucchini Pasta with Spinach, Olives, and Asiago	Summer Tuna Avocado Salad	BLT Dip
7	Cross-Country Scrambler	Parmesan-Crusted Chicken	Mediterranean Cucumber Salad	Sausage Balls
8	Turkish Egg Bowl	Three-Cheese Zucchini Boats	Coconut Milk-Braised Squid	English Cucumber Tea Sandwiches
9	Sausage and Gruyère Breakfast Casserole	Asparagus and Fennel Frittata	Crispy Bacon Salad with Mozzarella & Tomato	Cheese Chips and Guacamole
10	Buffalo Chicken Breakfast Muffins	Fried Chicken Breasts	Salmon Salad Cups	Olive Pâté
11	Jalapeño Popper Stuffed Omelet	Herbed Ricotta–Stuffed Mushrooms	Parmesan Mackerel with Coriander	Edana's Macadamia Crack Bars
12	Soft-Scrambled Eggs	Cauliflower Steak with Gremolata	Zucchini Pasta Salad	Creamed Onion Spinach
13	Prosciutto Baked Eggs with Spinach	Slow Cooker Chicken Thighs with Sun-Dried Tomatoes	Bacon and Spinach Salad	Southern Pimento Cheese Dip
14	Pancake Cake	Broccoli Crust Pizza	Parchment-Baked Cod and Asparagus with Beurre Blanc	Thyme Sautéed Radishes
15	Chocolate Raspberry Smoothie	Tangy Asparagus and Broccoli	Special Sauce Cobb Salad	Oregano Sausage Balls
16	Sausage & Squash Omelet with Swiss Chard	Greek Chicken Stir-Fry	Taco Salad	Bacon-Studded Pimento Cheese
17	Pork Sausage Eggs with Mustard Sauce	White Cheddar and Mushroom Soufflés	Grandma Kitty's Tuna Salad	Bacon-Studded Pimento Cheese
18	All Day Any Day Hash	Cheese Stuffed Zucchini	Olive Garden Salad	Seasonal Fruit Crumble

DAYS	BREAKFAST	LUNCH	DINNER	SNACK/DESSERT
19	Breakfast Sammies	Chicken Pesto Pizzas	Broccoli & Raspberry "Bacon" Salad	Berry Chia Pudding
20	Coconut & Walnut Chia Pudding	Stuffed Eggplant	Shrimp Caesar Salad	Paleo Egg Rolls
21	Baklava Hot Porridge	Pesto Vegetable Skewers	Calamari Salad	Goat'S Cheese & Hazelnut Dip
22	Waffles with Sausage Gravy	Cobb Salad	Vintage Three Bean Salad	Liver Bites
23	Southwestern Ham Egg Cups	Baked Zucchini	Scallops with Creamy Bacon Sauce	Almond and Chocolate Chia Pudding
24	Smoked Ham and Egg Muffins	Greek Stuffed Eggplant	Cheeseburger Salad	Low-Carb Granola Bars
25	Bacon Crackers	Porchetta-Style Chicken Breasts	Spinach Turnip Salad with Bacon	Rosemary Chicken Wings
26	Cheesy Cauliflower Grits	Spinach Cheese Casserole	Friday Night Fish Fry	Avocado Feta Dip
27	Slow-Cooked Granola with Nuts	Cauliflower Tikka Masala	Kale Salad with Spicy Lime-Tahini Dressing	Bone Broth Fat Bombs
28	Counterfeit Bagels	Merry Christmas Chicken	Avocado Salad with Arugula and Red Onion	Buffalo Bill's Chicken Dip
29	Blender Cinnamon Pancakes with Cacao Cream Topping	Zucchini Lasagna	Coconut Crab Patties	Everything Bagel Cream Cheese Dip
30	Liver Sausages & Onions	Zucchini-Ricotta Tart	Traditional Greek Salad	Queso Dip

Chapter 1 Breakfasts

Slow-Cooked Granola with Nuts

Prep time: 5 minutes | Cook time: 2 hours 30 minutes | Serves 10

1 cup raw almonds
1 cup pumpkin seeds
1 cup raw walnuts
1 cup raw cashews
1 tablespoon coconut oil

¼ cup unsweetened coconut chips
1 teaspoon sea salt
1 teaspoon cinnamon

1. In a large bowl, stir together the almonds, pumpkin seeds, walnuts, cashews and coconut oil. Make sure all the nuts are coated with the coconut oil. Place the nut mixture in the Instant Pot and cover the pot with a paper towel. 2. Lock the lid. Select the Slow Cook mode and set the cooking time for 1 hour on More. When the timer goes off, stir the nuts. Set the timer for another hour. 3. Again, when the timer goes off, stir the nut mixture and add the coconut chips. Set the timer for another 30 minutes. The cashews should become a nice golden color. 4. When the timer goes off, transfer the nut mixture to a baking pan to cool and sprinkle with the sea salt and cinnamon. Serve.

Per Serving:
calories: 311 | fat: 27.6g | protein: 10.2g | carbs: 10.8g | net carbs: 6.7g | fiber: 4.1g

Blender Cinnamon Pancakes with Cacao Cream Topping

Prep time: 10 minutes | Cook time: 10 minutes | Serves 4

Cinnamon Pancakes:
2 cups pecans
4 large eggs
1 tablespoon cinnamon
½ teaspoon baking soda
1 teaspoon fresh lemon juice or apple cider vinegar
1 tablespoon virgin coconut oil or ghee
Cacao Cream Topping:

1 cup coconut cream
1½ tablespoons raw cacao powder
Optional: low-carb sweetener, to taste
To Serve:
9 medium strawberries, sliced
1 tablespoon unsweetened shredded coconut

1. To make the pancakes: Place the pecans in a blender and process until powdered. Add all of the remaining ingredients apart from the ghee. Blend again until smooth. 2. Place a nonstick pan greased with 1 teaspoon of the coconut oil over low heat. Using a ¼-cup (60 ml) measure per pancake, cook in batches of 2 to 3 small pancakes over low heat until bubbles begin to form on the pancakes. Use a spatula to flip over, then cook for 30 to 40 seconds and place on a plate. Grease the pan with more coconut oil between batches. Transfer the pancakes to a plate. 3. To make the cacao cream topping: Place the coconut cream in a bowl. Add the cacao powder and sweetener, if using. Whisk until well combined and creamy. 4. Serve the pancakes with the cacao cream, sliced strawberries and a sprinkle of shredded coconut. You can enhance the flavor of the shredded coconut by toasting it in a dry pan for about 1 minute.

Per Serving:
calories: 665 | fat: 65g | protein: 14g | carbs: 17g | fiber: 9g | sodium: 232mg

Coffee Smoothie

Prep time: 5 minutes | Cook time: 0 minutes | serves 2

1 cup unsweetened hemp milk
½ cup ice
⅓ cup cold-brew coffee
½ avocado
2 tablespoons cacao powder

1 scoop plant-based, low-carb protein powder (such as Truvani or Sunwarrior brands) (optional)
2 or 3 drops liquid stevia

1. Combine all the ingredients in a blender and blend on high until creamy and smooth. 2. Divide between tall serving glasses and enjoy chilled.

Per Serving:
calories: 130 | fat: 9g | protein: 3g | carbs: 8g | net carbs: 4g | fiber: 4g

Counterfeit Bagels

Prep time: 15 minutes | Cook time: 17 minutes | Serves 10

1½ cups blanched almond flour
1 tablespoon baking powder
2½ cups shredded whole milk mozzarella cheese
2 ounces full-fat cream cheese, softened

2 large eggs, whisked
2 tablespoons Everything but the Bagel seasoning
1 tablespoon unsalted butter, melted

1 Preheat oven to 400°F. Line a baking sheet with parchment paper. 2 In a small bowl, mix almond flour and baking powder. 3 In a medium microwave-safe bowl, mix mozzarella cheese, cream cheese, and whisked eggs. 4 Microwave cheese mixture 1 minute. Stir and microwave again 30 seconds. Let mixture cool until okay to handle. 5 Combine dry ingredients into cheese mixture. Work quickly, stirring with a sturdy spatula or bamboo spoon to create dough. Shape dough into approximately ¾"-thick snakes, and then form into ten bagels. 6 Place bagels on prepared baking sheet and sprinkle tops with seasoning. Bake 15 minutes until browning on top. 7 Remove bagels from oven, brush with melted butter, and serve.

Per Serving:
calories: 236 | fat: 18g | protein: 11g | carbs: 5g | net carbs: 3g | fiber: 2g

Jalapeño Popper Stuffed Omelet

Prep time: 10 minutes | Cook time: 10 minutes | Serves 1

1 ounce (28 g) cream cheese, softened at room temperature
4 tablespoons (1 ounce / 28 g) shredded Cheddar cheese, divided into 2 tablespoons and 2 tablespoons
2 tablespoons cooked bacon bits
1½ teaspoons thinly sliced green onions
1½ teaspoons finely diced seeded jalapeño pepper (about ⅛ medium)
2 large eggs
2 tablespoons heavy cream
¼ teaspoon sea salt
⅛ teaspoon black pepper
1 tablespoon butter

1. In a medium bowl, mash together the cream cheese, 2 tablespoons of the Cheddar, and the bacon bits. Stir in the green onions and jalapeño. Set the cream cheese mixture aside. 2. In another medium bowl, whisk together the eggs, heavy cream, sea salt, and black pepper. 3. In a medium skillet, melt the butter over medium heat. Pour in the egg mixture. Cover and cook for 1 to 2 minutes, until mostly cooked through. You can lift with a spatula to get more of the egg underneath if needed, but don't stir or scramble. 4. Drop dollops of the cream cheese mixture onto half of the omelet, distributing as evenly as possible. Use a spatula to fold the omelet over. Sprinkle the remaining 2 tablespoons Cheddar cheese on top. 5. Reduce the heat to medium-low. Cover and cook for a couple of minutes, until the cheese melts on top and inside.
Per Serving:
calories: 416 | fat: 35g | protein: 22g | carbs: 3g | net carbs: 3g | fiber: 0g

Prosciutto Baked Eggs with Spinach

Prep time: 5 minutes | Cook time: 20 minutes | Serves 6

1 (12 ounces / 340 g) bag frozen spinach, thawed and drained
6 ounces (170 g) prosciutto, very thinly sliced (about 12 large, ultra-thin slices)
1 tablespoon avocado oil
6 cloves garlic, minced
¼ cup finely chopped sun-dried tomatoes
⅛ teaspoon sea salt
Pinch of black pepper
12 large eggs

1. Preheat the oven to 350°F (180°C). 2. Place the thawed spinach into a kitchen towel and squeeze well over the sink, getting rid of as much liquid as possible. Set aside. 3. Line 12 cups of a muffin tin with a thin layer of prosciutto, overlapping the prosciutto pieces slightly if necessary. Wrap around the sides first, then patch any holes and the bottom. Set aside. 4. In a large skillet, heat the oil over medium-high heat. Add the minced garlic and sauté for about 30 seconds, until fragrant. Add the spinach and sun-dried tomatoes. Season with the sea salt and black pepper. Sauté for 5 minutes. 5. Divide the spinach mixture evenly among the prosciutto-lined muffin cups. Crack an egg into each muffin cup. 6. Transfer the pan to the oven and bake until the eggs are done to your liking, approximately as follows: a. Runny yolks: 13 to 15 minutes b. Semi-firm yolks: 16 to 18 minutes c. Firm yolks: 18 to 20 minutes 7. Allow the egg muffins to cool in the pan for a few minutes before removing.
Per Serving:
calories: 314 | fat: 22g | protein: 20g | carbs: 7g | net carbs: 5g | fiber: 2g

Soft-Scrambled Eggs

Prep time: 5 minutes | Cook time: 7 minutes | Serves 4

6 eggs
2 tablespoons heavy cream
1 teaspoon salt
¼ teaspoon pepper
2 tablespoons butter
2 ounces (57 g) cream cheese, softened

1. In large bowl, whisk eggs, heavy cream, salt, and pepper. Press the Sauté button and then press the Adjust button to set heat to Less. 2. Gently push eggs around pot with rubber spatula. When they begin to firm up, add butter and softened cream cheese. Continue stirring slowly in a figure-8 pattern until eggs are fully cooked, approximately 7 minutes total.
Per Serving:
calories: 232 | fat: 18g | protein: 10g | carbs: 2g | net carbs: 2g | fiber: 0g

Pancake Cake

Prep time: 10 minutes | Cook time: 7 minutes |
Serves 4

½ cup blanched finely ground almond flour
¼ cup powdered erythritol
½ teaspoon baking powder
2 tablespoons unsalted butter,
softened
1 large egg
½ teaspoon unflavored gelatin
½ teaspoon vanilla extract
½ teaspoon ground cinnamon

1. In a large bowl, mix almond flour, erythritol, and baking powder. Add butter, egg, gelatin, vanilla, and cinnamon. Pour into a round baking pan. 2. Place pan into the air fryer basket. 3. Adjust the temperature to 300°F (149°C) and set the timer for 7 minutes. 4. When the cake is completely cooked, a toothpick will come out clean. Cut cake into four and serve.

Chocolate Raspberry Smoothie

Prep time: 5 minutes | Cook time: 0 minutes | Serves 1

¾ cup water
½ packed cup frozen raspberries
4 large ice cubes (approximately ½ cup)
¼ cup full-fat coconut, nut, or dairy milk
¼ medium avocado, peeled
2 tablespoons cacao powder
2 tablespoons ground chia or flax seeds
2 scoops grass-fed collagen peptides
¼ teaspoon pure vanilla extract
⅛ teaspoon green stevia, or 2 or 3 drops stevia extract (optional)
Pinch of sea salt
Cacao nibs, for garnish (optional)
Whole fresh raspberries, for garnish (optional)

1. Place all the ingredients in a blender and blend until smooth. If you prefer a thinner smoothie, add more water or milk to your liking. 2. Garnish with cacao nibs and fresh raspberries, if desired.
Per Serving:
calories: 444 | fat: 27g | protein: 28g | carbs: 27g | net carbs: 8g | fiber: 19g

Sausage and Gruyère Breakfast Casserole

Prep time: 15 minutes | Cook time: 50 minutes | Makes 8

¾ pound unseasoned ground pork
1 bunch scallions, chopped
½ teaspoon red pepper flakes
Pinch of ground cloves
1 teaspoon pink Himalayan salt
¼ teaspoon ground black pepper
1 tablespoon chopped fresh

sage
1 teaspoon chopped fresh marjoram
8 large eggs
¼ cup heavy whipping cream
1¼ cups shredded Gruyère cheese (about 5 ounces), divided

1. Preheat the oven to 350°F and grease a 1¾-quart baking dish with coconut oil spray. 2. In a large skillet over medium-high heat, partially cook the pork, stirring to break it up, about 5 minutes. Add the scallions, red pepper flakes, cloves, salt, and pepper and stir to combine. Continue to cook until the pork is fully cooked and browned, an additional 5 minutes. 3. Add the sage and marjoram and stir to combine—now you have your own seasoned breakfast sausage! Pour the cooked sausage into the greased baking dish. 4. In a bowl, whisk together the eggs, cream, and 1 cup of the shredded cheese. Pour over the sausage in the casserole dish. 5. Sprinkle the remaining Gruyère over the top of the casserole and bake for 40 minutes, or until the eggs are fully set in the center and the top is golden brown.

Per Serving:
calories: 282 | fat: 22g | protein: 19g | carbs: 1g | net carbs: 1g | fiber: 0g

Rosti with Bacon, Mushrooms, and Green Onions

Prep time: 10 minutes | Cook time: 25 minutes | Serves 2

2 slices bacon, diced
2 tablespoons coconut oil or lard
1 cup mushrooms, thinly sliced
¼ cup chopped green onions, plus more for garnish (optional)

¼ teaspoon minced garlic
1 cup shredded cabbage
1 large egg
½ teaspoon fine sea salt
⅛ teaspoon freshly ground black pepper

1. Place the bacon in a large skillet over medium heat and fry until cooked and crispy. Reserve a little bit of the cooked bacon for garnish, if desired. Add the coconut oil, mushrooms, green onions, and garlic. Sauté for 5 minutes, or until the mushrooms are golden. 2. In a large bowl, mix the shredded cabbage, egg, salt, and pepper. Transfer to the skillet with the bacon mixture. Spread out the cabbage mixture in the pan and press it down to form a large pancake. Cook over medium heat until the bottom is crispy and golden brown, about 5 minutes. Flip with a large spatula and cook for another 10 minutes, or until the cabbage softens. 3. Remove from the heat and serve. Store extras in an airtight container in the fridge for up to 4 days. To reheat, fry in a skillet with a tablespoon of Paleo fat or coconut oil on both sides until crispy, about 3 minutes a side. Garnish with green onions and/or reserved bacon, if desired.

Per Serving:
calories: 275 | fat: 24g | protein: 10g | carbs: 5g | net carbs: 3g | fiber: 2g

Cross-Country Scrambler

Prep time: 5 minutes | Cook time: 28 minutes | Serves 2

8 strips bacon (about 8 oz/225 g)
1 packed cup spiral-sliced butternut squash (about 5¼ oz/150 g)
½ green bell pepper, diced

6 large eggs, beaten
½ cup (40 g) sliced green onions (green parts only)
¼ teaspoon ground black pepper

1. Cook the bacon in a large frying pan over medium heat until crispy, about 15 minutes. Remove the bacon from the pan, leaving the grease in the pan. When the bacon has cooled, crumble it. 2. Add the squash and bell pepper to the pan with the bacon grease. Cover and cook over medium-low heat for 8 minutes, or until the vegetables are fork-tender. 3. Add the beaten eggs, green onions, and black pepper. Mix with a large spoon until fully incorporated. 4. Cook, uncovered, for 5 minutes, stirring every minute, or until the eggs are cooked to your liking. Once complete, fold in half of the crumbled bacon. 5. Divide evenly between 2 plates, top with remaining crumbled bacon, and dig in!

Per Serving:
calories: 395 | fat: 27g | protein: 26g | carbs: 12g | net carbs: 9g | fiber: 3g

Heart-Healthy Hazelnut-Collagen Shake

Prep time: 5 minutes | Cook time: 0 minutes | Serves 1

1½ cups unsweetened almond milk
2 tablespoons hazelnut butter
2 tablespoons grass-fed collagen powder
½–1 teaspoon cinnamon

⅛ teaspoon LoSalt or pink Himalayan salt
⅛ teaspoon sugar-free almond extract
1 tablespoon macadamia oil or hazelnut oil

1. Place all of the ingredients in a blender and pulse until smooth and frothy. Serve immediately.

Per Serving:
calories: 507 | fat: 41g | protein: 3g | carbs: 35g | fiber: 12g | sodium: 569mg

Mocha Protein Keto Coffee

Prep time: 5 minutes | Cook time: 1 minutes | Serves 1

12 ounces hot brewed coffee
2 tablespoons heavy whipping cream
1 tablespoon unsalted butter
1 tablespoon cocoa powder

1 scoop chocolate-flavored protein powder
1 scoop unflavored collagen peptides
10 drops of liquid stevia

1. Place all the ingredients in a blender and blend until smooth and frothy. Pour into a 16-ounce mug and serve immediately, or pour it into a Thermos and take it on the go!

Per Serving:
calories: 361 | fat: 24g | protein: 37g | carbs: 4g | net carbs: 2g | fiber: 2g

Cheesy Cauliflower Grits

Prep time: 5 minutes | Cook time: 15 minutes | Serves 4

¼ cup heavy cream
4 tablespoons unsalted butter, divided
1 teaspoon salt
½ teaspoon garlic powder
¼ teaspoon freshly ground

black pepper
2 cups riced cauliflower
¾ cup shredded Cheddar cheese
¼ cup shredded Parmesan cheese

1. In a medium saucepan over high heat, combine the heavy cream, 2 tablespoons of butter, salt, garlic powder, and pepper and bring to just below a boil. Add the riced cauliflower and reduce heat to low. 2. Simmer, stirring occasionally, for 8 to 10 minutes, until the cauliflower is tender, most of the water from the vegetable has evaporated, and the mixture is thick and creamy. 3. Remove from the heat and stir in the shredded cheeses and remaining 2 tablespoons of butter. Serve warm.

Per Serving:
calories: 280 | fat: 26g | protein: 8g | carbs: 5g | net carbs: 4g | fiber: 1g

Liver Sausages & Onions

Prep time: 10 minutes | Cook time: 26 minutes | Serves 6

SAUSAGES:
8 ounces (225 g) chicken livers
1 tablespoon apple cider vinegar
1 pound (455 g) ground beef
1 pound (455 g) ground pork
2½ teaspoons dried rubbed sage
1¼ teaspoons dried rosemary leaves
1 teaspoon dried thyme leaves

1 teaspoon finely ground sea salt
¾ teaspoon ground black pepper
4 cloves garlic, minced
¼ cup (60 ml) avocado oil, or ¼ cup (55 g) coconut oil or ghee, for the pan
2 medium-sized white onions, thinly sliced

1. Place the chicken livers in a medium-sized bowl and cover with water. Add the vinegar. Cover and place in the fridge to soak for 24 to 48 hours. 2. Rinse and drain the livers, then place them in a blender or food processor. Blend until smooth. 3. Transfer the pureed livers to a large mixing bowl and add the remaining ingredients for the sausages. Mix thoroughly with your hands to combine. 4. Heat the oil in a large frying pan over medium-low heat. 5. While the oil is heating, form the liver mixture into patties: Using a ¼-cup (60-ml) scoop, scoop up portions of the mixture and roll between your hands to form into 12 balls about 1¾ inches (4.5 cm) in diameter. Place the balls in the hot pan and press down until they're ½ inch (1.25 cm) thick. Do not overcrowd the pan; you may have to cook the sausages in two batches if they don't all fit comfortably. 6. Cook the sausages for 8 minutes per side, or until no longer pink in the center. 7. Place the cooked sausages on a serving plate. Set in a 180°F (82°C) oven to keep warm, if you wish. 8. Once the sausages are done, place the sliced onions in the same pan and cook for 10 minutes, or until translucent, stirring every minute or so. 9. Transfer the cooked onions to the serving plate with the sausages and enjoy.

Per Serving:
calories: 392 | fat: 22g | protein: 43g | carbs: 6g | net carbs: 4g | fiber: 2g

Southwestern Ham Egg Cups

Prep time: 5 minutes | Cook time: 12 minutes | Serves 2

4 (1-ounce / 28-g) slices deli ham
4 large eggs
2 tablespoons full-fat sour cream
¼ cup diced green bell pepper

2 tablespoons diced red bell pepper
2 tablespoons diced white onion
½ cup shredded medium Cheddar cheese

1. Place one slice of ham on the bottom of four baking cups. 2. In a large bowl, whisk eggs with sour cream. Stir in green pepper, red pepper, and onion. 3. Pour the egg mixture into ham-lined baking cups. Top with Cheddar. Place cups into the air fryer basket. 4. Adjust the temperature to 320°F (160°C) and bake for 12 minutes or until the tops are browned. 5. Serve warm.

Smoked Ham and Egg Muffins

Prep time: 5 minutes | Cook time: 25 minutes | Serves 9

2 cups chopped smoked ham
⅓ cup grated Parmesan cheese
¼ cup almond flour
9 eggs

⅓ cup mayonnaise, sugar-free
¼ teaspoon garlic powder
¼ cup chopped onion
Sea salt to taste

1. Preheat your oven to 370°F. 2. Lightly grease nine muffin pans with cooking spray and set aside. Place the onion, ham, garlic powder, and salt, in a food processor, and pulse until ground. Stir in the mayonnaise, almond flour, and Parmesan cheese. Press this mixture into the muffin cups. 3. Make sure it goes all the way up the muffin sides so that there will be room for the egg. Bake for 5 minutes. Crack an egg into each muffin cup. Return to the oven and bake for 20 more minutes or until the tops are firm to the touch and eggs are cooked. Leave to cool slightly before serving.

Per Serving:
calories: 165 | fat: 11g | protein: 14g | carbs: 2g | net carbs: 1g | fiber: 1g

Bacon Crackers

Prep time: 10 minutes | Cook time: 20 minutes | Makes 60 crackers

13 strips bacon (about 13 ounces/370 g), preferably thick-cut

1. Preheat the oven to 400°F (205°C) and line a rimmed baking sheet with parchment paper or a silicone baking mat. 2. Cut the strips of bacon into roughly 2-inch (5-cm) squares, about 6 per strip. Place the squares on the prepared baking sheet, leaving a small gap between crackers. 3. Bake the crackers until crisp, about 15 minutes if using regular bacon or 20 minutes if using thick-cut bacon. 4. Allow the crackers to cool on the baking sheet for 10 minutes. Transfer to a serving plate and enjoy.

Per Serving:
calories: 258 | fat: 25g | protein: 8g | carbs: 1g | net carbs: 1g | fiber: 0g

Easy Egg Scramble

Prep time: 10 minutes | Cook time: 15 minutes | Serves 2

1 tablespoon unsalted butter	1/3 cup cooked chopped bacon
1 cup sliced white mushrooms	2 large fresh basil leaves,
4 large eggs	chopped
3 ounces goat cheese, crumbled	Salt and pepper
(about 1/3 cup)	

1 In a medium-sized skillet, melt the butter over medium-high heat. Add the mushrooms and sauté until tender, 4 to 5 minutes. 2 Add the eggs and scramble, stirring constantly, until almost fully cooked, 4 to 5 minutes. 3 Sprinkle the goat cheese, bacon, and basil over the eggs and mushrooms; toss a few times. Season to taste with salt and pepper and serve.

Per Serving:
calories: 381 | fat: 28g | protein: 30g | carbs: 2g | net carbs: 2g | fiber: 0g

Quick Low-Carb Avocado Toasts

Prep time: 10 minutes | Cook time: 10 minutes | Makes 4 toasts

Quick Bread Base:	2 tablespoons water
1/4 cup (28 g/1 oz) flax meal	Avocado Topping:
2 tablespoons (16 g/0.6 oz)	1 large ripe avocado
coconut flour	1/4 small red onion or 1 spring
2 teaspoons (2 g) psyllium	onion, minced
powder	1 tablespoon extra-virgin olive
1/8 teaspoon baking soda	oil
Optional: 1/2 teaspoon dried	1 tablespoon fresh lemon juice
herbs, 1/4 teaspoon paprika or	Salt, black pepper, and/or chile
ground turmeric	flakes, to taste
Salt and black pepper, to taste	2 teaspoons chopped fresh
1/4 teaspoon apple cider vinegar	herbs, such as parsley or chives
1 teaspoon extra-virgin olive oil	Optional: 2 ounces (57 g)
or ghee, plus more for greasing	smoked salmon and/or poached
1 large egg	egg

Make the bread base: Combine all the dry ingredients in a bowl. Add the wet ingredients. Combine and set aside for 5 minutes. Divide the mixture between two wide ramekins lightly greased with the olive oil and microwave on high for about 2 minutes, checking every 30 to 60 seconds to avoid overcooking. (If the bread ends up too dry, you can "rehydrate" it: Pour 1 tablespoon [15 ml] of water evenly over it, then return it to the microwave for 30 seconds.) Let it cool slightly, then cut widthwise. Place on a dry nonstick pan and toast for 1 to 2 minutes per side. Set aside. Make the topping: In a bowl, mash the avocado with the onion, oil, lemon juice, salt, pepper, and chile flakes. To serve, spread the avocado mixture on top of the sliced bread and add fresh herbs. Optionally, top with smoked salmon. Store the bread separately from the topping at room temperature in a sealed container for 1 day, in the fridge for up to 5 days, or freeze for up to 3 months. Refrigerate the topping in a sealed jar for up to 3 days.

Per Serving:
calories: 112 | fat: 10g | protein: 3g | carbs: 4g | fiber: 3g | sodium: 71mg

Pork Sausage Eggs with Mustard Sauce

Prep time: 20 minutes | Cook time: 12 minutes | Serves 8

1 pound (454 g) pork sausage	Smoky Mustard Sauce:
8 soft-boiled or hard-boiled	1/4 cup mayonnaise
eggs, peeled	2 tablespoons sour cream
1 large egg	1 tablespoon Dijon mustard
2 tablespoons milk	1 teaspoon chipotle hot sauce
1 cup crushed pork rinds	

1. Preheat the air fryer to 390°F (199°C). 2. Divide the sausage into 8 portions. Take each portion of sausage, pat it down into a patty, and place 1 egg in the middle, gently wrapping the sausage around the egg until the egg is completely covered. (Wet your hands slightly if you find the sausage to be too sticky.) Repeat with the remaining eggs and sausage. 3. In a small shallow bowl, whisk the egg and milk until frothy. In another shallow bowl, place the crushed pork rinds. Working one at a time, dip a sausage-wrapped egg into the beaten egg and then into the pork rinds, gently rolling to coat evenly. Repeat with the remaining sausage-wrapped eggs. 4. Arrange the eggs in a single layer in the air fryer basket, and lightly spray with olive oil. Air fry for 10 to 12 minutes, pausing halfway through the baking time to turn the eggs, until the eggs are hot and the sausage is cooked through. 5. To make the sauce: In a small bowl, combine the mayonnaise, sour cream, Dijon, and hot sauce. Whisk until thoroughly combined. Serve with the Scotch eggs.

All Day Any Day Hash

Prep time: 10 minutes | Cook time: 25 minutes | Serves 4

1/4 cup (55 g) coconut oil or	thinly sliced
ghee	1/3 cup (25 g) crushed pork rinds
2/3 cup (100 g) sliced white	2 tablespoons chopped fresh
onions	parsley leaves
3 cloves garlic, minced	1 teaspoon fresh thyme leaves
3 medium turnips (about 1	1/4 teaspoon finely ground sea
lb/455 g), peeled and cubed	salt
2 medium carrots (about 5	1/8 teaspoon ground black
oz/140 g), diced	pepper
1 red bell pepper, diced	1/2 cup (120 ml) creamy Italian
8 ounces (225 g) boneless steak,	dressing

1. Heat the oil in a large frying pan over medium heat. Add the onions and garlic and cook until the onions are translucent, 5 to 7 minutes. 2. Add the turnips, carrots, bell pepper, and steak. Toss to coat, cover, and cook for 15 to 18 minutes, stirring every 3 minutes, until the turnips are fork-tender and the steak is cooked to your liking. Remove the pan from the heat. 3. Add the crushed pork rinds, parsley, thyme, salt, and pepper and toss to coat. 4. Divide the hash evenly among 4 bowls and drizzle each bowl with 2 tablespoons of dressing just before serving.

Per Serving:
calories: 512 | fat: 37g | protein: 27g | carbs: 17g | net carbs: 13g | fiber: 4g

Turmeric Scrambled Eggs

Prep time: 5 minutes | Cook time: 5 minutes | Serves 2

3 large eggs	Salt, to taste
2 tablespoons heavy cream (optional)	Freshly ground black pepper, to taste
1 teaspoon ground turmeric	1 tablespoon butter

1. In a small bowl, lightly beat the eggs with the cream. Add the turmeric, salt, and pepper. 2. Melt the butter in a skillet over medium heat. When it just starts to bubble, gently pour in the egg mixture. Stir frequently as eggs begin to set, and cook for 2 to 3 minutes. 3. Remove from the heat, taste and add more pepper and salt if needed, and serve.

Per Serving:
calories: 213 | fat: 18g | protein: 10g | carbs: 2g | net carbs: 2g | fiber: 0g

Green Eggs and Ham

Prep time: 5 minutes | Cook time: 10 minutes | Serves 2

1 large Hass avocado, halved and pitted	½ teaspoon fine sea salt
2 thin slices ham	¼ teaspoon ground black pepper
2 large eggs	¼ cup shredded Cheddar cheese (omit for dairy-free)
2 tablespoons chopped green onions, plus more for garnish	

1. Preheat the air fryer to 400°F (204°C). 2. Place a slice of ham into the cavity of each avocado half. Crack an egg on top of the ham, then sprinkle on the green onions, salt, and pepper. 3. Place the avocado halves in the air fryer cut side up and air fry for 10 minutes, or until the egg is cooked to your desired doneness. Top with the cheese (if using) and air fry for 30 seconds more, or until the cheese is melted. Garnish with chopped green onions. 4. Best served fresh. Store extras in an airtight container in the fridge for up to 4 days. Reheat in a preheated 350°F (177°C) air fryer for a few minutes, until warmed through.

Per Serving:
calories: 316 | fat: 25g | protein: 16g | carbs: 10g | sugars: 1g | fiber: 7g | sodium: 660mg

Bacon and Mushroom Quiche Lorraine

Prep time: 10 minutes | Cook time: 37 minutes | Serves 4

4 strips bacon, chopped	milk
2 cups sliced button mushrooms	¼ cup sliced green onions
½ cup diced onions	½ teaspoon sea salt
8 large eggs	¼ teaspoon ground black pepper
1½ cups shredded Swiss cheese	
1 cup unsweetened almond	2 tablespoons coconut flour

1. Press the Sauté button on the Instant Pot and add the bacon. Sauté for 4 minutes, or until crisp. Transfer the bacon to a plate lined with paper towel to drain, leaving the drippings in the pot. 2. Add the mushrooms and diced onions to the pot and sauté for 3 minutes, or until the onions are tender. Remove the mixture from the pot to a large bowl. Wipe the Instant Pot clean. 3. Set a trivet in the Instant Pot and pour in 1 cup water. 4. In a medium bowl, stir together the eggs, cheese, almond milk, green onions, salt and pepper. Pour the egg mixture into the bowl with the mushrooms and onions. Stir to combine. Fold in the coconut flour. Pour the mixture into a greased round casserole dish. Spread the cooked bacon on top. 5. Place the casserole dish onto the trivet in the Instant Pot. 6. Lock the lid, select the Manual mode and set the cooking time for 30 minutes on High Pressure. When the timer goes off, do a natural pressure release for 15 minutes, then release any remaining pressure. Open the lid. 7. Remove the casserole dish from the Instant Pot. 8. Let cool for 15 to 30 minutes before cutting into 4 pieces. Serve immediately.

Per Serving:
calories: 433 | fat: 29.1g | protein: 32.0g | carbs: 6.9g | net carbs: 4.8g | fiber: 2.1g

Rocket Fuel Hot Chocolate

Prep time: 5 minutes | Cook time: 0 minutes | Makes 2

2 cups (475 ml) milk (nondairy or regular), hot	powder, or ghee
2 tablespoons cocoa powder	1 tablespoon coconut butter
2 tablespoons collagen peptides or protein powder	1 tablespoon erythritol, or 4 drops liquid stevia
2 tablespoons coconut oil, MCT oil, unflavored MCT oil	Pinch of ground cinnamon (optional)

1. Place all the ingredients in a blender and blend for 10 seconds, or until the ingredients are fully incorporated. 2. Divide between 2 mugs, sprinkle with cinnamon if you'd like, and enjoy!

Per Serving:
calories: 357 | fat: 29g | protein: 13g | carbs: 11g | net carbs: 7g | fiber: 4g

Buffalo Chicken Breakfast Muffins

Prep time: 7 minutes | Cook time: 13 to 16 minutes | Serves 10

6 ounces (170 g) shredded cooked chicken	as Frank's RedHot
3 ounces (85 g) blue cheese, crumbled	1 teaspoon minced garlic
2 tablespoons unsalted butter, melted	6 large eggs
⅓ cup Buffalo hot sauce, such	Sea salt and freshly ground black pepper, to taste
	Avocado oil spray

1. In a large bowl, stir together the chicken, blue cheese, melted butter, hot sauce, and garlic. 2. In a medium bowl or large liquid measuring cup, beat the eggs. Season with salt and pepper. 3. Spray 10 silicone muffin cups with oil. Divide the chicken mixture among the cups, and pour the egg mixture over top. 4. Place the cups in the air fryer and set to 300°F (149°C). Bake for 13 to 16 minutes, until the muffins are set and cooked through. (Depending on the size of your air fryer, you may need to cook the muffins in batches.)

Per Serving:
calories: 129 | fat: 9g | protein: 10g | carbs: 1g | net carbs: 1g | fiber: 0g

Herbed Buttery Breakfast Steak

Prep time: 5 minutes | Cook time: 1 minute | Serves 2

½ cup water
1 pound (454 g) boneless beef sirloin steak
½ teaspoon salt
½ teaspoon black pepper
1 clove garlic, minced
2 tablespoons butter, softened
¼ teaspoon dried rosemary
¼ teaspoon dried parsley
Pinch of dried thyme

1. Pour the water into the Instant Pot and put the trivet in the pot. 2. Rub the steak all over with salt and black pepper. Place the steak on the trivet. 3. In a small bowl, stir together the remaining ingredients. Spread half of the butter mixture over the steak. 4. Set the lid in place. Select the Manual mode and set the cooking time for 1 minute on Low Pressure. When the timer goes off, perform a quick pressure release. Carefully open the lid. 5. Remove the steak from the pot. Top with the remaining half of the butter mixture. Serve hot.

Per Serving:
calories: 426 | fat: 25.1g | protein: 46.8g | carbs: 0.6g | net carbs: 0.4g | fiber: 0.2g

Green Monster Smoothie

Prep time: 3 minutes | Cook time: 0 minutes | Serves 1

1 cup ice
1 cup chopped fresh spinach
½ cup fresh raspberries
2 (1-gram) packets 0g net carb
sweetener
1 cup unsweetened almond milk (or dairy alternative milk of your choice)

1. Pulse all ingredients in a food processor or blender 30–60 seconds until ice is blended.

Per Serving:
calories: 67 | fat: 3g | protein: 3g | carbs: 10g | net carbs: 4g | fiber: 6g

Waffles with Sausage Gravy

Prep time: 5 minutes | Cook time: 15 minutes | Serves 4

Sausage Gravy:
1 pound (454 g) ground pork (or ground beef or turkey)
1 teaspoon dried sage
½ teaspoon dried thyme
½ teaspoon garlic powder
¼ teaspoon kosher salt
¼ teaspoon black pepper
About 1¼ cups full-fat coconut
milk
Waffles:
2 large eggs
1 tablespoon melted coconut oil
½ cup full-fat coconut milk
¾ cup almond flour or nut pulp
¼ teaspoon salt
½ teaspoon baking soda
1½ teaspoons arrowroot powder

1. Heat a large skillet over medium heat and add the ground pork. Break up with a fork as it cooks. 2. When the pork is mostly cooked, in about 5 minutes, add the spices and stir well. Cook until fully browned, another 2 to 3 minutes. Add the coconut milk and allow to come to a simmer, then turn the heat to low. 3. In a medium bowl, whisk the eggs with the coconut oil and coconut milk. Add the pulp, salt, baking soda, and arrowroot powder, and mix well. The waffle batter will be thicker than a traditional batter; if needed, add a little water a tablespoon at a time until it is pourable. 4. Pour some batter into a waffle maker set on medium-low heat. (Alternatively, use a lightly greased pan or griddle and make pancakes.) Remove the waffle from the waffle maker when cooked through and continue to make waffles with the remaining batter. 5. Serve the waffles with the gravy on top.

Per Serving:
calories: 644 | fat: 56g | protein: 28g | carbs: 7g | net carbs: 3g | fiber: 4g

Baklava Hot Porridge

Prep time: 5 minutes | Cook time: 5 minutes | Serves 2

2 cups riced cauliflower
¾ cup unsweetened almond, flax, or hemp milk
4 tablespoons extra-virgin olive oil, divided
2 teaspoons grated fresh orange peel (from ½ orange)
½ teaspoon ground cinnamon
½ teaspoon almond extract or vanilla extract
⅛ teaspoon salt
4 tablespoons chopped walnuts, divided
1 to 2 teaspoons liquid stevia, monk fruit, or other sweetener of choice (optional)

1. In medium saucepan, combine the riced cauliflower, almond milk, 2 tablespoons olive oil, grated orange peel, cinnamon, almond extract, and salt. Stir to combine and bring just to a boil over medium-high heat, stirring constantly. 2. Remove from heat and stir in 2 tablespoons chopped walnuts and sweetener (if using). Stir to combine. 3. Divide into bowls, topping each with 1 tablespoon of chopped walnuts and 1 tablespoon of the remaining olive oil.

Per Serving:
calories: 414 | fat: 38g | protein: 6g | carbs: 16g | fiber: 4g | sodium: 252mg

Mexican Breakfast Beef Chili

Prep time: 5 minutes | Cook time: 45 minutes | Serves 4

2 tablespoons coconut oil
1 pound (454 g) ground grass-fed beef
1 (14-ounce / 397-g) can sugar-free or low-sugar diced tomatoes
½ cup shredded full-fat Cheddar cheese (optional)
1 teaspoon hot sauce
½ teaspoon chili powder
½ teaspoon crushed red pepper
½ teaspoon ground cumin
½ teaspoon kosher salt
½ teaspoon freshly ground black pepper

1. Set the Instant Pot to Sauté and melt the oil. 2. Pour in ½ cup of filtered water, then add the beef, tomatoes, cheese, hot sauce, chili powder, red pepper, cumin, salt, and black pepper to the Instant Pot, stirring thoroughly. 3. Close the lid, set the pressure release to Sealing, and hit Cancel to stop the current program. Select Manual, set the Instant Pot to 45 minutes on High Pressure and let cook. 4. Once cooked, let the pressure naturally disperse from the Instant Pot for about 10 minutes, then carefully switch the pressure release to Venting. 5. Open the Instant Pot, serve, and enjoy!

Per Serving:
calories: 351 | fat: 19g | protein: 39g | carbs: 6g | net carbs: 4g | fiber: 2g

Turkish Egg Bowl

Prep time: 10 minutes | Cook time: 15 minutes | Serves 2

2 tablespoons ghee
½–1 teaspoon red chile flakes
2 tablespoons extra-virgin olive oil
1 cup full-fat goat's or sheep's milk yogurt
1 clove garlic, minced

1 tablespoon fresh lemon juice
Salt and black pepper, to taste
Dash of vinegar
4 large eggs
Optional: pinch of sumac
2 tablespoons chopped fresh cilantro or parsley

1. In a skillet, melt the ghee over low heat. Add the chile flakes and let it infuse while you prepare the eggs. Remove from the heat and mix with the extra-virgin olive oil. Set aside. Combine the yogurt, garlic, lemon juice, salt, and pepper. 2. Poach the eggs. Fill a medium saucepan with water and a dash of vinegar. Bring to a boil over high heat. Crack each egg individually into a ramekin or a cup. Using a spoon, create a gentle whirlpool in the water; this will help the egg white wrap around the egg yolk. Slowly lower the egg into the water in the center of the whirlpool. Turn off the heat and cook for 3 to 4 minutes. Use a slotted spoon to remove the egg from the water and place it on a plate. Repeat for all remaining eggs. 3. To assemble, place the yogurt mixture in a bowl and add the poached eggs. Drizzle with the infused oil, and garnish with cilantro. Add a pinch of sumac, if using. Eat warm.

Per Serving:
calories: 576 | fat: 46g | protein: 27g | carbs: 17g | fiber: 4g | sodium: 150mg

Breakfast Sammies

Prep time: 15 minutes | Cook time: 20 minutes | Serves 5

Biscuits:
6 large egg whites
2 cups blanched almond flour, plus more if needed
1½ teaspoons baking powder
½ teaspoon fine sea salt
¼ cup (½ stick) very cold unsalted butter (or lard for dairy-free), cut into ¼-inch pieces

Eggs:
5 large eggs
½ teaspoon fine sea salt
¼ teaspoon ground black pepper
5 (1-ounce / 28-g) slices Cheddar cheese (omit for dairy-free)
10 thin slices ham

1. Spray the air fryer basket with avocado oil. Preheat the air fryer to 350ºF (177ºC). Grease two pie pans or two baking pans that will fit inside your air fryer. 2. Make the biscuits: In a medium-sized bowl, whip the egg whites with a hand mixer until very stiff. Set aside. 3. In a separate medium-sized bowl, stir together the almond flour, baking powder, and salt until well combined. Cut in the butter. Gently fold the flour mixture into the egg whites with a rubber spatula. If the dough is too wet to form into mounds, add a few tablespoons of almond flour until the dough holds together well. 4. Using a large spoon, divide the dough into 5 equal portions and drop them about 1 inch apart on one of the greased pie pans. (If you're using a smaller air fryer, work in batches if necessary.) Place the pan in the air fryer and bake for 11 to 14 minutes, until the biscuits are golden brown. Remove from the air fryer and set aside to cool. 5. Make the eggs: Set the air fryer to 375ºF (191ºC).

Crack the eggs into the remaining greased pie pan and sprinkle with the salt and pepper. Place the eggs in the air fryer to bake for 5 minutes, or until they are cooked to your liking. 6. Open the air fryer and top each egg yolk with a slice of cheese (if using). Bake for another minute, or until the cheese is melted. 7. Once the biscuits are cool, slice them in half lengthwise. Place 1 cooked egg topped with cheese and 2 slices of ham in each biscuit. 8. Store leftover biscuits, eggs, and ham in separate airtight containers in the fridge for up to 3 days. Reheat the biscuits and eggs on a baking sheet in a preheated 350ºF (177ºC) air fryer for 5 minutes, or until warmed through.

Per Serving:
calories: 454 | fat: 35g | protein: 27g | carbs: 8g | net carbs: 4g | fiber: 4g

Bacon Cheese Egg with Avocado

Prep time: 15 minutes | Cook time: 20 minutes | Serves 4

6 large eggs
¼ cup heavy whipping cream
1½ cups chopped cauliflower
1 cup shredded medium Cheddar cheese
1 medium avocado, peeled and

pitted
8 tablespoons full-fat sour cream
2 scallions, sliced on the bias
12 slices sugar-free bacon, cooked and crumbled

1. In a medium bowl, whisk eggs and cream together. Pour into a round baking dish. 2. Add cauliflower and mix, then top with Cheddar. Place dish into the air fryer basket. 3. Adjust the temperature to 320ºF (160ºC) and set the timer for 20 minutes. 4. When completely cooked, eggs will be firm and cheese will be browned. Slice into four pieces. 5. Slice avocado and divide evenly among pieces. Top each piece with 2 tablespoons sour cream, sliced scallions, and crumbled bacon.

Per Serving:
calories: 506 | fat: 40g | protein: 28g | carbs: 10g | net carbs: 6g | fiber: 4g

Sausage & Squash Omelet with Swiss Chard

Prep time: 10 minutes | Cook time: 10 minutes | Serves 1

2 eggs
1 cup Swiss chard, chopped
4 oz sausage, chopped
2 tablespoons ricotta cheese

4 ounces roasted squash
1 tablespoon olive oil
Salt and black pepper, to taste
Fresh parsley to garnish

1. Beat the eggs in a bowl, season with salt and pepper; stir in the swiss chard and the ricotta cheese. 2. In another bowl, mash the squash and add to the egg mixture. Heat ¼ tbsp of olive oil in a pan over medium heat. Add sausage and cook until browned on all sides, turning occasionally. 3. Drizzle the remaining olive oil. Pour the egg mixture over. Cook for about 2 minutes per side until the eggs are thoroughly cooked and lightly browned. Remove the pan and run a spatula around the edges of the omelet; slide it onto a warm platter. Fold in half, and serve sprinkled with fresh parsley.

Per Serving:
calories: 744 | fat: 62g | protein: 32g | carbs: 15g | net carbs: 12g | fiber: 3g

Egg Roll in a Bowl

Prep time: 10 minutes | Cook time: 10 minutes | Serves 2

2 large eggs
2 tablespoons sesame oil, divided
2 tablespoons soy sauce, divided
2 tablespoons extra-virgin olive oil
6 ounces (170 g) ground pork
1 tablespoon chopped fresh ginger (or 1 teaspoon ground ginger)
2 cloves garlic, minced
2 cups finely chopped cabbage

(or bagged coleslaw mix; no dressing)
2 ribs celery, diced
½ small red bell pepper, diced
2 tablespoons lime juice, divided
2 scallions, minced (green and white parts)
2 tablespoons mayonnaise
1 teaspoon sriracha or other hot sauce
½ teaspoon garlic powder

1. In a small bowl, beat together the eggs, 1 tablespoon of sesame oil, and 1 tablespoon of soy sauce and set aside. 2. Heat the olive oil in a large skillet over medium heat. Sauté the ground pork, breaking it apart, until browned and no longer pink, 4 to 5 minutes. Add the ginger and garlic and sauté for an additional 30 seconds. 3. Add the cabbage, celery, and bell pepper and sauté, stirring constantly, until the vegetables are wilted and fragrant, another 2 to 3 minutes. 4. Push the vegetables and pork to one side of the skillet and add the egg mixture to the other side. Reduce heat to low and scramble the egg until cooked through, 1 to 2 minutes. Remove the skillet from the heat and mix the egg into the pork and cabbage. 5. In a small bowl, whisk together the remaining 1 tablespoon of sesame oil, the remaining 1 tablespoon of soy sauce, 1 tablespoon of lime juice, and the scallions. Pour over the cooked pork mixture and stir to combine well, reserving the bowl. 6. In the same small bowl, combine the remaining 1 tablespoon of lime juice, the mayonnaise, sriracha, and garlic powder. 7. Divide the pork mixture evenly between two bowls and drizzle each with half of the spicy mayo. Serve warm.

Per Serving:
calories: 695 | fat: 61g | protein: 25g | carbs: 16g | net carbs: 10g | fiber: 4g

Hashed Zucchini & Bacon Breakfast

Prep time: 10 minutes | Cook time: 15 minutes | Serves 1

1medium zucchini, diced
2bacon slices
1 egg
1 tablespoon coconut oil

½ small onion, chopped
1 tablespoon chopped parsley
¼ teaspoon salt

1. Place the bacon in a skillet and cook for a few minutes, until crispy. Remove and set aside. 2. Warm the coconut oil and cook the onion until soft, for about 3-4 minutes, occasionally stirring. Add the zucchini, and cook for 10 more minutes until zucchini is brown and tender, but not mushy. Transfer to a plate and season with salt. 3. Crack the egg into the same skillet and fry over medium heat. Top the zucchini mixture with the bacon slices and a fried egg. Serve hot, sprinkled with parsley.

Per Serving:
calories: 440 | fat: 39g | protein: 15g | carbs: 10g | net carbs: 7g | fiber: 3g

Golden Gate Granola

Prep time: 10 minutes | Cook time: 1 hour | Makes 4 cups

¼ cup (½ stick) unsalted butter
¼ cup powdered erythritol
¼ teaspoon plus 10 drops of liquid stevia
1 teaspoon ground cinnamon
½ teaspoon vanilla extract

1 cup raw almonds
1 cup raw hazelnuts
1 cup unsweetened coconut flakes
½ cup raw pumpkin seeds
¼ cup hemp hearts

1. Preheat the oven to 275°F and line a rimmed baking sheet with parchment paper or a silicone baking mat. 2. In a small saucepan over medium heat, combine the butter, erythritol, stevia, cinnamon, and vanilla extract. Stirring occasionally, heat until the butter and erythritol are melted and dissolved. Remove from the heat and set aside. 3. In a large bowl, combine the nuts, coconut flakes, pumpkin seeds, and hemp hearts. Pour the melted butter mixture over the nut mixture and toss using a rubber spatula, making sure that everything is well coated. 4. Pour the granola onto the lined baking sheet and spread it out into an even layer. Bake for 1 hour, stirring every 15 minutes or so, until dark golden brown. 5. Let the granola cool in the pan for at least 1 hour to allow it to harden and form clumps. Store in a sealed jar or zip-top plastic bag for up to 3 weeks. It does not need to be refrigerated.

Per Serving:
calories: 200 | fat: 18g | protein: 5g | carbs: 5g | net carbs: 2g | fiber: 3g

Waffle Breakfast Sandwiches

Prep time: 10 minutes | Cook time: 20 minutes | Serves 2

Waffles
2 large eggs
⅓ cup blanched almond flour
½ tablespoon coconut flour
¼ teaspoon baking powder
Pinch of salt
¼ teaspoon vanilla extract
4 drops liquid stevia

Sandwich Fillings
4 slices bacon
2 large eggs
2 slices cheddar cheese or other cheese of choice (optional) ½ avocado, sliced
Salt and pepper

1 Preheat a waffle maker to medium-high heat. 2 Make the waffles: In a medium-sized mixing bowl, beat the eggs. Add the almond flour, coconut flour, baking powder, salt, vanilla, and stevia and mix until smooth. 3 Pour the batter into the preheated waffle maker and close the lid; cook for 3 to 5 minutes, until light golden brown and slightly crisp. Remove the cooked waffle and set aside. 4 Make the sandwich fillings: In a skillet over medium heat, fry the bacon until crispy. Remove the bacon and set aside, leaving the bacon fat in the skillet. 5 Crack the eggs into the skillet with the bacon fat (cooked over easy so that the yolks are runny). 6 After flipping the eggs, cover each with a slice of cheese, if using, and cover the pan with a lid to help melt the cheese. 7 To assemble the sandwiches, cut the waffle into quarters. Place a quarter waffle on each plate and top each with 2 slices of bacon and a cheese-topped egg. Top each stack with avocado slices and season with salt and pepper to taste. Top each sandwich with one of the remaining waffle quarters.

Per Serving:
calories: 393 | fat: 31g | protein: 24g | carbs: 9g | net carbs: 4g | fiber: 5g

Kale-Avocado Egg Skillet

Prep time: 5 minutes | Cook time: 10 minutes | Serves 2

2 tablespoons olive oil, divided
2 cups sliced mushrooms
5 ounces fresh kale, stemmed and sliced into ribbons

1 avocado, sliced
4 large eggs
Pink Himalayan salt
Freshly ground black pepper

1. In a large skillet over medium heat, heat 1 tablespoon of olive oil. 2. Add the mushrooms to the pan, and sauté for about 3 minutes. 3. In a medium bowl, massage the kale with the remaining 1 tablespoon of olive oil for 1 to 2 minutes to help tenderize it. Add the kale to the skillet on top of the mushrooms, then place the slices of avocado on top of the kale. 4. Using a spoon, create 4 wells for the eggs. Crack one egg into each well. Season the eggs and kale with pink Himalayan salt and pepper. 5. Cover the skillet and cook for about 5 minutes, or until the eggs reach your desired degree of doneness. 6. Serve hot.

Per Serving:
calories: 407 | fat: 34g | protein: 18g | carbs: 13g | net carbs: 6g | fiber: 7g

Starbucks Egg Bites

Prep time: 5 minutes | Cook time: 30 minutes | Serves 6

5 large eggs, whisked
1 cup shredded Swiss cheese
1 cup full-fat cottage cheese
⅛ teaspoon salt

⅛ teaspoon black pepper
2 strips no-sugar-added bacon, cooked and crumbled

1 Preheat oven to 350°F. 2 In a large bowl, whisk together eggs, Swiss cheese, cottage cheese, salt, and pepper. 3 Pour six equal amounts of mixture into well-greased muffin tins (or use cupcake liners). 4 Top with bacon bits. 5 Bake 30 minutes until eggs are completely cooked. 6 Remove Starbucks Egg Bites from oven and serve warm.
Per Serving:
PER SERVING:
CALORIES: 182 , FAT: 11G , PROTEIN: 16G , SODIUM:321MG , FIBER:0G , CARBOHYDRATE:3G , SUGAR:1G

Coconut & Walnut Chia Pudding

Prep time: 10 minutes | Cook time: 10 minutes | Serves 1

½ tsp vanilla extract
½ cup water
1tbsp chia seeds
2tbsp hemp seeds
1tbsp flax seed meal

2tbsp almond meal
2 tbsp shredded coconut
¼ tsp granulated stevia
1 tbsp walnuts, chopped

1Put chia seeds, hemp seeds, flaxseed meal, almond meal, granulated stevia, and shredded coconut in a nonstick saucepan and pour over the water. Simmer over medium heat, occasionally stirring, until creamed and thickened, for about 3-4 minutes. Stir in vanilla. When the pudding is ready, spoon into a serving bowl, sprinkle with walnuts and serve warm.
Per Serving:
Per serving: Kcal 334, Fat: 29g, Net Carbs: 1.5g Protein: 15g

Cheese Ciabatta with Pepperoni

Prep time: 10 minutes | Cook time: 10 minutes | Serves 6

10 ounces cream cheese, melted
2 ½ cups mozzarella cheese, shredded
4 large eggs, beaten
3 tablespoons Romano cheese,

grated
½ cup pork rinds, crushed
2 ½ teaspoons baking powder
½ cup tomato puree
12 large slices pepperoni

1. Combine eggs, mozzarella cheese and cream cheese. Place in baking powder, pork rinds, and Romano cheese. Form into 6 chiabatta shapes. Set a nonstick pan over medium heat. Cook each ciabatta for 2 minutes per side. Sprinkle tomato puree over each one and top with pepperoni slices to serve.
Per Serving:
calories: 466 | fat: 41g | protein: 20g | carbs: 6g | net carbs: 6g | fiber: 0g

Pork and Quill Egg Cups

Prep time: 15 minutes | Cook time: 15 minutes | Serves 4

10 ounces (283 g) ground pork
1 jalapeño pepper, chopped
1 tablespoon butter, softened
1 teaspoon dried dill

½ teaspoon salt
1 cup water
4 quill eggs

1. In a bowl, stir together all the ingredients, except for the quill eggs and water. Transfer the meat mixture to the silicone muffin molds and press the surface gently. 2. Pour the water and insert the trivet in the Instant Pot. Put the meat cups on the trivet. 3. Crack the eggs over the meat mixture. 4. Set the lid in place. Select the Manual mode and set the cooking time for 15 minutes on High Pressure. When the timer goes off, do a quick pressure release. Carefully open the lid. 5. Serve warm.
Per Serving:
calories: 142 | fat: 6.3g | protein: 20.0g | carbs: 0.3g | net carbs: 0.1g | fiber: 0.2g

Smoked Salmon Rolls with Dill Cream Cheese

Prep time: 10 minutes | Cook time: 0 minutes | Serves 3

3 tbsp cream cheese, softened
1 small lemon, zested and juiced
3 tsp chopped fresh dill

Salt and black pepper to taste
3 (7-inch) low carb tortillas
6 slices smoked salmon

1. In a bowl, mix the cream cheese, lemon juice, zest, dill, salt, and black pepper. 2. Lay each tortilla on a plastic wrap (just wide enough to cover the tortilla), spread with cream cheese mixture, and top each (one) with two salmon slices. Roll up the tortillas and secure both ends by twisting. 3. Refrigerate for 2 hours, remove plastic, cut off both ends of each wrap, and cut wraps into wheels.
Per Serving:
Per serving: Kcal 250, Fat 16g, Net Carbs 7g, Protein 18g

Cauliflower and Cheese Quiche

Prep time: 10 minutes | Cook time: 10 minutes | Serves 2

1 cup chopped cauliflower
¼ cup shredded Cheddar cheese
5 eggs, beaten

1 teaspoon butter
1 teaspoon dried oregano
1 cup water

1. Grease the instant pot baking pan with butter from inside. 2. Pour water in the instant pot. 3. Sprinkle the cauliflower with dried oregano and put it in the prepared baking pan. Flatten the vegetables gently. 4. After this, add eggs and stir the vegetables. 5. Top the quiche with shredded cheese and transfer it in the instant pot. Close and seal the lid. Cook the quiche on Manual mode (High Pressure) for 10 minutes. Make a quick pressure release.

Per Serving:
calories: 246 | fat: 18g | protein: 18g | carbs: 4g | net carbs: 2g | fiber: 2g

Mediterranean Frittata

Prep time: 10 minutes | Cook time: 15 minutes | Serves 2

4 large eggs
2 tablespoons fresh chopped herbs, such as rosemary, thyme, oregano, basil or 1 teaspoon dried herbs
¼ teaspoon salt
Freshly ground black pepper
4 tablespoons extra-virgin olive oil, divided

1 cup fresh spinach, arugula, kale, or other leafy greens
4 ounces (113 g) quartered artichoke hearts, rinsed, drained, and thoroughly dried
8 cherry tomatoes, halved
½ cup crumbled soft goat cheese

1. Preheat the oven to broil on low. 2. In small bowl, combine the eggs, herbs, salt, and pepper and whisk well with a fork. Set aside. 3. In a 4- to 5-inch oven-safe skillet or omelet pan, heat 2 tablespoons olive oil over medium heat. Add the spinach, artichoke hearts, and cherry tomatoes and sauté until just wilted, 1 to 2 minutes. 4. Pour in the egg mixture and let it cook undisturbed over medium heat for 3 to 4 minutes, until the eggs begin to set on the bottom. 5. Sprinkle the goat cheese across the top of the egg mixture and transfer the skillet to the oven. 6. Broil for 4 to 5 minutes, or until the frittata is firm in the center and golden brown on top. 7. Remove from the oven and run a rubber spatula around the edge to loosen the sides. Invert onto a large plate or cutting board and slice in half. Serve warm and drizzled with the remaining 2 tablespoons olive oil.

Per Serving:
calories: 520 | fat: 44g | protein: 22g | carbs: 10g | fiber: 5g | sodium: 665mg

Breakfast Pizza

Prep time: 5 minutes | Cook time: 8 minutes | Serves 1

2 large eggs
¼ cup unsweetened, unflavored almond milk (or unflavored hemp milk for nut-free)
¼ teaspoon fine sea salt
⅛ teaspoon ground black pepper

¼ cup diced onions
¼ cup shredded Parmesan cheese (omit for dairy-free)
6 pepperoni slices (omit for vegetarian)
¼ teaspoon dried oregano leaves
¼ cup pizza sauce, warmed, for serving

1. Preheat the air fryer to 350°F (177°C). Grease a cake pan. 2. In a small bowl, use a fork to whisk together the eggs, almond milk, salt, and pepper. Add the onions and stir to mix. Pour the mixture into the greased pan. Top with the cheese (if using), pepperoni slices (if using), and oregano. 3. Place the pan in the air fryer and bake for 8 minutes, or until the eggs are cooked to your liking. 4. Loosen the eggs from the sides of the pan with a spatula and place them on a serving plate. Drizzle the pizza sauce on top. Best served fresh.

Chapter 2 Poultry

Bacon Lovers' Stuffed Chicken

Prep time: 10 minutes | Cook time: 20 minutes | Serves 4

4 (5-ounce / 142-g) boneless, skinless chicken breasts, pounded to ¼ inch thick
2 (5.2-ounce / 147-g) packages Boursin cheese (or Kite Hill brand chive cream cheese style

spread, softened, for dairy-free)
8 slices thin-cut bacon or beef bacon
Sprig of fresh cilantro, for garnish (optional)

1. Spray the air fryer basket with avocado oil. Preheat the air fryer to 400°F (204°C). 2. Place one of the chicken breasts on a cutting board. With a sharp knife held parallel to the cutting board, make a 1-inch-wide incision at the top of the breast. Carefully cut into the breast to form a large pocket, leaving a ½-inch border along the sides and bottom. Repeat with the other 3 chicken breasts. 3. Snip the corner of a large resealable plastic bag to form a ¾-inch hole. Place the Boursin cheese in the bag and pipe the cheese into the pockets in the chicken breasts, dividing the cheese evenly among them. 4. Wrap 2 slices of bacon around each chicken breast and secure the ends with toothpicks. Place the bacon-wrapped chicken in the air fryer basket and air fry until the bacon is crisp and the chicken's internal temperature reaches 165°F (74°C), about 18 to 20 minutes, flipping after 10 minutes. Garnish with a sprig of cilantro before serving, if desired. 5. Store leftovers in an airtight container in the refrigerator for up to 4 days. Reheat in a preheated 400°F (204°C) air fryer for 5 minutes, or until warmed through.
Per Serving:
calories: 634 | fat: 49g | protein: 43g | carbs: 3g | net carbs: 3g | fiber: 0g

Tandoori Chicken

Prep time: 30 minutes | Cook time: 15 minutes | Serves 4

1 pound (454 g) chicken tenders, halved crosswise
¼ cup plain Greek yogurt
1 tablespoon minced fresh ginger
1 tablespoon minced garlic
¼ cup chopped fresh cilantro or parsley
1 teaspoon kosher salt
½ to 1 teaspoon cayenne pepper

1 teaspoon ground turmeric
1 teaspoon garam masala
1 teaspoon sweet smoked paprika
1 tablespoon vegetable oil or melted ghee
2 teaspoons fresh lemon juice
2 tablespoons chopped fresh cilantro

1. In a large glass bowl, toss together the chicken, yogurt, ginger, garlic, cilantro, salt, cayenne, turmeric, garam masala, and paprika to coat. Marinate at room temperature for 30 minutes, or cover and refrigerate for up to 24 hours. 2. Place the chicken in a single layer in the air fryer basket. (Discard remaining marinade.) Spray the chicken with oil. Set the air fryer to 350°F (177°C) for 15 minutes.

Halfway through the cooking time, spray the chicken with more vegetable oil spray, and toss gently to coat. Cook for 5 minutes more. 3. Transfer the chicken to a serving platter. Sprinkle with lemon juice and toss to coat. Sprinkle with the cilantro and serve.
Per Serving:
calories: 191 | fat: 9g | protein: 24g | carbs: 3g | net carbs: 2g | fiber: 1g

Chicken and Bacon Rolls

Prep time: 10 minutes | Cook time: 35 minutes | Serves 4

1 tbsp fresh chives, chopped
8 ounces blue cheese
2 pounds chicken breasts, skinless, boneless, halved

12 bacon slices
2 tomatoes, chopped
Salt and ground black pepper, to taste

1 Set a pan over medium heat, place in the bacon, cook until halfway done, remove to a plate. In a bowl, stir together blue cheese, chives, tomatoes, pepper and salt. Use a meat tenderizer to flatten the chicken breasts, season and lay blue cheese mixture on top. Roll them up, and wrap each in a bacon slice. Place the wrapped chicken breasts in a greased baking dish, and roast in the oven at 370°F for 30 minutes. Serve on top of wilted kale.
Per Serving:
Per serving: Kcal 623, Fat 48g, Net Carbs 5g, Protein 38g

Bacon-Wrapped Stuffed Chicken Breasts

Prep time: 15 minutes | Cook time: 30 minutes | Serves 4

½ cup chopped frozen spinach, thawed and squeezed dry
¼ cup cream cheese, softened
¼ cup grated Parmesan cheese
1 jalapeño, seeded and chopped
½ teaspoon kosher salt
1 teaspoon black pepper

2 large boneless, skinless chicken breasts, butterflied and pounded to ½-inch thickness
4 teaspoons salt-free Cajun seasoning
6 slices bacon

1. In a small bowl, combine the spinach, cream cheese, Parmesan cheese, jalapeño, salt, and pepper. Stir until well combined. 2. Place the butterflied chicken breasts on a flat surface. Spread the cream cheese mixture evenly across each piece of chicken. Starting with the narrow end, roll up each chicken breast, ensuring the filling stays inside. Season chicken with the Cajun seasoning, patting it in to ensure it sticks to the meat. 3. Wrap each breast in 3 slices of bacon. Place in the air fryer basket. Set the air fryer to 350°F (177°C) for 30 minutes. Use a meat thermometer to ensure the chicken has reached an internal temperature of 165°F (74°C). 4. Let the chicken stand 5 minutes before slicing each rolled-up breast in half to serve

Uncle Marty's Chicken

Prep time: 10 minutes | Cook time: 20 minutes | Serves 4

1½ pounds (680 g) boneless skinless chicken breasts, halved lengthwise
Salt, to taste
Freshly ground black pepper, to taste
2 eggs
3 tablespoons heavy (whipping) cream
2 cups almond flour
1 tablespoon dried oregano
1 tablespoon garlic powder
¼ cup olive oil

1. Cover the chicken in plastic wrap and use a meat tenderizer or heavy skillet to flatten each piece—pound it pretty vigorously so it is as thin as possible. Season with salt and pepper. 2. In a shallow dish, whisk together the eggs and cream. 3. In another shallow dish, season the almond flour with lots of salt and pepper and stir in the oregano and garlic powder. 4. Place a large skillet over medium-high heat and add the olive oil. 5. Dip each piece of chicken first in the egg wash and then in the almond flour. Coat both sides of the chicken with the flour and carefully transfer the chicken to the hot oil. Cook for about 5 minutes per side or until the almond flour starts to turn golden brown. 6. Remove from the skillet and place on a paper towel-lined platter (you can also transfer the pieces to a baking sheet and keep them warm in a 250ºF (121ºC) oven until ready to serve). Refrigerate leftovers in an airtight container for up to 1 week. Reheat in a skillet over medium heat until warmed through.

Per Serving:
calories: 456 | fat: 28g | protein: 45g | carbs: 6g | net carbs: 4g | fiber: 2g

Chicken Florentine

Prep time: 10 minutes | Cook time: 30 minutes | Serves 4

1 pound (454 g) boneless skinless chicken breasts
Salt, to taste
Freshly ground black pepper, to taste
3 tablespoons butter, divided
¼ white onion, diced
2 garlic cloves, minced
1 cup chicken broth
1 cup heavy (whipping) cream
10 ounces (283 g) fresh spinach, chopped
½ cup grated Parmesan cheese

1. Preheat the oven to 200ºF (93ºC). 2. Season the chicken with salt and pepper. In a large skillet over medium heat, melt 1½ tablespoons of butter. Add the chicken and cook for about 5 minutes per side or until browned. Transfer the chicken to an ovenproof dish and keep it warm in the low oven. 3. Return the skillet to the heat and melt the remaining 1½ tablespoons of butter. 4. Add the onion and garlic. Sauté for 5 to 7 minutes until the onion is softened and translucent. 5. Add the chicken broth. Increase the heat to medium high and simmer for about 3 minutes until reduced slightly 6. Stir in the cream and spinach. Cook for 3 to 4 minutes. Transfer the sauce to the baking dish with the chicken. Top with the Parmesan. Increase the oven temperature to 350ºF (180ºC). Cook for about 5 minutes or until the Parmesan browns slightly. Refrigerate leftovers in an airtight container for up to 5 days.

Per Serving:
calories: 489 | fat: 36g | protein: 36g | carbs: 6g | net carbs: 4g | fiber: 2g

Porchetta-Style Chicken Breasts

Prep time: 10 minutes | Cook time: 15 minutes | Serves 4

½ cup fresh parsley leaves
¼ cup roughly chopped fresh chives
4 cloves garlic, peeled
2 tablespoons lemon juice
3 teaspoons fine sea salt
1 teaspoon dried rubbed sage
1 teaspoon fresh rosemary leaves
1 teaspoon ground fennel
½ teaspoon red pepper flakes
4 (4-ounce / 113-g) boneless, skinless chicken breasts, pounded to ¼ inch thick
8 slices bacon
Sprigs of fresh rosemary, for garnish (optional)

1. Spray the air fryer basket with avocado oil. Preheat the air fryer to 340ºF (171ºC). 2. Place the parsley, chives, garlic, lemon juice, salt, sage, rosemary, fennel, and red pepper flakes in a food processor and purée until a smooth paste forms. 3. Place the chicken breasts on a cutting board and rub the paste all over the tops. With a short end facing you, roll each breast up like a jelly roll to make a log and secure it with toothpicks. 4. Wrap 2 slices of bacon around each chicken breast log to cover the entire breast. Secure the bacon with toothpicks. 5. Place the chicken breast logs in the air fryer basket and air fry for 5 minutes, flip the logs over, and cook for another 5 minutes. Increase the heat to 390ºF (199ºC) and cook until the bacon is crisp, about 5 minutes more. 6. Remove the toothpicks and garnish with fresh rosemary sprigs, if desired, before serving. Store leftovers in an airtight container in the refrigerator for up to 4 days or in the freezer for up to a month. Reheat in a preheated 350ºF (177ºC) air fryer for 5 minutes, then increase the heat to 390ºF (199ºC) and cook for 2 minutes to crisp the bacon.

Merry Christmas Chicken

Prep time: 10 minutes | Cook time: 23 minutes | Serves 4

4 (4.2-ounce) boneless, skinless chicken breasts
1 medium red bell pepper, seeded and chopped
1 medium green bell pepper, seeded and chopped
4 ounces full-fat cream cheese, softened
¼ teaspoon salt
¼ teaspoon black pepper
¼ teaspoon paprika
¼ teaspoon dried parsley

1. Preheat oven to 375ºF. 2. Place wax paper on both sides of chicken breasts. Use a rolling pin, kitchen mallet, or cast iron skillet to pound chicken until thin (less than ¼"). 3. In a medium microwave-safe bowl, microwave bell peppers 3 minutes. 4. In a separate medium bowl, mix cream cheese and softened bell peppers. Add salt and pepper. 5. Cover a large baking sheet with foil. Coat evenly with cooking spray. Lay flattened breasts on baking sheet. 6. Place one-quarter of the cream cheese mixture into the center of each pounded chicken and roll. Secure with a wet toothpick. 7. Garnish chicken with paprika and parsley to continue Christmas theme. 8. Bake 20 minutes. Serve warm.

Per Serving:
calories: 240 | fat: 11g | protein: 28g | carbs: 5g | net carbs: 4g | fiber: 1g

Chicken Breasts with Spinach & Artichoke

Prep time: 10 minutes | Cook time: 55 minutes | Serves 4

4 ounces cream cheese	1 tbsp onion powder
4 chicken breasts	1 tbsp garlic powder
8 oz canned artichoke hearts, chopped	Salt and ground black pepper, to taste
1 cup spinach	4 ounces Monterrey Jack
½ cup Pecorino cheese, grated	cheese, shredded

1. Lay the chicken breasts on a lined baking sheet, season with pepper and salt, set in the oven at 350ºF, and bake for 35 minutes. In a bowl, combine the artichokes with onion powder, Pecorino cheese, salt, spinach, cream cheese, garlic powder, and pepper. 2Remove the chicken from the oven, cut each piece in half, divide artichokes mixture on top, spread with Monterrey cheese, set in the oven at 350ºF, and bake for 20 minutes.

Per Serving:
Per serving: Kcal 431, Fat 21g, Net Carbs 3.5g, Protein 36g

Parmesan-Crusted Chicken

Prep time: 15 minutes | Cook time: 13 minutes | Serves 2

1 tomato, sliced	1 teaspoon butter
8 ounces (227 g) chicken fillets	4 tablespoons water, for sprinkling
2 ounces (57 g) Parmesan, sliced	1 cup water, for cooking

1. Pour water and insert the steamer rack in the instant pot. 2. Then grease the baking mold with butter. 3. Slice the chicken fillets into halves and put them in the mold. 4. Sprinkle the chicken with water and top with tomato and Parmesan. 5. Cover the baking mold with foil and place it on the rack. 6. Close and seal the lid. 7. Cook the meal in Manual mode for 13 minutes. Then allow the natural pressure release for 10 minutes.

Per Serving:
calories: 329 | fat: 16g | protein: 42g | carbs: 2g | net carbs: 2g | fiber: 0g

Fried Chicken Breasts

Prep time: 30 minutes | Cook time: 12 to 14 minutes | Serves 4

1 pound (454 g) boneless, skinless chicken breasts	cheese
¾ cup dill pickle juice	½ teaspoon sea salt
¾ cup finely ground blanched almond flour	½ teaspoon freshly ground black pepper
¾ cup finely grated Parmesan	2 large eggs
	Avocado oil spray

1. Place the chicken breasts in a zip-top bag or between two pieces of plastic wrap. Using a meat mallet or heavy skillet, pound the chicken to a uniform ½-inch thickness. 2. Place the chicken in a large bowl with the pickle juice. Cover and allow to brine in the refrigerator for up to 2 hours. 3. In a shallow dish, combine the almond flour, Parmesan cheese, salt, and pepper. In a separate, shallow bowl, beat the eggs. 4. Drain the chicken and pat it dry with paper towels. Dip in the eggs and then in the flour mixture, making sure to press the coating into the chicken. Spray both sides of the coated breasts with oil. 5. Spray the air fryer basket with oil and put the chicken inside. Set the temperature to 400ºF (204ºC) and air fry for 6 to 7 minutes. 6. Carefully flip the breasts with a spatula. Spray the breasts again with oil and continue cooking for 6 to 7 minutes more, until golden and crispy.

Per Serving:
calories: 319 | fat: 17g | protein: 37g | carbs: 5g | fiber: 3g | sodium: 399mg

Greek Chicken Stir-Fry

Prep time: 15 minutes | Cook time: 15 minutes | Serves 2

1 (6-ounce / 170-g) chicken breast, cut into 1-inch cubes	and sliced
½ medium zucchini, chopped	1 tablespoon coconut oil
½ medium red bell pepper, seeded and chopped	1 teaspoon dried oregano
¼ medium red onion, peeled	½ teaspoon garlic powder
	¼ teaspoon dried thyme

1. Place all ingredients into a large mixing bowl and toss until the coconut oil coats the meat and vegetables. Pour the contents of the bowl into the air fryer basket. 2. Adjust the temperature to 375ºF (191ºC) and air fry for 15 minutes. 3. Shake the basket halfway through the cooking time to redistribute the food. Serve immediately.

Per Serving:
calories: 183 | fat: 9g | protein: 20g | carbs: 4g | fiber: 1g | sodium: 44mg

Chicken Pesto Pizzas

Prep time: 10 minutes | Cook time: 12 minutes | Serves 4

1 pound (454 g) ground chicken thighs	¼ cup basil pesto
¼ teaspoon salt	1 cup shredded Mozzarella cheese
⅛ teaspoon ground black pepper	4 grape tomatoes, sliced

1. Cut four squares of parchment paper to fit into your air fryer basket. 2. Place ground chicken in a large bowl and mix with salt and pepper. Divide mixture into four equal sections. 3. Wet your hands with water to prevent sticking, then press each section into a 6-inch circle onto a piece of ungreased parchment. Place each chicken crust into air fryer basket, working in batches if needed. 4. Adjust the temperature to 350ºF (177ºC) and air fry for 10 minutes, turning crusts halfway through cooking. 5. Spread 1 tablespoon pesto across the top of each crust, then sprinkle with ¼ cup Mozzarella and top with 1 sliced tomato. Continue cooking at 350ºF (177ºC) for 2 minutes. Cheese will be melted and brown when done. Serve warm.

Per Serving:
calories: 302 | fat: 18g | protein: 32g | carbs: 2g | fiber: 0g | sodium: 398mg

Lemon-Basil Turkey Breasts

Prep time: 30 minutes | Cook time: 58 minutes | Serves 4

2 tablespoons olive oil
2 pounds (907 g) turkey breasts, bone-in, skin-on
Coarse sea salt and ground black pepper, to taste
1 teaspoon fresh basil leaves, chopped
2 tablespoons lemon zest, grated

1. Rub olive oil on all sides of the turkey breasts; sprinkle with salt, pepper, basil, and lemon zest. 2. Place the turkey breasts skin side up on the parchment-lined air fryer basket. 3. Cook in the preheated air fryer at 330°F (166°C) for 30 minutes. Now, turn them over and cook an additional 28 minutes. 4. Serve with lemon wedges, if desired. Bon appétit!

Per Serving:
calories: 417 | fat: 23g | protein: 50g | carbs: 0g | fiber: 0g | sodium: 134mg

Chicken Thighs with Broccoli & Green Onions

Prep time: 10 minutes | Cook time: 25 minutes | Serves 2

2 chicken thighs, skinless, boneless, cut into strips
1 tablespoon olive oil
1 teaspoon red pepper flakes
1 teaspoon onion powder
1 tablespoon fresh ginger, grated
¼ cup tamari sauce
½ teaspoon garlic powder
½ cup water
½ cup erythritol
½ teaspoon xanthan gum
½ cup green onions, chopped
1 small head broccoli, cut into florets

1. Set a pan over medium heat and warm oil, cook in the chicken and ginger for 4 minutes. Stir in the water, onion powder, pepper flakes, garlic powder, tamari sauce, xanthan gum, and erythritol, and cook for 15 minutes. Add in the green onions and broccoli, cook for 6 minutes. Serve hot.

Per Serving:
calories: 386 | fat: 26g | protein: 32g | carbs: 6g | net carbs: 4g | fiber: 2g

Cacio e Pepe Spaghetti Squash with Grilled Chicken Thighs

Prep time: 5 minutes | Cook time: 50 minutes | Serves 6

1 medium spaghetti squash (about 3 pounds / 1.4 kg)
¼ cup (½ stick) butter
1 cup finely grated hard cheese, such as Parmigiano-Reggiano or Pecorino Romano, plus extra for garnish
½ teaspoon ground black pepper
Sea salt, to taste
2 pounds (907 g) bone-in, skin-on chicken thighs, grilled or baked, then sliced

1. Preheat the oven to 375°F (190°C). 2. Make the spaghetti squash noodles: Slice the spaghetti squash in half crosswise. Scoop out the seeds, then sprinkle the cut sides with salt and pepper. Place both halves face down on a rimmed baking sheet and roast for 35 to 45 minutes, until the flesh of the squash is translucent and the skin begins to soften and easily separates from the "noodles" inside. 3. Allow the squash to cool enough that you can handle it (or carefully use tongs to hold it while still hot), then scoop out the "noodles" into a large serving bowl. Set aside. 4. Melt the butter in a large skillet and add the spaghetti squash noodles, cheese, and pepper, tossing everything together until the cheese begins to melt and coats the noodles. 5. Garnish with a pinch or two of sea salt and more black pepper and grated cheese, and serve with the chicken thighs.

Per Serving:
calories: 561 | fat: 41g | protein: 40g | carbs: 8g | net carbs: 8g | fiber: 0g

Curry Chicken Salad

Prep time: 10 minutes | Cook time: 0 minutes | Serves 4

1½ pounds boneless, skinless chicken thighs, cooked
⅓ cup mayonnaise, homemade or store-bought
2 tablespoons sour cream
Juice of ½ lemon
1½ tablespoons minced fresh
chives, plus extra for garnish
1½ teaspoons curry powder
¼ teaspoon pink Himalayan salt
¼ teaspoon ground black pepper
2 stalks celery, chopped

1. Chop the cooked chicken into bite-sized pieces and set aside. 2. Put the mayo, sour cream, lemon juice, chives, curry powder, salt, and pepper in a medium-sized mixing bowl and stir to combine. 3. Add the chicken pieces and celery to the mayo mixture and toss to coat thoroughly. Serve garnished with additional chives, if desired.

Per Serving:
calories: 339 | fat: 14g | protein: 25g | carbs: 2g | net carbs: 1g | fiber: 1g

Lemon Chicken

Prep time: 5 minutes | Cook time: 20 to 25 minutes | Serves 4

8 bone-in chicken thighs, skin on
1 tablespoon olive oil
1½ teaspoons lemon-pepper seasoning
½ teaspoon paprika
½ teaspoon garlic powder
¼ teaspoon freshly ground black pepper
Juice of ½ lemon

1. Preheat the air fryer to 360°F (182°C). 2. Place the chicken in a large bowl and drizzle with the olive oil. Top with the lemon-pepper seasoning, paprika, garlic powder, and freshly ground black pepper. Toss until thoroughly coated. 3. Working in batches if necessary, arrange the chicken in a single layer in the basket of the air fryer. Pausing halfway through the cooking time to turn the chicken, air fry for 20 to 25 minutes, until a thermometer inserted into the thickest piece registers 165°F (74°C). 4. Transfer the chicken to a serving platter and squeeze the lemon juice over the top.

Per Serving:
calories: 399 | fat: 19g | protein: 56g | carbs: 1g | fiber: 0g | sodium: 367mg

Chicken Paella with Chorizo

Prep time: 15 minutes | Cook time: 45 minutes | Serves 6

18 chicken drumsticks
12 oz chorizo, chopped
1 white onion, chopped
4 oz jarred piquillo peppers, finely diced
2 tbsp olive oil
½ cup chopped parsley
1tsp smoked paprika

2tbsp tomato puree
½ cup white wine
1cup chicken broth
2cups cauli rice
1 cup chopped green beans
1 lemon, cut in wedges
Salt and pepper, to taste

1Preheat the oven to 350ºF. 2Heat the olive oil in a cast iron pan over medium heat, meanwhile season the chicken with salt and black pepper, and fry in the hot oil on both sides for 10 minutes to lightly brown. After, remove onto a plate with a perforated spoon. 3Then, add the chorizo and onion to the hot oil, and sauté for 4 minutes. Include the tomato puree, piquillo peppers, and paprika, and let simmer for 2 minutes. Add the broth, and bring the ingredients to boil for 6 minutes until slightly reduced. 4Stir in the cauli rice, white wine, green beans, half of the parsley, and lay the chicken on top. Transfer the pan to the oven and continue cooking for 20-25 minutes. Let the paella sit to cool for 10 minutes before serving garnished with the remaining parsley and lemon wedges.

Per Serving:
Per serving: Kcal 440, Fat 28g, Net Carbs 3g, Protein 22g

Chicken Scarpariello with Spicy Sausage

Prep time: 10 minutes | Cook time: 45 minutes | Serves 6

1 pound boneless chicken thighs
Sea salt, for seasoning
Freshly ground black pepper, for seasoning
3 tablespoons good-quality olive oil, divided
½ pound Italian sausage (sweet

or hot)
1 tablespoon minced garlic
1 pimiento, chopped
¼ cup dry white wine
1 cup chicken stock
2 tablespoons chopped fresh parsley

1. Preheat the oven. Set the oven temperature to 425°F. 2. Brown the chicken and sausage. Pat the chicken thighs dry with paper towels and season them lightly with salt and pepper. In a large oven-safe skillet over medium-high heat, warm 2 tablespoons of the olive oil. Add the chicken thighs and sausage to the skillet and brown them on all sides, turning them carefully, about 10 minutes. 3. Bake the chicken and sausage. Place the skillet in the oven and bake for 25 minutes or until the chicken is cooked through. Take the skillet out of the oven, transfer the chicken and sausage to a plate, and put the skillet over medium heat on the stovetop. 4. Make the sauce. Warm the remaining 1 tablespoon of olive oil, add the garlic and pimiento, and sauté for 3 minutes. Add the white wine and deglaze the skillet by using a spoon to scrape up any browned bits from the bottom of the skillet. Pour in the chicken stock and bring it to a boil, then reduce the heat to low and simmer until the sauce reduces by about half, about 6 minutes. 5. Finish and serve. Return the chicken and sausage to the skillet, toss it to coat it with the sauce, and serve it topped with the parsley.

Per Serving:
calories: 370 | fat: 30g | protein: 19g | carbs: 3g | net carbs: 3g | fiber: 0g

Coconut Chicken

Prep time: 10 minutes | Cook time: 25 minutes | Serves 4

2 tablespoons olive oil
4 (4-ounce) chicken breasts, cut into 2-inch chunks
½ cup chopped sweet onion
1 cup coconut milk

1 tablespoon curry powder
1 teaspoon ground cumin
1 teaspoon ground coriander
¼ cup chopped fresh cilantro

1. In a small bowl, whisk together the olive oil, rosemary, garlic, and salt. 2. Place the racks in a sealable freezer bag and pour the olive oil mixture into the bag. Massage the meat through the bag so it is coated with the marinade. Press the air out of the bag and seal it. 3. Marinate the lamb racks in the refrigerator for 1 to 2 hours. 4. Preheat the oven to 450°F. 5. Place a large ovenproof skillet over medium-high heat. Take the lamb racks out of the bag and sear them in the skillet on all sides, about 5 minutes in total. 6. Arrange the racks upright in the skillet, with the bones interlaced, and roast them in the oven until they reach your desired doneness, about 20 minutes for medium-rare or until the internal temperature reaches 125°F. 7. Let the lamb rest for 10 minutes and then cut the racks into chops. 8. Serve 4 chops per person.

Per Serving:
calories: 354 | fat: 30g | protein: 21g | carbs: 0g | net carbs: 0g | fiber: 0g

Cobb Salad

Prep time: 15 minutes | Cook time: 8 minutes | Serves 4

8 slices reduced-sodium bacon
8 chicken breast tenders (about 1½ pounds / 680 g)
8 cups chopped romaine lettuce
1 cup cherry tomatoes, halved
¼ red onion, thinly sliced
2 hard-boiled eggs, peeled and sliced
Avocado-Lime Dressing:
½ cup plain Greek yogurt

¼ cup almond milk
½ avocado
Juice of ½ lime
3 scallions, coarsely chopped
1 clove garlic
2 tablespoons fresh cilantro
⅛ teaspoon ground cumin
Salt and freshly ground black pepper, to taste

1. Preheat the air fryer to 400°F (204ºC). 2. Wrap a piece of bacon around each piece of chicken and secure with a toothpick. Working in batches if necessary, arrange the bacon-wrapped chicken in a single layer in the air fryer basket. Air fry for 8 minutes until the bacon is browned and a thermometer inserted into the thickest piece of chicken register 165°F (74ºC). Let cool for a few minutes, then slice into bite-size pieces. 3. To make the dressing: In a blender or food processor, combine the yogurt, milk, avocado, lime juice, scallions, garlic, cilantro, and cumin. Purée until smooth. Season to taste with salt and freshly ground pepper. 4. To assemble the salad, in a large bowl, combine the lettuce, tomatoes, and onion. Drizzle the dressing over the vegetables and toss gently until thoroughly combined. Arrange the chicken and eggs on top just before serving.

Per Serving:
calories: 630 | fat: 44g | protein: 48g | carbs: 10g | net carbs: 6g | fiber: 4g

Cheese Stuffed Chicken Breasts with Spinach

Prep time: 10 minutes | Cook time: 20 minutes | Serves 4

	Breading:
4 chicken breasts, boneless and skinless	2 eggs
½ cup mozzarella cheese	⅓ cup almond flour
⅓ cup Parmesan cheese	2 tbsp olive oil
6 ounces cream cheese	½ tsp parsley
2 cups spinach, chopped	⅓ cup Parmesan cheese
A pinch of nutmeg	A pinch of onion powder
½ tsp minced garlic	

1Pound the chicken until it doubles in size. Mix the cream cheese, spinach, mozzarella, nutmeg, salt, black pepper, and Parmesan cheese in a bowl. Divide the mixture between the chicken breasts and spread it out evenly. Wrap the chicken in a plastic wrap. Refrigerate for 15 minutes. 2Heat the oil in a pan and preheat the oven to 370ºF. Beat the eggs and combine all other breading ingredients in a bowl. Dip the chicken in egg first, then in the breading mixture. Cook in the pan until browned. Place on a lined baking sheet and bake for 20 minutes.

Per Serving:
Per serving: Kcal 491, Fat: 36g, Net Carbs: 3.5g, Protein: 38g

Chicken Kiev

Prep time: 15 minutes | Cook time: 25 minutes | Serves 4

1 cup (2 sticks) unsalted butter, softened (or butter-flavored coconut oil for dairy-free)	1 teaspoon fine sea salt, divided
2 tablespoons lemon juice	4 (4-ounce / 113-g) boneless, skinless chicken breasts
2 tablespoons plus 1 teaspoon chopped fresh parsley leaves, divided, plus more for garnish	2 large eggs
	2 cups pork dust
2 tablespoons chopped fresh tarragon leaves	1 teaspoon ground black pepper
	Sprig of fresh parsley, for garnish
3 cloves garlic, minced	Lemon slices, for serving

1. Spray the air fryer basket with avocado oil. Preheat the air fryer to 350ºF (177ºC). 2. In a medium-sized bowl, combine the butter, lemon juice, 2 tablespoons of the parsley, the tarragon, garlic, and ¼ teaspoon of the salt. Cover and place in the fridge to harden for 7 minutes. 3. While the butter mixture chills, place one of the chicken breasts on a cutting board. With a sharp knife held parallel to the cutting board, make a 1-inch-wide incision at the top of the breast. Carefully cut into the breast to form a large pocket, leaving a ½-inch border along the sides and bottom. Repeat with the other 3 breasts. 4. Stuff one-quarter of the butter mixture into each chicken breast and secure the openings with toothpicks. 5. Beat the eggs in a small shallow dish. In another shallow dish, combine the pork dust, the remaining 1 teaspoon of parsley, the remaining ¾ teaspoon of salt, and the pepper. 6. One at a time, dip the chicken breasts in the egg, shake off the excess egg, and dredge the breasts in the pork dust mixture. Use your hands to press the pork dust onto each breast to form a nice crust. If you desire a thicker coating, dip it again in the egg and pork dust. As you finish, spray each coated chicken breast with avocado oil and place it in the air fryer basket. 7. Roast the chicken in the air fryer for 15 minutes, flip the breasts, and cook for another 10 minutes, or until the internal temperature of the chicken is 165ºF (74ºC) and the crust is golden brown. 8. Serve garnished with chopped fresh parsley and a parsley sprig, with lemon slices on the side. 9. Store leftovers in an airtight container in the refrigerator for up to 4 days or in the freezer for up to a month. Reheat in a preheated 350ºF (177ºC) air fryer for 5 minutes, or until heated through.

Per Serving:
calories: 569 | fat: 40g | protein: 48g | carbs: 3g | net carbs: 3g | fiber: 0g

Cilantro Chicken Breasts with Mayo-Avocado Sauce

Prep time: 10 minutes | Cook time: 16 minutes | Serves 4

For the Sauce	4chicken breasts
1 avocado, pitted	Pink salt and black pepper to taste
½ cup mayonnaise	
Salt to taste	1 cup chopped cilantro leaves
For the Chicken	½ cup chicken broth
3tbsp ghee	

1Spoon the avocado, mayonnaise, and salt into a small food processor and puree until a smooth sauce is derived. Pour sauce into a jar and refrigerate while you make the chicken. 2Melt ghee in a large skillet, season chicken with salt and black pepper and fry for 4 minutes on each side to golden brown. Remove chicken to a plate. 3Pour the broth in the same skillet and add the cilantro. Bring to simmer covered for 3 minutes and add the chicken. Cover and cook on low heat for 5 minutes until the liquid has reduced and chicken is fragrant. Dish chicken only into serving plates and spoon the mayoavocado sauce over.

Per Serving:
Per serving: Kcal 398, Fat 32g, Net Carbs 4g, Protein 24g

Pork Rind Fried Chicken

Prep time: 30 minutes | Cook time: 20 minutes | Serves 4

¼ cup buffalo sauce	¼ teaspoon ground black pepper
4 (4-ounce / 113-g) boneless, skinless chicken breasts	2 ounces (57 g) plain pork rinds, finely crushed
½ teaspoon paprika	
½ teaspoon garlic powder	

1. Pour buffalo sauce into a large sealable bowl or bag. Add chicken and toss to coat. Place sealed bowl or bag into refrigerator and let marinate at least 30 minutes up to overnight. 2. Remove chicken from marinade but do not shake excess sauce off chicken. Sprinkle both sides of thighs with paprika, garlic powder, and pepper. 3. Place pork rinds into a large bowl and press each chicken breast into pork rinds to coat evenly on both sides. 4. Place chicken into ungreased air fryer basket. Adjust the temperature to 400ºF (204ºC) and roast for 20 minutes, turning chicken halfway through cooking. Chicken will be golden and have an internal temperature of at least 165ºF (74ºC) when done. Serve warm.

Per Serving:
calories: 217 | fat: 8g | protein: 35g | carbs: 1g | fiber: 0g | sodium: 400mg

Cheesy Bacon and Broccoli Chicken

Prep time: 10 minutes | Cook time: 1 hour | Serves 2

2 tablespoons ghee
2 boneless skinless chicken breasts
Pink Himalayan salt
Freshly ground black pepper
4 bacon slices

6 ounces cream cheese, at room temperature
2 cups frozen broccoli florets, thawed
½ cup shredded Cheddar cheese

1. Preheat the oven to 375°F. 2. Choose a baking dish that is large enough to hold both chicken breasts and coat it with the ghee. 3. Pat dry the chicken breasts with a paper towel, and season with pink Himalayan salt and pepper. 4. Place the chicken breasts and the bacon slices in the baking dish, and bake for 25 minutes. 5. Transfer the chicken to a cutting board and use two forks to shred it. Season it again with pink Himalayan salt and pepper. 6. Place the bacon on a paper towel–lined plate to crisp up, and then crumble it. 7. In a medium bowl, mix to combine the cream cheese, shredded chicken, broccoli, and half of the bacon crumbles. Transfer the chicken mixture to the baking dish, and top with the Cheddar and the remaining half of the bacon crumbles. 8. Bake until the cheese is bubbling and browned, about 35 minutes, and serve.

Per Serving:
calories: 935 | fat: 66g | protein: 75g | carbs: 10g | net carbs: 8g | fiber: 3g

Baked Cheesy Mushroom Chicken

Prep time: 5 minutes | Cook time: 15 minutes | Serves 4

1 tablespoon butter
2 cloves garlic, smashed
½ cup chopped yellow onion
1 pound (454 g) chicken breasts, cubed
10 ounces (283 g) button mushrooms, thinly sliced
1 cup chicken broth
½ teaspoon shallot powder

½ teaspoon turmeric powder
½ teaspoon dried basil
½ teaspoon dried sage
½ teaspoon cayenne pepper
⅓ teaspoon ground black pepper
Kosher salt, to taste
½ cup heavy cream
1 cup shredded Colby cheese

1. Set your Instant Pot to Sauté and melt the butter. 2. Add the garlic, onion, chicken, and mushrooms and sauté for about 4 minutes, or until the vegetables are softened. 3. Add the remaining ingredients except the heavy cream and cheese to the Instant Pot and stir to incorporate. 4. Lock the lid. Select the Meat/Stew mode and set the cooking time for 6 minutes at High Pressure. 5. When the timer beeps, perform a natural pressure release for 10 minutes, then release any remaining pressure. Carefully remove the lid. 6. Stir in the heavy cream until heated through. Pour the mixture into a baking dish and scatter the cheese on top. 7. Bake in the preheated oven at 400°F (205°C) until the cheese bubbles. 8. Allow to cool for 5 minutes and serve.

Per Serving:
calories: 439 | fat: 29g | protein: 34g | carbs: 10g | net carbs: 8g | fiber: 2g

Tex-Mex Chicken Roll-Ups

Prep time: 10 minutes | Cook time: 14 to 17 minutes | Serves 8

2 pounds (907 g) boneless, skinless chicken breasts or thighs
1 teaspoon chili powder
½ teaspoon smoked paprika
½ teaspoon ground cumin
Sea salt and freshly ground

black pepper, to taste
6 ounces (170 g) Monterey Jack cheese, shredded
4 ounces (113 g) canned diced green chiles
Avocado oil spray

1. Place the chicken in a large zip-top bag or between two pieces of plastic wrap. Using a meat mallet or heavy skillet, pound the chicken until it is about ¼ inch thick. 2. In a small bowl, combine the chili powder, smoked paprika, cumin, and salt and pepper to taste. Sprinkle both sides of the chicken with the seasonings. 3. Sprinkle the chicken with the Monterey Jack cheese, then the diced green chiles. 4. Roll up each piece of chicken from the long side, tucking in the ends as you go. Secure the roll-up with a toothpick. 5. Set the air fryer to 350°F (177°C). Spray the outside of the chicken with avocado oil. Place the chicken in a single layer in the basket, working in batches if necessary, and roast for 7 minutes. Flip and cook for another 7 to 10 minutes, until an instant-read thermometer reads 160°F (71°C). 6. Remove the chicken from the air fryer and allow it to rest for about 5 minutes before serving.

Per Serving:
calories: 220 | fat: 10g | protein: 31g | carbs: 1g | fiber: 0g | sodium: 355mg

Buffalo Chicken Wings

Prep time: 10 minutes | Cook time: 20 to 25 minutes | Serves 4

2 tablespoons baking powder
1 teaspoon smoked paprika
Sea salt and freshly ground black pepper, to taste
2 pounds (907 g) chicken wings or chicken drumettes
Avocado oil spray
⅓ cup avocado oil

½ cup Buffalo hot sauce, such as Frank's RedHot
¼ cup (4 tablespoons) unsalted butter
2 tablespoons apple cider vinegar
1 teaspoon minced garlic

1. In a large bowl, stir together the baking powder, smoked paprika, and salt and pepper to taste. Add the chicken wings and toss to coat. 2. Set the air fryer to 400°F (204°C). Spray the wings with oil. 3. Place the wings in the basket in a single layer, working in batches, and air fry for 20 to 25 minutes. Check with an instant-read thermometer and remove when they reach 155°F (68°C). Let rest until they reach 165°F (74°C). 4. While the wings are cooking, whisk together the avocado oil, hot sauce, butter, vinegar, and garlic in a small saucepan over medium-low heat until warm. 5. When the wings are done cooking, toss them with the Buffalo sauce. Serve warm.

Cheese Stuffed Chicken

Prep time: 15 minutes | Cook time: 20 minutes | Serves 4

12 ounces (340 g) chicken fillet
4 ounces (113 g) provolone cheese, sliced
1 tablespoon cream cheese
½ teaspoon dried cilantro
½ teaspoon smoked paprika
1 cup water, for cooking

1. Beat the chicken fillet well and rub it with dried cilantro and smoked paprika. 2. Then spread it with cream cheese and top with Provolone cheese. 3. Roll the chicken fillet into the roll and wrap in the foil. 4. Pour water and insert the rack in the instant pot. 5. Place the chicken roll on the rack. Close and seal the lid. 6. Cook it on Manual mode (High Pressure) for 20 minutes. 7. Make a quick pressure release and slice the chicken roll into the servings.

Per Serving:
calories: 271 | fat: 15g | protein: 32g | carbs: 1g | net carbs: 1g | fiber: 0g

Mezze Cake

Prep time: 10 minutes | Cook time: 35 minutes | Serves 2 to 4

Nonstick cooking spray
2 coconut wraps (one of them is optional)
1 small eggplant, thinly sliced lengthwise
Salt, to taste
1 zucchini, thinly sliced lengthwise
1 (8-ounce / 227-g) jar sun-dried tomatoes packed in olive oil (do not discard oil), chopped or whole
½ (14-ounce / 397-g) can
quartered artichoke hearts
½ cup cauliflower rice
¼ cup black olives, pitted and coarsely chopped
2 precooked sugar-free chicken sausages, cut into bite-size pieces
1 tablespoon dried oregano or marjoram
½ tablespoon garlic powder
Freshly ground black pepper, to taste

1. Preheat the oven to 350ºF (180ºC). Coat a shallow baking dish with nonstick spray and place a coconut wrap in the bottom. 2. Sprinkle the eggplant with ½ teaspoon of salt and let sit for 5 minutes to let the moisture come to the surface. Get a damp towel and wipe off the salt and excess water from the eggplant. 3. Lay the eggplant slices on top of the coconut wrap, then lay the zucchini slices on top of the eggplant. Next add the sun-dried tomatoes and drizzle in the olive oil they're packed in. Sprinkle in the artichoke hearts, then add the cauliflower rice. Scatter the olives on top, then shower the chicken sausage over all the vegetables. Season everything with the oregano, garlic powder, salt, and pepper. 4. Place another coconut wrap over the top of everything, if desired, and bake this vegetable layer "cake" in the oven for about 25 minutes, or until the vegetables are a bit wilted. 5. Turn the oven to broil and cook for another 5 minutes, or until the top is crisp. 6. Remove from the oven and let cool before slicing and serving.

Per Serving:
calories: 510 | fat: 38g | protein: 17g | carbs: 25g | net carbs: 13g | fiber: 12g

Lemon Threaded Chicken Skewers

Prep time: 10 minutes | Cook time: 12 minutes | Serves 4

3 chicken breasts, cut into cubes
2 tbsp olive oil, divided
2/3 jar preserved lemon, flesh removed, drained
2 cloves garlic, minced
½ cup lemon juice
Salt and black pepper to taste
1tsp rosemary leaves to garnish
2to 4 lemon wedges to garnish

1First, thread the chicken onto skewers and set aside. 2In a wide bowl, mix half of the oil, garlic, salt, pepper, and lemon juice, and add the chicken skewers, and lemon rind. Cover the bowl and let the chicken marinate for at least 2 hours in the refrigerator. 3When the marinating time is almost over, preheat a grill to 350ºF, and remove the chicken onto the grill. Cook for 6 minutes on each side. 4Remove and serve warm garnished with rosemary leaves and lemons wedges.

Per Serving:
Per serving: Kcal 350, Fat 11g, Net Carbs 3.5g, Protein 34g

My Favorite Creamy Pesto Chicken

Prep time: 10 minutes | Cook time: 20 minutes | Serves 4

CHICKEN:
¼ cup (60 ml) avocado oil
1 pound (455 g) boneless, skinless chicken breasts, thinly sliced
1 small white onion, thinly sliced
½ cup (105 g) sun-dried tomatoes, drained and chopped
¾ teaspoon dried oregano leaves
½ teaspoon dried thyme leaves
⅛ teaspoon red pepper flakes
PESTO CREAM SAUCE:
2 cloves garlic
¼ cup (37 g) pine nuts
¼ cup (17 g) nutritional yeast
½ cup (120 ml) chicken bone broth
½ cup (120 ml) full-fat coconut milk
½ teaspoon finely ground sea salt
½ teaspoon ground black pepper
½ ounce (14 g) fresh basil leaves and stems
2 medium zucchinis, spiral sliced, raw or cooked, for serving

1. Heat the oil in a large frying pan over medium heat. When hot, add the chicken, onion, sun-dried tomatoes, oregano, thyme, and red pepper flakes. Sauté for 5 minutes, or until fragrant. 2. Meanwhile, place all the ingredients for the pesto cream sauce, except the basil, in a food processor or blender. Blend on high until smooth, about 30 seconds. Add the basil and pulse to break it up slightly, but before the sauce turns a bright green color—don't pulverize the basil! 3. Pour the sauce into the pan and toss the chicken to coat. Reduce the heat to low, cover, and cook for 15 minutes, stirring every couple of minutes, until the chicken is cooked through. 4. Divide the spiral-sliced zucchini among 4 dinner plates and top with equal portions of the chicken and sauce. Dig in!

Per Serving:
calories: 455 | fat: 29g | protein: 32g | carbs: 16g | net carbs: 11g | fiber: 4g

Slow Cooker Chicken Thighs with Sun-Dried Tomatoes

Prep time: 10 minutes | Cook time: 10 minutes | Serves 4

¼ cup olive oil, divided
4 (4-ounce) boneless chicken thighs
Sea salt, for seasoning
Freshly ground black pepper, for seasoning
1 (28-ounce) can sodium-free diced tomatoes
½ cup chicken stock

4 ounces julienned oil-packed sun-dried tomatoes
2 tablespoons minced garlic
2 tablespoons dried oregano
Pinch red pepper flakes
2 tablespoons chopped fresh parsley

1. Grease the slow cooker. Coat the bowl of the slow cooker with 1 tablespoon of the olive oil. 2. Brown the chicken. Pat the chicken thighs dry with paper towels and season them lightly with salt and pepper. In a large skillet over medium-high heat, warm the remaining 3 tablespoons of olive oil. Add the chicken thighs and brown them, turning them once, about 10 minutes in total. 3. Cook in the slow cooker. Put the tomatoes, chicken stock, sun-dried tomatoes, garlic, oregano, and red pepper flakes into the slow cooker and stir to combine the ingredients. Add the chicken, making sure it is covered by the sauce, place the lid on the slow cooker, and cook it on high heat for 4 to 6 hours or on low heat for 6 to 8 hours. 4. Serve. Divide the chicken thighs and sauce between four bowls and top with the parsley.

Per Serving:
calories: 468 | fat: 36g | protein: 24g | carbs: 12g | net carbs: 6g | fiber: 6g

Chapter 3 Beef, Pork, and Lamb

BLTA Cups

Prep time: 5 minutes | Cook time: 20 minutes | Serves 2

12 bacon slices
¼ head romaine lettuce, chopped
½ avocado, diced
½ cup halved grape tomatoes
2 tablespoons sour cream

1. Preheat the oven to 400°F. You will need a muffin tin. (I use a jumbo muffin tin, but you can use a standard muffin tin if that's what you have.) 2. Turn a muffin tin upside down, and lay it on a baking sheet. Make a cross with 2 bacon strip halves over the upside-down muffin tin. Take 2 more bacon strip halves and put them around the perimeter of the crossed halves. Take 1 full bacon strip and circle it around the base of the upside down tin and then use a toothpick to hold that piece together tightly. Repeat to make 4 cups total. 3. Bake for 20 minutes, or until the bacon is crispy. Transfer to a cooling rack and let rest for at least 10 minutes. 4. Once the bacon cups have become firm, carefully remove them from the muffin cups and place two cups on each of two plates. Fill the cups evenly with the romaine, add the avocado, tomatoes, and a dollop of sour cream, and serve.

Per Serving:
2 bowls :calories: 354 | fat: 28g | protein: 20g | carbs: 7g | net carbs: 3g | fiber: 4g

Korean Beef and Pickled Vegetable Bowls

Prep time: 15 minutes | Cook time: 10 minutes | Serves 6

1 tablespoon vegetable oil
5 garlic cloves, thinly sliced
1 tablespoon julienned fresh ginger
2 dried red chiles
1 cup sliced onions
1 pound (454 g) 80% lean ground beef
1 tablespoon gochujang, adjusted to taste
1 cup fresh basil leaves, divided
1 tablespoon coconut aminos
1 teaspoon Swerve
2 tablespoons freshly squeezed

lime juice
1 teaspoon salt
1 teaspoon freshly ground pepper
¼ cup water
1 teaspoon sesame oil
For the Pickled Vegetables:
1 cucumber, peeled, coarsely grated
1 turnip, coarsely grated
¼ cup white vinegar
½ teaspoon salt
½ teaspoon Swerve

1. Select Sauté mode of the Instant Pot. When the pot is hot, add the oil and heat until it is shimmering. 2. Add the garlic, ginger, and chiles and sauté for 1 minute. 3. Add the onions and sauté for 1 minute. 4. Add the ground beef and cooking for 4 minutes.. 5. Add the gochujang, ½ cup of basil, coconut aminos, sweetener, lime juice, salt, pepper, water, and sesame oil, and stir to combine. 6. Lock the lid. Select Manual mode. Set the time for 4 minutes on High Pressure. 7. When cooking is complete, let the pressure release naturally for 5 minutes, then release any remaining pressure. Unlock the lid and stir in the remaining ½ cup of basil. 8. Meanwhile, put the cucumber and turnip in a medium bowl and mix with the vinegar, salt, and sweetener. To serve, portion the basil beef into individual bowls and serve with the pickled salad.

Per Serving:
calories: 298 | fat: 20.0g | protein: 22.0g | carbs: 8.0g | net carbs: 7.0g | fiber: 1.0g

Steak Bites with Garlic Dipping Sauce

Prep time: 5 minutes | Cook time: 10 minutes | Serves 4

Steak Bites:
1 pound (454 g) sirloin steak
1 teaspoon salt
¼ teaspoon pepper
4 tablespoons butter
Dipping Sauce:
½ cup mayonnaise
1 teaspoon lemon juice
1 roasted garlic clove, mashed
⅛ teaspoon red pepper flakes

1. Cut steak into 1-inch cubes. Sprinkle with salt and pepper. Press the Sauté button and add butter to Instant Pot. When butter is melted, add steak and sear each side until desired doneness, about 10 minutes. Press the Cancel button and place steak bites into dish. 2. In medium bowl, mix mayo, lemon juice, roasted garlic, and red pepper flakes. Serve steak bites with dipping sauce.

Per Serving:
calories: 518 | fat: 43g | protein: 23g | carbs: 1g | net carbs: 1g | fiber: 0g

Grilled Herbed Pork Kebabs

Prep time: 10 minutes | Cook time: 15 minutes | Serves 4

¼ cup good-quality olive oil
1 tablespoon minced garlic
2 teaspoons dried oregano
1 teaspoon dried basil
1 teaspoon dried parsley
½ teaspoon sea salt
¼ teaspoon freshly ground black pepper
1 (1-pound) pork tenderloin, cut into 1½-inch pieces

1. Marinate the pork. In a medium bowl, stir together the olive oil, garlic, oregano, basil, parsley, salt, and pepper. Add the pork pieces and toss to coat them in the marinade. Cover the bowl and place it in the refrigerator for 2 to 4 hours. 2. Make the kebabs. Divide the pork pieces between four skewers, making sure to not crowd the meat. 3. Grill the kebabs. Preheat your grill to medium-high heat. Grill the skewers for about 12 minutes, turning to cook all sides of the pork, until the pork is cooked through. 4. Serve. Rest the skewers for 5 minutes. Divide the skewers between four plates and serve them immediately.

Per Serving:
calories: 261 | fat: 18g | protein: 24g | carbs: 1g | net carbs: 1g | fiber: 0g

Zoodle, Bacon, Spinach, and Halloumi Gratin

Prep time: 10 minutes | Cook time: 25 minutes | Serves 4

2 large zucchinis, spiralized	1 cup heavy cream
4 slices bacon, chopped	½ cup sugar-free tomato sauce
2 cups baby spinach	1 cup grated mozzarella cheese
4 ounces halloumi cheese, cut into cubes	½ teaspoon dried Italian mixed herbs
2 cloves garlic, minced	Salt and black pepper to taste

1. Preheat the oven to 350°F. Place the cast iron pan over medium heat and fry the bacon for 4 minutes, then add garlic and cook for 1 minute. 2. In a bowl, mix the heavy cream, tomato sauce, and 1/6 cup water and add it to the pan. Stir in the zucchini, spinach, halloumi, Italian herbs, salt, and pepper. Sprinkle the mozzarella cheese on top, and transfer the pan to the oven. Bake for 20 minutes or until the cheese is golden. Serve the gratin warm.

Per Serving:
calories: 350 | fat: 27g | protein: 16g | carbs: 5g | net carbs: 4g | fiber: 1g

Pork and Mushroom Bake

Prep time: 5 minutes | Cook time: 45 minutes | Serves 6

1 onion, chopped	½ cup sliced mushrooms
2(10.5-oz) cans mushroom soup	Salt and ground pepper, to taste
6 pork chops	

1. Preheat the oven to 370°F. 2. Season the pork chops with salt and black pepper, and place in a baking dish. Combine the mushroom soup, mushrooms, and onion, in a bowl. Pour this mixture over the pork chops. Bake for 45 minutes.

Per Serving:
calories: 302 | fat: 10g | protein: 42g | carbs: 9g | net carbs: 8g | fiber: 1g

Meatballs in Creamy Almond Sauce

Prep time: 15 minutes | Cook time: 35 minutes | Serves 4 to 6

8 ounces (227 g) ground veal or pork	½ teaspoon ground nutmeg
8 ounces (227 g) ground beef	2 teaspoons chopped fresh flat-leaf Italian parsley, plus ¼ cup, divided
½ cup finely minced onion, divided	½ cup extra-virgin olive oil, divided
1 large egg, beaten	¼ cup slivered almonds
¼ cup almond flour	1 cup dry white wine or chicken broth
1½ teaspoons salt, divided	
1 teaspoon garlic powder	¼ cup unsweetened almond butter
½ teaspoon freshly ground black pepper	

1. In a large bowl, combine the veal, beef, ¼ cup onion, and the egg and mix well with a fork. In a small bowl, whisk together the almond flour, 1 teaspoon salt, garlic powder, pepper, and nutmeg. Add to the meat mixture along with 2 teaspoons chopped parsley and incorporate well. Form the mixture into small meatballs, about 1 inch in diameter, and place on a plate. Let sit for 10 minutes at room temperature. 2. In a large skillet, heat ¼ cup oil over medium-high heat. Add the meatballs to the hot oil and brown on all sides, cooking in batches if necessary, 2 to 3 minutes per side. Remove from skillet and keep warm. 3. In the hot skillet, sauté the remaining ¼ cup minced onion in the remaining ¼ cup olive oil for 5 minutes. Reduce the heat to medium-low and add the slivered almonds. Sauté until the almonds are golden, another 3 to 5 minutes. 4. In a small bowl, whisk together the white wine, almond butter, and remaining ½ teaspoon salt. Add to the skillet and bring to a boil, stirring constantly. Reduce the heat to low, return the meatballs to skillet, and cover. Cook until the meatballs are cooked through, another 8 to 10 minutes. 5. Remove from the heat, stir in the remaining ¼ cup chopped parsley, and serve the meatballs warm and drizzled with almond sauce.

Per Serving:
calories: 447 | fat: 36g | protein: 20g | carbs: 7g | fiber: 2g | sodium: 659mg

Pork Lettuce Cups

Prep time: 10 minutes | Cook time: 14 minutes | Serves 6

2 pounds (907 g) ground pork	1head Iceberg lettuce
1 tablespoon ginger- garlic paste	2sprigs green onion, chopped
Pink salt and chili pepper to taste	1 red bell pepper, seeded and chopped
1 teaspoon ghee	½ cucumber, finely chopped

1. Put the pork with ginger-garlic paste, salt, and chili pepper seasoning in a saucepan. Cook for 10 minutes over medium heat while breaking any lumps until the pork is no longer pink. Drain liquid and add the ghee, melt and brown the meat for 4 minutes, continuously stirring. Turn the heat off. 2. Pat the lettuce dry with a paper towel and in each leaf, spoon two to three tablespoons of pork, top with green onions, bell pepper, and cucumber. Serve with soy drizzling sauce.

Per Serving:
calories: 311 | fat: 24g | protein: 19g | carbs: 6g | net carbs: 4g | fiber: 2g

Paprika Pork Ribs

Prep time: 10 minutes | Cook time: 30 minutes | Serves 4

1 pound (454 g) pork ribs	3 tablespoons avocado oil
1 tablespoon ground paprika	1 teaspoon salt
1 teaspoon ground turmeric	½ cup beef broth

1. Rub the pork ribs with ground paprika, turmeric, salt, and avocado oil. 2. Then pour the beef broth in the instant pot. 3. Arrange the pork ribs in the instant pot. Close and seal the lid. 4. Cook the pork ribs for 30 minutes on Manual mode (High Pressure). 5. When the time is finished, make a quick pressure release and chop the ribs into servings.

Per Serving:
calories: 335 | fat: 22g | protein: 31g | carbs: 2g | net carbs: 1g | fiber: 1g

Cilantro Lime Shredded Pork

Prep time: 5 minutes | Cook time: 30 minutes | Serves 4

1 tablespoon chili adobo sauce
1 tablespoon chili powder
2 teaspoons salt
1 teaspoon garlic powder
1 teaspoon cumin
½ teaspoon pepper
1 (2½ to 3 pounds / 1.1 to 1.4 kg) cubed pork butt
1 tablespoon coconut oil
2 cups beef broth
1 lime, cut into wedges
¼ cup chopped cilantro

1. In a small bowl, mix adobo sauce, chili powder, salt, garlic powder, cumin, and pepper. 2. Press the Sauté button on Instant Pot and add coconut oil to pot. Rub spice mixture onto cubed pork butt. Place pork into pot and sear for 3 to 5 minutes per side. Add broth. 3. Press the Cancel button. Lock Lid. Press the Manual button and adjust time to 30 minutes. 4. When timer beeps, let pressure naturally release until the float valve drops, and unlock lid. 5. Shred pork with fork. Pork should easily fall apart. For extra-crispy pork, place single layer in skillet on stove over medium heat. Cook for 10 to 15 minutes or until water has cooked out and pork becomes brown and crisp. Serve warm with fresh lime wedges and cilantro garnish.

Per Serving:
calories: 570 | fat: 36g | protein: 55g | carbs: 3g | net carbs: 2g | fiber: 1g

Chile Verde Pulled Pork with Tomatillos

Prep time: 15 minutes | Cook time: 1 hour 3 minutes | Serves 6

2 pounds (907 g) pork shoulder, cut into 6 equal-sized pieces
1 teaspoon sea salt
½ teaspoon ground black pepper
2 jalapeño peppers, deseeded and stemmed
1 pound (454 g) tomatillos, husks removed and quartered
3 garlic cloves
1 tablespoon lime juice
3 tablespoons fresh cilantro, chopped
1 medium white onion, chopped
1 teaspoon ground cumin
½ teaspoon dried oregano
1⅔ cups chicken broth
1½ tablespoons olive oil

1. Season the pork pieces with the salt and pepper. Gently rub the seasonings into the pork cuts. Set aside. 2. Combine the jalapeños, tomatillos, garlic cloves, lime juice, cilantro, onions, cumin, oregano, and chicken broth in the blender. Pulse until well combined. Set aside. 3. Select Sauté mode and add the olive oil to the pot. Once the oil is hot, add the pork cuts and sear for 4 minutes per side or until browned. 4. Pour the jalapeño sauce over the pork and lightly stir to coat well. 5. Lock the lid. Select Manual mode and set cooking time for 55 minutes on High Pressure. 6. When cooking is complete, allow the pressure to release naturally for 10 minutes and then release the remaining pressure. 7. Open the lid. Transfer the pork pieces to a cutting board and use two forks to shred the pork. 8. Transfer the shredded pork back to the pot and stir to combine the pork with the sauce. Transfer to a serving platter. Serve warm.

Per Serving:
calories: 381 | fat: 24.8g | protein: 29.3g | carbs: 11.1g | net carbs: 8.3g | fiber: 2.8g

Beefy Poppers

Prep time: 15 minutes | Cook time: 15 minutes | Makes 8 poppers

8 medium jalapeño peppers, stemmed, halved, and seeded
1 (8-ounce / 227-g) package cream cheese (or Kite Hill brand cream cheese style spread for dairy-free), softened
2 pounds (907 g) ground beef
(85% lean)
1 teaspoon fine sea salt
½ teaspoon ground black pepper
8 slices thin-cut bacon
Fresh cilantro leaves, for garnish

1. Spray the air fryer basket with avocado oil. Preheat the air fryer to 400ºF (204ºC). 2. Stuff each jalapeño half with a few tablespoons of cream cheese. Place the halves back together again to form 8 jalapeños. 3. Season the ground beef with the salt and pepper and mix with your hands to incorporate. Flatten about ¼ pound (113 g) of ground beef in the palm of your hand and place a stuffed jalapeño in the center. Fold the beef around the jalapeño, forming an egg shape. Wrap the beef-covered jalapeño with a slice of bacon and secure it with a toothpick. 4. Place the jalapeños in the air fryer basket, leaving space between them (if you're using a smaller air fryer, work in batches if necessary), and air fry for 15 minutes, or until the beef is cooked through and the bacon is crispy. Garnish with cilantro before serving. 5. Store leftovers in an airtight container in the fridge for 3 days or in the freezer for up to a month. Reheat in a preheated 350ºF (177ºC) air fryer for 4 minutes, or until heated through and the bacon is crispy.

Parmesan-Crusted Steak

Prep time: 30 minutes | Cook time: 12 minutes | Serves 6

½ cup (1 stick) unsalted butter, at room temperature
1 cup finely grated Parmesan cheese
¼ cup finely ground blanched almond flour
1½ pounds (680 g) New York strip steak
Sea salt and freshly ground black pepper, to taste

1. Place the butter, Parmesan cheese, and almond flour in a food processor. Process until smooth. Transfer to a sheet of parchment paper and form into a log. Wrap tightly in plastic wrap. Freeze for 45 minutes or refrigerate for at least 4 hours. 2. While the butter is chilling, season the steak liberally with salt and pepper. Let the steak rest at room temperature for about 45 minutes. 3. Place the grill pan or basket in your air fryer, set it to 400ºF (204ºC), and let it preheat for 5 minutes. 4. Working in batches, if necessary, place the steak on the grill pan and air fry for 4 minutes. Flip and cook for 3 minutes more, until the steak is brown on both sides. 5. Remove the steak from the air fryer and arrange an equal amount of the Parmesan butter on top of each steak. Return the steak to the air fryer and continue cooking for another 5 minutes, until an instant-read thermometer reads 120ºF (49ºC) for medium-rare and the crust is golden brown (or to your desired doneness). 6. Transfer the cooked steak to a plate; let rest for 10 minutes before serving.

Per Serving:
calories: 319 | fat: 20g | protein: 32g | carbs: 3g | net carbs: 2g | fiber: 1g

Beef Cotija Cheeseburger

Prep time: 10 minutes | Cook time: 14 minutes | Serves 4

1 pound (454 g) ground beef	Salt and black pepper to taste
1 teaspoon dried parsley	1 cup cotija cheese, shredded
½ teaspoon Worcestershire sauce	4 low carb buns, halved

1. Preheat a grill to 400ºF and grease the grate with cooking spray. 2. Mix the beef, parsley, Worcestershire sauce, salt, and black pepper with your hands until evenly combined. Make medium sized patties out of the mixture, about 4 patties. Cook on the grill for 7 minutes one side to be cooked through and no longer pink. 3. Flip the patties and top with cheese. Cook for 7 minutes, until the cheese melts. Remove the patties and sandwich into two halves of a bun each. Serve with a tomato dipping sauce and zucchini fries.

Per Serving:
calories: 324 | fat: 23g | protein: 29g | carbs: 2g | net carbs: 2g | fiber: 0g

Garlic Balsamic London Broil

Prep time: 30 minutes | Cook time: 8 to 10 minutes | Serves 8

2 pounds (907 g) London broil	2 tablespoons olive oil
3 large garlic cloves, minced	Sea salt and ground black pepper, to taste
3 tablespoons balsamic vinegar	½ teaspoon dried hot red pepper flakes
3 tablespoons whole-grain mustard	

1. Score both sides of the cleaned London broil. 2. Thoroughly combine the remaining ingredients; massage this mixture into the meat to coat it on all sides. Let it marinate for at least 3 hours. 3. Set the air fryer to 400ºF (204ºC); Then cook the London broil for 15 minutes. Flip it over and cook another 10 to 12 minutes. Bon appétit!

Per Serving:
calories: 240 | fat: 15g | protein: 23g | carbs: 2g | fiber: 0g | sodium: 141mg

Steak with Bell Pepper

Prep time: 30 minutes | Cook time: 20 to 23 minutes | Serves 6

¼ cup avocado oil	steak or flank steak, thinly sliced against the grain
¼ cup freshly squeezed lime juice	1 red bell pepper, cored, seeded, and cut into ½-inch slices
2 teaspoons minced garlic	1 green bell pepper, cored, seeded, and cut into ½-inch slices
1 tablespoon chili powder	
½ teaspoon ground cumin	
Sea salt and freshly ground black pepper, to taste	1 large onion, sliced
1 pound (454 g) top sirloin	

1. In a small bowl or blender, combine the avocado oil, lime juice, garlic, chili powder, cumin, and salt and pepper to taste. 2. Place the sliced steak in a zip-top bag or shallow dish. Place the bell peppers and onion in a separate zip-top bag or dish. Pour half the marinade over the steak and the other half over the vegetables. Seal both bags and let the steak and vegetables marinate in the refrigerator for at least 1 hour or up to 4 hours. 3. Line the air fryer basket with an air fryer liner or aluminum foil. Remove the vegetables from their bag or dish and shake off any excess marinade. Set the air fryer to 400ºF (204ºC). Place the vegetables in the air fryer basket and cook for 13 minutes. 4. Remove the steak from its bag or dish and shake off any excess marinade. Place the steak on top of the vegetables in the air fryer, and cook for 7 to 10 minutes or until an instant-read thermometer reads 120ºF (49ºC) for medium-rare (or cook to your desired doneness). 5. Serve with desired fixings, such as keto tortillas, lettuce, sour cream, avocado slices, shredded Cheddar cheese, and cilantro.

Per Serving:
calories: 252 | fat: 18g | protein: 17g | carbs: 6g | fiber: 2g | sodium: 81mg

Baby Back Ribs

Prep time: 5 minutes | Cook time: 25 minutes | Serves 4

2 pounds (907 g) baby back ribs	¼ teaspoon ground cayenne pepper
2 teaspoons chili powder	½ cup low-carb, sugar-free barbecue sauce
1 teaspoon paprika	
½ teaspoon onion powder	
½ teaspoon garlic powder	

1. Rub ribs with all ingredients except barbecue sauce. Place into the air fryer basket. 2. Adjust the temperature to 400ºF (204ºC) and roast for 25 minutes. 3. When done, ribs will be dark and charred with an internal temperature of at least 185ºF (85ºC). Brush ribs with barbecue sauce and serve warm.

Per Serving:
calories: 571 | fat: 36g | protein: 45g | carbs: 17g | fiber: 1g | sodium: 541mg

Eggplant Pork Lasagna

Prep time: 20 minutes | Cook time: 30 minutes | Serves 6

2 eggplants, sliced	1 tablespoon unsweetened tomato purée
1 teaspoon salt	1 teaspoon butter, softened
10 ounces (283 g) ground pork	1 cup chicken stock
1 cup Mozzarella, shredded	

1. Sprinkle the eggplants with salt and let sit for 10 minutes, then pat dry with paper towels. 2. In a mixing bowl, mix the ground pork, butter, and tomato purée. 3. Make a layer of the sliced eggplants in the bottom of the Instant Pot and top with ground pork mixture. 4. Top the ground pork with Mozzarella and repeat with remaining ingredients. 5. Pour in the chicken stock. Close the lid. Select Manual mode and set cooking time for 30 minutes on High Pressure. 6. When timer beeps, use a natural pressure release for 10 minutes, then release the remaining pressure and open the lid. 7. Cool for 10 minutes and serve.

Per Serving:
calories: 136 | fat: 3.6g | protein: 15.7g | carbs: 11.5g | net carbs: 4.9g | fiber: 6.6g

Buttery Pork Chops

Prep time: 5 minutes | Cook time: 12 minutes | Serves 4

4 (4-ounce / 113-g) boneless
pork chops
½ teaspoon salt
¼ teaspoon ground black

pepper
2 tablespoons salted butter,
softened

1. Sprinkle pork chops on all sides with salt and pepper. Place chops into ungreased air fryer basket in a single layer. Adjust the temperature to 400°F (204°C) and air fry for 12 minutes. Pork chops will be golden and have an internal temperature of at least 145°F (63°C) when done. 2. Use tongs to remove cooked pork chops from air fryer and place onto a large plate. Top each chop with ½ tablespoon butter and let sit 2 minutes to melt. Serve warm.

Per Serving:
calories: 211 | fat: 12g | protein: 25g | carbs: 0g | net carbs: 0g | fiber: 0g

Beef Cauliflower Curry

Prep time: 10 minutes | Cook time: 21 minutes | Serves 6

1 tbsp olive oil
1 ½ lb ground beef
1 tbsp ginger-garlic paste
1 tsp garam masala
1 (7 oz) can whole tomatoes

1 head cauliflower, cut into
florets
Pink salt and chili pepper to
taste
¼ cup water

1. Heat oil in a saucepan over medium heat, add the beef, ginger-garlic paste and season with garam masala. Cook for 5 minutes while breaking any lumps. 2. Stir in the tomatoes and cauliflower, season with salt and chili pepper, and cook covered for 6 minutes. Add the water and bring to a boil over medium heat for 10 minutes or until the water has reduced by half. Adjust taste with salt. Spoon the curry into serving bowls and serve with shirataki rice.

Per Serving:
Per serving: Kcal 374, Fat 33g, Net Carbs 2g, Protein 22g

Steaks with Walnut-Blue Cheese Butter

Prep time: 30 minutes | Cook time: 10 minutes | Serves 6

½ cup unsalted butter, at room
temperature
½ cup crumbled blue cheese
2 tablespoons finely chopped
walnuts
1 tablespoon minced fresh
rosemary

1 teaspoon minced garlic
¼ teaspoon cayenne pepper
Sea salt and freshly ground
black pepper, to taste
1½ pounds (680 g) New
York strip steaks, at room
temperature

1. In a medium bowl, combine the butter, blue cheese, walnuts, rosemary, garlic, and cayenne pepper and salt and black pepper to taste. Use clean hands to ensure that everything is well combined. Place the mixture on a sheet of parchment paper and form it into a log. Wrap it tightly in plastic wrap. Refrigerate for at least 2 hours or freeze for 30 minutes. 2. Season the steaks generously with salt and pepper. 3. Place the air fryer basket or grill pan in the air fryer. Set the air fryer to 400°F (204°C) and let it preheat for 5 minutes. 4. Place the steaks in the basket in a single layer and air fry for

5 minutes. Flip the steaks, and cook for 5 minutes more, until an instant-read thermometer reads 120°F (49°C) for medium-rare (or as desired). 5. Transfer the steaks to a plate. Cut the butter into pieces and place the desired amount on top of the steaks. Tent a piece of aluminum foil over the steaks and allow to sit for 10 minutes before serving. 6. Store any remaining butter in a sealed container in the refrigerator for up to 2 weeks.

Per Serving:
calories: 283 | fat: 18g | protein: 30g | carbs: 1g | net carbs: 1g | fiber: 0g

Mississippi Pork Butt Roast

Prep time: 10 minutes | Cook time: 6 hours | Serves 7

1 tablespoon ranch dressing
mix
1½ pound (680 g) pork butt
roast, chopped

1 cup butter
1 chili pepper, chopped
½ cup water

1. Put all ingredients in the instant pot. 2. Close the instant pot and cook the meal for 6 hours on Low Pressure. 3. When the time is over, shred the meat gently and transfer in the serving plate.

Per Serving:
calories: 414 | fat: 38g | protein: 17g | carbs: 0g | net carbs: 0g | fiber: 0g

Steak au Poivre for Two

Prep time: 5 minutes | Cook time: 15 minutes | Serves 2

¼ cup plus 1 tablespoon Paleo
fat, such as lard, coconut oil, or
avocado oil, divided
1 (8-ounce / 227-g) rib-eye
steak
1 tablespoon coarsely ground
black peppercorns, plus more

for garnish (optional)
1½ teaspoons fine sea salt
2 tablespoons chopped green
onions or shallots
¼ cup beef bone broth,
homemade or store-bought
¼ cup full-fat coconut milk

1. Heat a cast-iron skillet over medium-high heat; once hot, place 1 tablespoon of the fat in the pan. While the pan is heating, prepare the steak: Pat the steak dry and season it well with the pepper and salt. 2. When the fat is hot, place the steak in the pan and sear for 3 minutes, then flip it over and sear the other side for 3 minutes. Remove from the skillet for a rare steak, or continue to cook until done to your liking. Thicker steaks will take longer. 3. When done to your liking, remove the steak from the pan and set on a cutting board to rest while you make the sauce. Leave the drippings in the pan. 4. Add the green onions to the pan and sauté over medium heat in the reserved drippings for 2 minutes. Add the remaining ¼ cup of fat and, using a whisk, scrape up the brown bits from the bottom of the pan. Add the broth and coconut milk and simmer for 5 minutes, whisking often. Once thickened a bit, remove from the heat. 5. Cut the steak into ½-inch slices. Place on a serving platter and pour the sauce over the steak. Garnish with coarsely ground peppercorns, if desired.

Per Serving:
calories: 630 | fat: 55g | protein: 21g | carbs: 2g | net carbs: 1g | fiber: 1g

Cottage Pie

Prep time: 20 minutes | Cook time: 30 minutes | Serves 4

Pie:
2 tablespoons extra-virgin olive oil
2 celery stalks, chopped
½ medium onion, chopped
2 garlic cloves, minced
1 pound (454 g) ground beef (80/20)
¼ cup chicken broth
1 tablespoon tomato paste
1 teaspoon pink Himalayan sea salt
1 teaspoon freshly ground black pepper
½ teaspoon ground white pepper

Topping:
2 (12-ounce / 340-g) packages cauliflower rice, cooked and drained
1 cup shredded low-moisture mozzarella cheese
2 tablespoons heavy (whipping) cream
2 tablespoons butter
½ teaspoon pink Himalayan sea salt
½ teaspoon freshly ground black pepper
¼ teaspoon ground white pepper
¼ teaspoon garlic powder

1. Preheat the oven to 400ºF (205ºC). 2. To make the pie: In a large sauté pan or skillet, heat the olive oil over medium heat. Add the celery and onion and cook for 8 to 10 minutes, until the onion is tender. 3. Add the garlic and cook for an additional minute, until fragrant. 4. Add the ground beef, breaking it up with a wooden spoon or spatula. Continue to cook the beef for 7 to 10 minutes, until fully browned. 5. Stir in the broth and tomato paste and stir to coat the meat. Sprinkle in the salt, black pepper, and white pepper. 6. Transfer the meat mixture to a 9-by-13-inch baking dish. 7. To make the topping: In a food processor, combine the cauliflower rice, mozzarella, cream, butter, salt, black pepper, white pepper, and garlic powder. Purée on high speed until the mixture is smooth, scraping down the sides of the bowl as necessary. 8. Spread the cauliflower mash over the top of the meat and smooth the top. 9. Bake for 10 minutes, until the topping is just lightly browned. Let cool for 5 minutes, then serve.

Per Serving:
calories: 564 | fat: 44g | protein: 30g | carbs: 13g | net carbs: 7g | fiber: 6g

Lamb Koobideh

Prep time: 15 minutes | Cook time: 30 minutes | Serves 4

1 pound (454 g) ground lamb
1 egg, beaten
1 tablespoon lemon juice
1 teaspoon ground turmeric
½ teaspoon garlic powder
1 teaspoon chives, chopped
½ teaspoon ground black pepper
1 cup water

1. In a mixing bowl, combine all the ingredients except for water. 2. Shape the mixture into meatballs and press into ellipse shape. 3. Pour the water and insert the trivet in the Instant Pot. 4. Put the prepared ellipse meatballs in a baking pan and transfer on the trivet. 5. Close the lid and select Manual mode. Set cooking time for 30 minutes on High Pressure. 6. When timer beeps, make a quick pressure release. Open the lid. 7. Serve immediately

Per Serving:
calories: 231 | fat: 9.5g | protein: 33.4g | carbs: 1.0g | net carbs: 0.7g | fiber: 0.3g

Beef Stroganoff

Prep time: 10 minutes | Cook time: 35 minutes | Serves 6

1 tablespoon coconut oil, lard, or other cooking fat
1½ pounds (680 g) beef sirloin, cut against the grain into thin strips
½ teaspoon sea salt, plus additional
¼ teaspoon freshly ground black pepper, plus additional
2 tablespoons butter or ghee
½ cup chopped onion
3 garlic cloves, minced
3 cups sliced mushrooms (about 8 ounces / 227 g)
1 teaspoon dried oregano
⅛ teaspoon cayenne pepper (optional)
1 cup bone broth
½ cup heavy (whipping) cream
½ cup sour cream
½ to 1 teaspoon xanthan or guar gum, for thickening
½ teaspoon garlic powder
½ teaspoon onion powder
Chopped fresh parsley, for garnish (optional)

1. In a large skillet, heat the oil over medium-high heat. 2. Season the beef strips with the salt and pepper and then add half of the beef to the pot and cook for 1 to 2 minutes on each side, just until browned. Remove to a large bowl and repeat with the remaining beef. 3. Once all the beef is browned and removed to the bowl, reduce the heat to medium and add the butter to the skillet along with the onion, garlic, and mushrooms. Season with the oregano and cayenne (if using). Season with a bit more salt and pepper. Cook the onions and mushrooms for 7 to 10 minutes, stirring occasionally, until tender. Remove the onion, mushrooms, and garlic to the bowl with the beef. 4. Add the bone broth to the skillet and bring to a boil. Once boiling, reduce the heat to low and slowly whisk in the cream, sour cream, xanthan or guar gum, garlic powder, and onion powder. Stir for 3 to 5 minutes until the broth starts to thicken. 5. Return the beef and vegetable mixture to the pot. Cook on low for another 5 to 10 minutes until the beef is cooked through and the sauce is thickened. Garnish with parsley (if using) and serve.

Per Serving:
calories: 326 | fat: 22g | protein: 27g | carbs: 5g | net carbs: 4g | fiber: 1g

Spice-Rubbed Pork Loin

Prep time: 5 minutes | Cook time: 20 minutes | Serves 6

1 teaspoon paprika
½ teaspoon ground cumin
½ teaspoon chili powder
½ teaspoon garlic powder
2 tablespoons coconut oil
1 (1½-pound / 680-g) boneless pork loin
½ teaspoon salt
¼ teaspoon ground black pepper

1. In a small bowl, mix paprika, cumin, chili powder, and garlic powder. 2. Drizzle coconut oil over pork. Sprinkle pork loin with salt and pepper, then rub spice mixture evenly on all sides. 3. Place pork loin into ungreased air fryer basket. Adjust the temperature to 400ºF (204ºC) and air fry for 20 minutes, turning pork halfway through cooking. Pork loin will be browned and have an internal temperature of at least 145ºF (63ºC) when done. Serve warm.

Per Serving:
calories: 192 | fat: 9g | protein: 26g | carbs: 1g | fiber: 0g | sodium: 257mg

Creamy Pork Liver

Prep time: 5 minutes | Cook time: 7 minutes | Serves 3

14 ounces (397 g) pork liver, chopped
1 teaspoon salt
1 teaspoon butter
½ cup heavy cream
3 tablespoons scallions, chopped

1. Rub the liver with the salt on a clean work surface. 2. Put the butter in the Instant Pot and melt on the Sauté mode. 3. Add the heavy cream, scallions, and liver. 4. Stir and close the lid. Select Manual mode and set cooking time for 12 minutes on High Pressure. 5. When timer beeps, perform a natural pressure release for 5 minutes, then release any remaining pressure. Open the lid. 6. Serve immediately.

Per Serving:
calories: 300 | fat: 14.5g | protein: 35.0g | carbs: 6.0g | net carbs: 5.8g | fiber: 0.2g

Nutmeg Pork Tenderloin

Prep time: 10 minutes | Cook time: 20 minutes | Serves 6

1 pound (454 g) pork tenderloin, sliced
½ cup apple cider vinegar
1 teaspoon ground nutmeg
1 tablespoon butter
½ cup water

1. Mix up the sliced pork tenderloin with ground nutmeg and put it in the instant pot. 2. Add water, butter, and apple cider vinegar. 3. Close and seal the lid and cook the meat on Manual mode (High Pressure) for 20 minutes. 4. When the time is finished, make a quick pressure release and open the lid.

Per Serving:
calories: 131 | fat: 5g | protein: 20g | carbs: 0g | net carbs: 0g | fiber: 0g

Spinach and Provolone Steak Rolls

Prep time: 10 minutes | Cook time: 12 minutes | Makes 8 rolls

1 (1-pound / 454-g) flank steak, butterflied
8 (1-ounce / 28-g, ¼-inch-thick) deli slices provolone cheese
1 cup fresh spinach leaves
½ teaspoon salt
¼ teaspoon ground black pepper

1. Place steak on a large plate. Place provolone slices to cover steak, leaving 1-inch at the edges. Lay spinach leaves over cheese. Gently roll steak and tie with kitchen twine or secure with toothpicks. Carefully slice into eight pieces. Sprinkle each with salt and pepper. 2. Place rolls into ungreased air fryer basket, cut side up. Adjust the temperature to 400ºF (204ºC) and air fry for 12 minutes. Steak rolls will be browned and cheese will be melted when done and have an internal temperature of at least 150ºF (66ºC) for medium steak and 180ºF (82ºC) for well-done steak. Serve warm.

Per Serving:
calorie: 155 | fat: 8g | protein: 19g | carbs: 1g | sugars: 0g | fiber: 0g | sodium: 351mg

Pepper Steak Stir-Fry

Prep time: 10 minutes | Cook time: 20 minutes | Serves 3

1 tablespoon extra-virgin olive oil, or more as needed
1 red bell pepper, cored, seeded, and cut into ½-inch-wide strips
1 green bell pepper, cored, seeded, and cut into ½-inch-wide strips
½ medium onion, thinly sliced
2 garlic cloves, minced
1 pound (454 g) flank steak, cut into ½-inch-wide strips
Pink Himalayan sea salt
Freshly ground black pepper
¼ cup coconut aminos or soy sauce
2 tablespoons granulated erythritol
1 teaspoon ground ginger
Cauliflower rice, cooked (optional)

1. In a large sauté pan or skillet, heat 1 tablespoon of olive oil over medium heat. Add the bell peppers, onion, and garlic and cook until tender, about 5 minutes. Transfer the vegetables to a bowl. 2. Season the steak with salt and pepper and transfer it to the skillet. If there is no oil left in the pan, add about 1 teaspoon olive oil. 3. Increase the temperature to medium high and cook the steak for 5 to 7 minutes, with 5 minutes being for medium and 7 minutes being for well done. 4. In a small bowl, mix the coconut aminos, erythritol, and ginger. 5. Return the pepper mixture to the pan and drizzle with the sauce. 6. Reduce the heat to medium low and simmer for about 5 minutes, until the sauce reduces by about half, then serve with the cauliflower rice, if desired.

Per Serving:
calories: 316 | fat: 16g | protein: 35g | carbs: 8g | net carbs: 6g | fiber: 2g

Pepperoni Pizza Casserole

Prep time: 10 minutes | Cook time: 30 minutes | Serves 4

1 tablespoon olive oil
¼ white onion, diced
1 pound (454 g) pepperoni, roughly chopped
2 teaspoons dried oregano
1 teaspoon red pepper flakes
2 eggs
½ cup heavy (whipping) cream
2 tablespoons tomato paste
1 cup shredded Mozzarella cheese, divided
Salt, to taste
Freshly ground black pepper, to taste

1. Preheat the oven to 350ºF (180ºC). 2. In a large skillet over medium heat, heat the olive oil. 3. Add the onion and sauté for 5 to 7 minutes until softened and translucent. 4. Stir in the pepperoni, oregano, and red pepper flakes and remove from the heat. 5. In a medium bowl, whisk the eggs, cream, tomato paste, and ½ cup of Mozzarella. Season with salt and pepper and whisk again. 6. Spread the pepperoni and onions in a 7-by-11-inch baking dish. Pour the egg mixture over it. Gently shake the dish and tap it on the counter to ensure the mixture makes it through to the bottom and sides of the dish. Top with the remaining ½ cup of Mozzarella. Bake for 25 minutes. Refrigerate leftovers in an airtight container for up to 1 week.

Per Serving:
calories: 772 | fat: 68g | protein: 36g | carbs: 4g | net carbs: 3g | fiber: 1g

Parmesan Herb Filet Mignon

Prep time: 20 minutes | Cook time: 13 minutes | Serves 4

1 pound (454 g) filet mignon	1 teaspoon dried rosemary
Sea salt and ground black	1 teaspoon dried thyme
pepper, to taste	1 tablespoon sesame oil
½ teaspoon cayenne pepper	1 small-sized egg, well-whisked
1 teaspoon dried basil	½ cup Parmesan cheese, grated

1. Season the filet mignon with salt, black pepper, cayenne pepper, basil, rosemary, and thyme. Brush with sesame oil. 2. Put the egg in a shallow plate. Now, place the Parmesan cheese in another plate. 3. Coat the filet mignon with the egg; then lay it into the Parmesan cheese. Set the air fryer to 360°F (182°C). 4. Cook for 10 to 13 minutes or until golden. Serve with mixed salad leaves and enjoy!

Per Serving:
calories: 252 | fat: 13g | protein: 32g | carbs: 1g | fiber: 0g | sodium: 96mg

Mexican-Style Shredded Beef

Prep time: 5 minutes | Cook time: 35 minutes | Serves 6

1 (2-pound / 907-g) beef chuck	pepper
roast, cut into 2-inch cubes	½ cup no-sugar-added chipotle
1 teaspoon salt	sauce
½ teaspoon ground black	

1. In a large bowl, sprinkle beef cubes with salt and pepper and toss to coat. Place beef into ungreased air fryer basket. Adjust the temperature to 400°F (204°C) and air fry for 30 minutes, shaking the basket halfway through cooking. Beef will be done when internal temperature is at least 160°F (71°C). 2. Place cooked beef into a large bowl and shred with two forks. Pour in chipotle sauce and toss to coat. 3. Return beef to air fryer basket for an additional 5 minutes at 400°F (204°C) to crisp with sauce. Serve warm.

Per Serving:
calories: 204 | fat: 9g | protein: 31g | carbs: 0g | fiber: 0g | sodium: 539mg

Onion Pork Kebabs

Prep time: 22 minutes | Cook time: 18 minutes | Serves 3

2 tablespoons tomato purée	3 cloves garlic, peeled and
½ fresh serrano, minced	finely minced
⅓ teaspoon paprika	1 teaspoon ground black
1 pound (454 g) pork, ground	pepper, or more to taste
½ cup green onions, finely	1 teaspoon salt, or more to taste
chopped	

1. Thoroughly combine all ingredients in a mixing dish. Then form your mixture into sausage shapes. 2. Cook for 18 minutes at 355°F (179°C). Mound salad on a serving platter, top with air-fried kebabs and serve warm. Bon appétit!

Per Serving:
calories: 216 | fat: 6g | protein: 35g | carbs: 4g | fiber: 1g | sodium: 855mg

Barbacoa Beef Roast

Prep time: 10 minutes | Cook time: 8 hours | Serves 2

1 pound beef chuck roast	1 (6-ounce) can green jalapeño
Pink Himalayan salt	chiles
Freshly ground black pepper	2 tablespoons apple cider
4 chipotle peppers in adobo	vinegar
sauce (I use La Costeña	½ cup beef broth
12-ounce can)	

1. With the crock insert in place, preheat the slow cooker to low. 2. Season the beef chuck roast on both sides with pink Himalayan salt and pepper. Put the roast in the slow cooker. 3. In a food processor (or blender), combine the chipotle peppers and their adobo sauce, jalapeños, and apple cider vinegar, and pulse until smooth. Add the beef broth, and pulse a few more times. Pour the chile mixture over the top of the roast. 4. Cover and cook on low for 8 hours. 5. Transfer the beef to a cutting board, and use two forks to shred the meat. 6. Serve hot.

Per Serving:
calories: 723 | fat: 46g | protein: 66g | carbs: 7g | net carbs: 2g | fiber: 5g

London Broil with Herb Butter

Prep time: 30 minutes | Cook time: 20 to 25 minutes | Serves 4

1½ pounds (680 g) London	softened
broil top round steak	1 tablespoon chopped fresh
¼ cup olive oil	parsley
2 tablespoons balsamic vinegar	¼ teaspoon salt
1 tablespoon Worcestershire	¼ teaspoon dried ground
sauce	rosemary or thyme
4 cloves garlic, minced	¼ teaspoon garlic powder
Herb Butter:	Pinch of red pepper flakes
6 tablespoons unsalted butter,	

1. Place the beef in a gallon-size resealable bag. In a small bowl, whisk together the olive oil, balsamic vinegar, Worcestershire sauce, and garlic. Pour the marinade over the beef, massaging gently to coat, and seal the bag. Let sit at room temperature for an hour or refrigerate overnight. 2. To make the herb butter: In a small bowl, mix the butter with the parsley, salt, rosemary, garlic powder, and red pepper flakes until smooth. Cover and refrigerate until ready to use. 3. Preheat the air fryer to 400°F (204°C). 4. Remove the beef from the marinade (discard the marinade) and place the beef in the air fryer basket. Pausing halfway through the cooking time to turn the meat, air fry for 20 to 25 minutes, until a thermometer inserted into the thickest part indicates the desired doneness, 125°F / 52°C (rare) to 150°F / 66°C (medium). Let the beef rest for 10 minutes before slicing. Serve topped with the herb butter.

Per Serving:
calories: 519 | fat: 38g | protein: 39g | carbs: 3g | net carbs: 3g | fiber: 0g

Sausage and Peppers

Prep time: 7 minutes | Cook time: 35 minutes | Serves 4

Oil, for spraying
2 pounds (907 g) hot or sweet Italian sausage links, cut into thick slices
4 large bell peppers of any color, seeded and cut into slices
1 onion, thinly sliced

1 tablespoon olive oil
1 tablespoon chopped fresh parsley
1 teaspoon dried oregano
1 teaspoon dried basil
1 teaspoon balsamic vinegar

1. Line the air fryer basket with parchment and spray lightly with oil. 2. In a large bowl, combine the sausage, bell peppers, and onion. 3. In a small bowl, whisk together the olive oil, parsley, oregano, basil, and balsamic vinegar. Pour the mixture over the sausage and peppers and toss until evenly coated. 4. Using a slotted spoon, transfer the mixture to the prepared basket, taking care to drain out as much excess liquid as possible. 5. Air fry at 350°F (177°C) for 20 minutes, stir, and cook for another 15 minutes, or until the sausage is browned and the juices run clear.

Per Serving:
calories: 378 | fat: 23g | protein: 39g | carbs: 6g | net carbs: 4g | fiber: 2g

Paprika Pork Chops

Prep time: 5 minutes | Cook time: 10 minutes | Serves 4

4 pork chops
Salt and black pepper, to taste
3 tablespoons paprika

¾ cup cumin powder
1 teaspoon chili powder

1. In a bowl, combine the paprika with black pepper, cumin, salt, and chili. Place in the pork chops and rub them well. Heat a grill over medium temperature, add in the pork chops, cook for 5 minutes, flip, and cook for 5 minutes. Serve with steamed veggies.

Per Serving:
calories: 355 | fat: 19g | protein: 42g | carbs: 3g | net carbs: 1g | fiber: 2g

Keto BLTs with Soft-Boiled Eggs

Prep time: 7 minutes | Cook time: 15 minutes | Makes 12 wraps

12 slices bacon
6 large eggs (omit for egg-free)
Coarse sea salt and freshly ground black pepper, to taste

12 thick slices tomato (about 3 tomatoes)
12 large lettuce leaves, such as romaine, green leaf, or Boston
¾ cup mayonnaise and/or baconnaise, homemade or store-bought

1. If using standard-sliced bacon, preheat the oven to 400°F (205°C); if using thick-cut bacon, preheat the oven to 375°F (190°C). Place the bacon on a wire rack set inside a rimmed baking sheet. Bake until crispy, 10 to 15 minutes, depending on how thick the bacon is. 2. Meanwhile, make the soft-boiled eggs: Place the eggs in a pot of simmering (not boiling) water, cover, and simmer for 6 minutes. Immediately rinse the eggs under cold water. Peel the eggs, then cut them in half and place on a large serving platter. Sprinkle the eggs with flaky sea salt and pepper. 3. Place the tomato slices on the serving platter with the eggs and sprinkle them with flaky sea salt. Then add the cooked bacon to the platter. 4. Place the lettuce leaves in a bowl and have mayo out for serving. 5. Let everyone assemble their wraps!

Per Serving:
calories: 461 | fat: 42g | protein: 16g | carbs: 5g | net carbs: 4g | fiber: 1g

Chapter 4 Fish and Seafood

Simple Fish Curry

Prep time: 10 minutes | Cook time: 25 minutes | Serves 4

2 tablespoons coconut oil
1½ tablespoons grated fresh ginger
2 teaspoons minced garlic
1 tablespoon curry powder
½ teaspoon ground cumin

2 cups coconut milk
16 ounces firm white fish, cut into 1-inch chunks
1 cup shredded kale
2 tablespoons chopped cilantro

1. Place a large saucepan over medium heat and melt the coconut oil. 2. Sauté the ginger and garlic until lightly browned, about 2 minutes. 3. Stir in the curry powder and cumin and sauté until very fragrant, about 2 minutes. 4. Stir in the coconut milk and bring the liquid to a boil. 5. Reduce the heat to low and simmer for about 5 minutes to infuse the milk with the spices. 6. Add the fish and cook until the fish is cooked through, about 10 minutes. 7. Stir in the kale and cilantro and simmer until wilted, about 2 minutes. 8. Serve.

Per Serving:
calories: 416 | fat: 31g | protein: 26g | carbs: 5g | net carbs: 4g | fiber: 1g

Basil Alfredo Sea Bass

Prep time: 15 minutes | Cook time: 30 minutes | Serves 4

Sea Bass:
4 (6-ounce / 170-g) sea bass pieces
2 tablespoons olive oil
Pesto:
1 cup tightly packed fresh basil leaves
¼ cup grated Parmesan cheese
3 tablespoons pine nuts, or walnuts
1 tablespoon water
½ teaspoon salt

Freshly ground black pepper, to taste
3 tablespoons olive oil
Alfredo Sauce:
2 tablespoons butter
1 tablespoon olive oil
1 garlic clove, minced
1 cup heavy (whipping) cream
¾ cup Parmesan cheese
Salt, to taste
Freshly ground black pepper, to taste

Make the Sea Bass 1. Preheat the oven to 375ºF (190ºC). 2. Rub the sea bass with the olive oil and place it in a baking dish or on a rimmed baking sheet. Bake for 20 to 25 minutes or until the fish is completely opaque and the flesh flakes easily with a fork. Make the Pesto 1. In a blender or food processor (I prefer a blender because I like this very finely chopped/blended), combine the basil, Parmesan, pine nuts, water, and salt. Season with pepper. 2. With the blender running, stream the olive oil in. Set aside. Make the Alfredo Sauce 1. In a small saucepan over medium heat, melt the butter and olive oil together. 2. Stir in the garlic and cream. Bring to a low simmer and cook for 5 to 7 minutes until thickened. 3. Slowly add the Parmesan, stirring well to mix as it melts. Continue to stir until smooth. Season with salt and pepper. Set aside. 4. In a small bowl, stir together ½ cup of pesto and ½ cup of Alfredo sauce. Spoon over the fish before serving. Refrigerate leftovers in an airtight container for up to 4 days.

Per Serving:
calories: 768 | fat: 64g | protein: 45g | carbs: 4g | net carbs: 4g | fiber: 0g

Coconut Milk-Braised Squid

Prep time: 10 minutes | Cook time: 20 minutes | Serves 3

1 pound (454 g) squid, sliced
1 teaspoon sugar-free tomato paste

1 cup coconut milk
1 teaspoon cayenne pepper
½ teaspoon salt

1. Put all ingredients from the list above in the instant pot. 2. Close and seal the lid and cook the squid on Manual (High Pressure) for 20 minutes. 3. When the cooking time is finished, do the quick pressure release. 4. Serve the squid with coconut milk gravy.

Per Serving:
calories: 326 | fat: 21g | protein: 25g | carbs: 10g | net carbs: 8g | fiber: 2g

Creamy Haddock

Prep time: 10 minutes | Cook time: 8 minutes | Serves 4

1 pound (454 g) haddock fillet
1 teaspoon cayenne pepper
1 teaspoon salt

1 teaspoon coconut oil
½ cup heavy cream

1. Grease a baking pan with coconut oil. 2. Then put haddock fillet inside and sprinkle it with cayenne pepper, salt, and heavy cream. Put the baking pan in the air fryer basket and cook at 375ºF (191ºC) for 8 minutes.

Calamari with Hot Sauce

Prep time: 10 minutes | Cook time: 6 minutes | Serves 2

10 ounces (283 g) calamari, trimmed

2 tablespoons keto hot sauce
1 tablespoon avocado oil

1. Slice the calamari and sprinkle with avocado oil. 2. Put the calamari in the air fryer and cook at 400ºF (204ºC) for 3 minutes per side. 3. Then transfer the calamari in the serving plate and sprinkle with hot sauce.

Crab Cakes

Prep time: 10 minutes | Cook time: 10 minutes | Serves 4

2 (6-ounce / 170-g) cans lump crab meat
¼ cup blanched finely ground almond flour
1 large egg
2 tablespoons full-fat mayonnaise
½ teaspoon Dijon mustard
½ tablespoon lemon juice
½ medium green bell pepper, seeded and chopped
¼ cup chopped green onion
½ teaspoon Old Bay seasoning

1. In a large bowl, combine all ingredients. Form into four balls and flatten into patties. Place patties into the air fryer basket. 2. Adjust the temperature to 350ºF (177ºC) and air fry for 10 minutes. 3. Flip patties halfway through the cooking time. Serve warm.

Friday Night Fish Fry

Prep time: 10 minutes | Cook time: 10 minutes | Serves 4

1 large egg
½ cup powdered Parmesan cheese (about 1½ ounces / 43 g)
1 teaspoon smoked paprika
¼ teaspoon celery salt
¼ teaspoon ground black pepper
4 (4-ounce / 113-g) cod fillets
Chopped fresh oregano or parsley, for garnish (optional)
Lemon slices, for serving (optional)

1. Spray the air fryer basket with avocado oil. Preheat the air fryer to 400ºF (204ºC). 2. Crack the egg in a shallow bowl and beat it lightly with a fork. Combine the Parmesan cheese, paprika, celery salt, and pepper in a separate shallow bowl. 3. One at a time, dip the fillets into the egg, then dredge them in the Parmesan mixture. Using your hands, press the Parmesan onto the fillets to form a nice crust. As you finish, place the fish in the air fryer basket. 4. Air fry the fish in the air fryer for 10 minutes, or until it is cooked through and flakes easily with a fork. Garnish with fresh oregano or parsley and serve with lemon slices, if desired. 5. Store leftovers in an airtight container in the refrigerator for up to 3 days. Reheat in a preheated 400ºF (204ºC) air fryer for 5 minutes, or until warmed through.
Per Serving:
calories: 165 | fat: 6g | protein: 25g | carbs: 2g | fiber: 0g | sodium: 392mg

Coconut Crab Patties

Prep time: 5 minutes | Cook time: 6 minutes | Serves 8

2 tablespoons coconut oil
1 tablespoon lemon juice
1 cup lump crab meat
2 teaspoons Dijon mustard
1 egg, beaten
1½ tablespoons coconut flour

1. In a bowl to the crabmeat, add all the ingredients, except for the oil; mix well to combine. Make patties out of the mixture. Melt the coconut oil in a skillet over medium heat. Add the crab patties and cook for about 2-3 minutes per side.
Per Serving:
calories: 209 | fat: 13g | protein: 17g | carbs: 6g | net carbs: 4g | fiber: 2g

Spicy Shrimp Fried Rice

Prep time: 15 minutes | Cook time: 15 minutes | Serves 4

¼ teaspoon cayenne pepper
¼ teaspoon chili powder
¼ teaspoon paprika
¼ teaspoon pink Himalayan salt
¼ teaspoon ground black pepper
1 pound medium-sized shrimp, peeled and deveined
2 tablespoons ghee, divided
4 cups riced cauliflower (see Tip)
½ medium-sized white onion, finely chopped
2 teaspoons minced fresh ginger
1 cup fresh broccoli florets, chopped
3 tablespoons soy sauce
1 tablespoon Sriracha sauce
1½ teaspoons unseasoned rice wine vinegar
2 large eggs
2 teaspoons toasted sesame oil
FOR GARNISH (OPTIONAL):
Sliced scallions
Black and white sesame seeds

1. Put the cayenne, chili powder, paprika, salt, and pepper in a medium-sized bowl. Mix to blend, then add the shrimp. Toss the shrimp in the seasoning blend until evenly coated. 2. Heat 1 tablespoon of the ghee in a large skillet over medium-high heat. Place the seasoned shrimp in the hot skillet and cook until pink, about 2 minutes on each side. Remove to a small bowl and set aside. 3. Add the remaining tablespoon of ghee to the hot skillet and pour in the riced cauliflower. Spread it out with a spatula so it lies flat on the surface of the skillet and cook until it crisps up, 3 to 5 minutes. 4. Stir the rice, then add the onion and ginger. Cook for 2 minutes, until the onion is slightly tender. Add the broccoli and cook for 1 to 2 minutes, until bright green in color. Add the soy sauce, Sriracha, and vinegar. Combine using the spatula. 5. Make a well in the center of the skillet and crack in the eggs. Scramble using the spatula, then combine with the rest of the contents of the skillet. 6. Add the shrimp and toss to combine. Drizzle with the sesame oil and garnish with sliced scallions and sesame seeds, if desired. Serve immediately. 7. Store leftovers in a sealed container in the refrigerator for up to 4 days. Reheat in the microwave for 60 to 90 seconds.
Per Serving:
calories: 283 | fat: 13g | protein: 32g | carbs: 13g | net carbs: 9g | fiber: 4g

Ahi Tuna Steaks

Prep time: 5 minutes | Cook time: 14 minutes | Serves 2

2 (6-ounce / 170-g) ahi tuna steaks
2 tablespoons olive oil
3 tablespoons everything bagel seasoning

1. Drizzle both sides of each steak with olive oil. Place seasoning on a medium plate and press each side of tuna steaks into seasoning to form a thick layer. 2. Place steaks into ungreased air fryer basket. Adjust the temperature to 400ºF (204ºC) and air fry for 14 minutes, turning steaks halfway through cooking. Steaks will be done when internal temperature is at least 145ºF (63ºC) for well-done. Serve warm.
Per Serving:
calories: 305 | fat: 14g | protein: 42g | carbs: 0g | fiber: 0g | sodium: 377mg

Grandma Kitty's Tuna Salad

Prep time: 10 minutes | Cook time: 0 minutes | Serves 4

3 (6-ounce / 170-g) cans white albacore tuna in water, well drained
3 large hard-boiled eggs
1 small dill pickle
1 teaspoon seasoned salt

1 teaspoon garlic salt
1 teaspoon freshly ground black pepper
¼ cup mayonnaise
¼ cup sour cream

1. Place the well-drained tuna into a medium bowl and use a fork to break up the chunks. 2. Chop the hard-boiled eggs and pickle, and add them to the tuna. 3. Add the seasoned salt, garlic salt, and pepper, and mix well. 4. Add the mayonnaise and sour cream, and mix well.

Per Serving:
¼ recipe: calories: 276 | fat: 12g | protein: 35g | carbs: 4g | net carbs: 4g | fiber: 0g

Turmeric Salmon

Prep time: 10 minutes | Cook time: 4 minutes | Serves 3

1 pound (454 g) salmon fillet
1 teaspoon ground black pepper
½ teaspoon salt

1 teaspoon ground turmeric
1 teaspoon lemon juice
1 cup water

1. In the shallow bowl, mix up salt, ground black pepper, and ground turmeric. 2. Sprinkle the salmon fillet with lemon juice and rub with the spice mixture. 3. Then pour water in the instant pot and insert the steamer rack. 4. Wrap the salmon fillet in the foil and place it on the rack. 5. Close and seal the lid. 6. Cook the fish on Manual mode (High Pressure) for 4 minutes. 7. Make a quick pressure release and cut the fish on servings.

Per Serving:
calories: 205 | fat: 9g | protein: 30g | carbs: 1g | net carbs: 1g | fiber: 0g

Shrimp Caesar Salad

Prep time: 30 minutes | Cook time: 4 to 6 minutes | Serves 4

12 ounces (340 g) fresh large shrimp, peeled and deveined
1 tablespoon plus 1 teaspoon freshly squeezed lemon juice, divided
4 tablespoons olive oil or avocado oil, divided
2 garlic cloves, minced, divided
¼ teaspoon sea salt, plus additional to season the marinade

¼ teaspoon freshly ground black pepper, plus additional to season the marinade
⅓ cup sugar-free mayonnaise
2 tablespoons freshly grated Parmesan cheese
1 teaspoon Dijon mustard
1 tinned anchovy, mashed
12 ounces (340 g) romaine hearts, torn

1. Place the shrimp in a large bowl. Add 1 tablespoon of lemon juice, 1 tablespoon of olive oil, and 1 minced garlic clove. Season with salt and pepper. Toss well and refrigerate for 15 minutes. 2. While the shrimp marinates, make the dressing: In a blender,

combine the mayonnaise, Parmesan cheese, Dijon mustard, the remaining 1 teaspoon of lemon juice, the anchovy, the remaining minced garlic clove, ¼ teaspoon of salt, and ¼ teaspoon of pepper. Process until smooth. With the blender running, slowly stream in the remaining 3 tablespoons of oil. Transfer the mixture to a jar; seal and refrigerate until ready to serve. 3. Remove the shrimp from its marinade and place it in the air fryer basket in a single layer. Set the air fryer to 400ºF (204ºC) and air fry for 2 minutes. Flip the shrimp and cook for 2 to 4 minutes more, until the flesh turns opaque. 4. Place the romaine in a large bowl and toss with the desired amount of dressing. Top with the shrimp and serve immediately.

Scallops with Creamy Bacon Sauce

Prep time: 5 minutes | Cook time: 20 minutes | Serves 2

4 bacon slices
1 cup heavy (whipping) cream
1 tablespoon butter
¼ cup grated Parmesan cheese
Pink Himalayan salt

Freshly ground black pepper
1 tablespoon ghee
8 large sea scallops, rinsed and patted dry

1. In a medium skillet over medium-high heat, cook the bacon on both sides until crispy, about 8 minutes. Transfer the bacon to a paper towel–lined plate. 2. Lower the heat to medium. Add the cream, butter, and Parmesan cheese to the bacon grease, and season with a pinch of pink Himalayan salt and pepper. Reduce the heat to low and cook, stirring constantly, until the sauce thickens and is reduced by 50 percent, about 10 minutes. 3. In a separate large skillet over medium-high heat, heat the ghee until sizzling. 4. Season the scallops with pink Himalayan salt and pepper, and add them to the skillet. Cook for just 1 minute per side. Do not crowd the scallops; if your pan isn't large enough, cook them in two batches. You want the scallops golden on each side. 5. Transfer the scallops to a paper towel–lined plate. 6. Divide the cream sauce between two plates, crumble the bacon on top of the cream sauce, and top with 4 scallops each. Serve immediately.

Per Serving:
calories: 782 | fat: 73g | protein:24 | carbs: 11g | net carbs: 10g | fiber: 0g

Sicilian-Style Zoodle Spaghetti

Prep time: 10 minutes | Cook time: 11 minutes | Serves 2

4 cups zoodles (spiralled zucchini)
2 ounces cubed bacon
4 ounces canned sardines, chopped

½ cup canned chopped tomatoes
1 tbsp capers
1 tbsp parsley
1 tsp minced garlic

1. Pour some of the sardine oil in a pan. Add garlic and cook for 1 minute. Add the bacon and cook for 2 more minutes. Stir in the tomatoes and let simmer for 5 minutes. Add zoodles and sardines and cook for 3 minutes.

Per Serving:
Per serving: Kcal 355, Fat: 31g, Net Carbs: 6g, Protein: 20g

Sour Cream Salmon with Parmesan

Prep time: 10 minutes | Cook time: 17 minutes | Serves 4

1 cup sour cream	season
½ tbsp minced dill	4 salmon steaks
½ lemon, zested and juiced	½ cup grated Parmesan cheese
Pink salt and black pepper to	

1. Preheat oven to 400°F and line a baking sheet with parchment paper; set aside. In a bowl, mix the sour cream, dill, lemon zest, juice, salt and black pepper, and set aside. 2. Season the fish with salt and black pepper, drizzle lemon juice on both sides of the fish and arrange them in the baking sheet. Spread the sour cream mixture on each fish and sprinkle with Parmesan. 3. Bake the fish for 15 minutes and after broil the top for 2 minutes with a close watch for a nice a brown color. Plate the fish and serve with buttery green beans.

Per Serving:
Per serving: Kcal 288, Fat 23.4g, Net Carbs 1.2g, Protein 16.2g

Apple Cider Mussels

Prep time: 10 minutes | Cook time: 2 minutes | Serves 5

2 pounds (907 g) mussels, cleaned, peeled	1 teaspoon ground cumin
1 teaspoon onion powder	1 tablespoon avocado oil
	¼ cup apple cider vinegar

1. Mix mussels with onion powder, ground cumin, avocado oil, and apple cider vinegar. 2. Put the mussels in the air fryer and cook at 395°F (202°C) for 2 minutes.

Per Serving:
calories: 187 | fat: 7g | protein: 22g | carbs: 7g | fiber: 0g | sodium: 521mg

Tuna Casserole

Prep time: 15 minutes | Cook time: 15 minutes | Serves 4

2 tablespoons salted butter	mayonnaise
¼ cup diced white onion	¼ teaspoon xanthan gum
¼ cup chopped white mushrooms	½ teaspoon red pepper flakes
2 stalks celery, finely chopped	2 medium zucchini, spiralized
½ cup heavy cream	2 (5-ounce / 142-g) cans
½ cup vegetable broth	albacore tuna
2 tablespoons full-fat	1 ounce (28 g) pork rinds, finely ground

1. In a large saucepan over medium heat, melt butter. Add onion, mushrooms, and celery and sauté until fragrant, about 3 to 5 minutes. 2. Pour in heavy cream, vegetable broth, mayonnaise, and xanthan gum. Reduce heat and continue cooking an additional 3 minutes, until the mixture begins to thicken. 3. Add red pepper flakes, zucchini, and tuna. Turn off heat and stir until zucchini noodles are coated. 4. Pour into a round baking dish. Top with ground pork rinds and cover the top of the dish with foil. Place into the air fryer basket. 5. Adjust the temperature to 370°F (188°C) and set the timer for 15 minutes. 6. When 3 minutes remain, remove the foil to brown the top of the casserole. Serve warm.

Cayenne Flounder Cutlets

Prep time: 15 minutes | Cook time: 10 minutes | Serves 2

1 egg	taste
1 cup Pecorino Romano cheese, grated	½ teaspoon cayenne pepper
Sea salt and white pepper, to	1 teaspoon dried parsley flakes
	2 flounder fillets

1. To make a breading station, whisk the egg until frothy. 2. In another bowl, mix Pecorino Romano cheese, and spices. 3. Dip the fish in the egg mixture and turn to coat evenly; then, dredge in the cracker crumb mixture, turning a couple of times to coat evenly. 4. Cook in the preheated air fryer at 390°F (199°C) for 5 minutes; turn them over and cook another 5 minutes. Enjoy!

Per Serving:
calories: 280 | fat: 13g | protein: 36g | carbs: 3g | fiber: 1g | sodium: 257mg

Lemon Pepper Shrimp

Prep time: 15 minutes | Cook time: 8 minutes | Serves 2

Oil, for spraying	1 tablespoon olive oil
12 ounces (340 g) medium raw shrimp, peeled and deveined	1 teaspoon lemon pepper
3 tablespoons lemon juice	¼ teaspoon paprika
	¼ teaspoon granulated garlic

1. Preheat the air fryer to 400°F (204°C). Line the air fryer basket with parchment and spray lightly with oil. 2. In a medium bowl, toss together the shrimp, lemon juice, olive oil, lemon pepper, paprika, and garlic until evenly coated. 3. Place the shrimp in the prepared basket. 4. Cook for 6 to 8 minutes, or until pink and firm. Serve immediately.

Per Serving:
calories: 211 | fat: 8g | protein: 34g | carbs: 2g | fiber: 0g | sodium: 203mg

Lemon Mahi-Mahi

Prep time: 5 minutes | Cook time: 14 minutes | Serves 2

Oil, for spraying	¼ teaspoon salt
2 (6-ounce / 170-g) mahi-mahi fillets	¼ teaspoon freshly ground black pepper
1 tablespoon lemon juice	1 tablespoon chopped fresh dill
1 tablespoon olive oil	2 lemon slices

1. Line the air fryer basket with parchment and spray lightly with oil. 2. Place the mahi-mahi in the prepared basket. 3. In a small bowl, whisk together the lemon juice and olive oil. Brush the mixture evenly over the mahi-mahi. 4. Sprinkle the mahi-mahi with the salt and black pepper and top with the dill. 5. Air fry at 400°F (204°C) for 12 to 14 minutes, depending on the thickness of the fillets, until they flake easily. 6. Transfer to plates, top each with a lemon slice, and serve.

Per Serving:
calories: 218 | fat: 8g | protein: 32g | carbs: 3g | fiber: 1g | sodium: 441mg

Garlic Tuna Casserole

Prep time: 7 minutes | Cook time: 9 minutes | Serves 4

1 cup grated Parmesan or shredded Cheddar cheese, plus more for topping
1 (8-ounce / 227-g) package cream cheese (1 cup), softened
½ cup chicken broth
1 tablespoon unsalted butter
½ small head cauliflower, cut into 1-inch pieces
1 cup diced onions

2 cloves garlic, minced, or more to taste
2 (4-ounce / 113-g) cans chunk tuna packed in water, drained
1½ cups cold water
For Garnish:
Chopped fresh flat-leaf parsley
Sliced green onions
Cherry tomatoes, halved
Ground black pepper

1. In a blender, add the Parmesan cheese, cream cheese, and broth and blitz until smooth. Set aside. 2. Set your Instant Pot to Sauté. Add and melt the butter. Add the cauliflower and onions and sauté for 4 minutes, or until the onions are softened. Fold in the garlic and sauté for an additional 1 minute. 3. Place the cheese sauce and tuna in a large bowl. Mix in the veggies and stir well. Transfer the mixture to a casserole dish. 4. Place a trivet in the bottom of your Instant Pot and add the cold water. Use a foil sling, lower the casserole dish onto the trivet. Tuck in the sides of the sling. 5. Lock the lid. Select the Manual mode and set the cooking time for 5 minutes for al dente cauliflower or 8 minutes for softer cauliflower at High Pressure. 6. Once cooking is complete, do a quick pressure release. Carefully open the lid. 7. Serve topped with the cheese and garnished with the parsley, green onions, cherry tomatoes, and freshly ground pepper.

Per Serving:
calories: 378 | fat: 26.8g | protein: 23.8g | carbs: 10.5g | net carbs: 9.3g | fiber: 1.2g

Pan-Fried Cod with Dill Caper Sauce

Prep time: 5 minutes | Cook time: 5 minutes | Serves 6

Dill Caper Sauce:
¼ cup drained capers
1 tablespoon chopped fresh dill
¼ cup extra-virgin olive oil
Juice from 1 small lemon
Salt and pepper, to taste
Fish:

1½ pounds (680 g) cod fillets, or any other mild white fish
Salt and pepper, to taste
1 tablespoon butter
2 teaspoons avocado oil
Juice of ½ lemon

1. Prepare the sauce first, even a day or two before. Combine the capers, dill, olive oil, and lemon juice in a jar with a tight-fitting lid. Shake vigorously. If you want to make it more of a sauce than a dressing, you can also pulse the mixture a few times in a food processor or with an immersion blender. Taste and add salt and pepper as needed. 2. Season both sides of the fish with salt and pepper. Heat a large skillet over medium heat. Add the butter and avocado oil, and heat until the butter bubbles; swirl the pan to combine. Add the fish and cook about 2 minutes, depending on thickness. Carefully flip to brown the other side and squeeze the lemon juice over the fish. Cook for 1 to 2 minutes more. Do not overcook. 3. Remove the fish from pan, transfer to a serving platter, and spoon 2 tablespoons sauce over each serving.

Per Serving:
calories: 336 | fat: 24g | protein: 19g | carbs: 10g | net carbs: 9g | fiber: 1g

Herb-Crusted Cod Steaks

Prep time: 5 minutes | Cook time: 4 minutes | Serves 4

1½ cups water
2 tablespoons garlic-infused oil
4 cod steaks, 1½-inch thick
Sea salt, to taste
½ teaspoon mixed peppercorns,

crushed
2 sprigs thyme
1 sprig rosemary
1 yellow onion, sliced

1. Pour the water into your Instant Pot and insert a trivet. 2. Rub the garlic-infused oil into the cod steaks and season with the salt and crushed peppercorns. 3. Lower the cod steaks onto the trivet, skin-side down. Top with the thyme, rosemary, and onion. 4. Lock the lid. Select the Manual mode and set the cooking time for 4 minutes at High Pressure. 5. When the timer beeps, perform a quick pressure release. Carefully remove the lid. 6. Serve immediately.

Per Serving:
calories: 149 | fat: 7.3g | protein: 18.0g | carbs: 2.0g | net carbs: 1.5g | fiber: 0.5g

Sushi

Prep time: 15 minutes | Cook time: 3 to 5 minutes | Serves 2 to 4

4 cups cauliflower rice
2 tablespoons grass-fed gelatin
1 tablespoon apple cider vinegar
1 teaspoon salt
2 to 4 nori sheets
½ pound (227 g) sushi-grade fish, thinly sliced
1 small avocado, halved, pitted, peeled, and thinly sliced
1 small cucumber (or any other

vegetable you'd like), thinly sliced
Sesame seeds, for topping (optional)
Coconut aminos or tamari, wasabi, sugar-free pickled ginger, sliced avocado, and/or avocado oil mayonnaise mixed with sugar-free hot sauce, for serving (optional)

1. In a shallow pot with a lid, combine the cauliflower with 3 tablespoons of water. Turn the heat to medium, cover the pot, and steam for 3 to 5 minutes. 2. Drain the cauliflower and transfer to a mixing bowl. Stir in the gelatin, vinegar, and salt. Stir together until the mixture is smooth and sticky. Set aside. 3. Fold a dish towel in half lengthwise and place it on your counter. Cover the towel in plastic wrap. 4. Place a nori sheet on top of the plastic wrap, then spread with a layer of the cauliflower rice. 5. Layer slices of fish, avocado, and cucumber over the cauliflower on the end of the nori sheet closest to you. 6. Starting at the end closest to you, gently roll the nori sheet over all the ingredients, using the towel as your rolling aid. (Emphasis on the word "gently" because you don't want to tear the nori sheet.) When you're done rolling, remove the towel and plastic wrap as you slide the roll onto a plate or cutting board. Using a sharp knife, cut the roll into equal pieces. Repeat steps 4 through 7 with the remaining nori and filling ingredients. 7. Sprinkle sesame seeds on top of your sushi, if desired, and serve with any of the other optional ingredients you'd like.

Per Serving:
calories: 295 | fat: 15g | protein: 30g | carbs: 10g | net carbs: 2g | fiber: 8g

Tuna Spinach Cakes

Prep time: 15 minutes | Cook time: 8 minutes | Serves 4

10 ounces (283 g) tuna, shredded
1 cup spinach
1 egg, beaten
1 teaspoon ground coriander
2 tablespoon coconut flakes
1 tablespoon avocado oil

1. Blend the spinach in the blender until smooth. 2. Then transfer it in the mixing bowl and add tuna, egg, and ground coriander. 3. Add coconut flakes and stir the mass with the help of the spoon. 4. Heat up avocado oil in the instant pot on Sauté mode for 2 minutes. 5. Then make the medium size cakes from the tuna mixture and place them in the hot oil. 6. Cook the tuna cakes on Sauté mode for 3 minutes. Then flip the on another side and cook for 3 minutes more or until they are light brown.

Per Serving:
calories: 163 | fat: 8g | protein:20g | carbs: 1g | net carbs: 0g | fiber: 1g

Nut-Crusted Baked Fish

Prep time: 10 minutes | Cook time: 20 minutes | Serves 4

½ cup extra-virgin olive oil, divided
1 pound (454 g) flaky white fish (such as cod, haddock, or halibut), skin removed
½ cup shelled finely chopped pistachios
½ cup ground flaxseed
Zest and juice of 1 lemon, divided
1 teaspoon ground cumin
1 teaspoon ground allspice
½ teaspoon salt (use 1 teaspoon if pistachios are unsalted)
¼ teaspoon freshly ground black pepper

1. Preheat the oven to 400°F(205°C). 2. Line a baking sheet with parchment paper or aluminum foil and drizzle 2 tablespoons olive oil over the sheet, spreading to evenly coat the bottom. 3. Cut the fish into 4 equal pieces and place on the prepared baking sheet. 4. In a small bowl, combine the pistachios, flaxseed, lemon zest, cumin, allspice, salt, and pepper. Drizzle in ¼ cup olive oil and stir well. 5. Divide the nut mixture evenly atop the fish pieces. Drizzle the lemon juice and remaining 2 tablespoons oil over the fish and bake until cooked through, 15 to 20 minutes, depending on the thickness of the fish.

Per Serving:
calories: 499 | fat: 41g | protein: 26g | carbs: 41g | fiber: 6g | sodium: 358mg

Fish Taco Bowl

Prep time: 10 minutes | Cook time: 12 minutes | Serves 4

½ teaspoon salt
¼ teaspoon garlic powder
¼ teaspoon ground cumin
4 (4-ounce / 113-g) cod fillets
4 cups finely shredded green cabbage
⅓ cup mayonnaise
¼ teaspoon ground black pepper
¼ cup chopped pickled jalapeños

1. Sprinkle salt, garlic powder, and cumin over cod and place into ungreased air fryer basket. Adjust the temperature to 350°F (177°C)

and air fry for 12 minutes, turning fillets halfway through cooking. Cod will flake easily and have an internal temperature of at least 145°F (63°C) when done. 2. In a large bowl, toss cabbage with mayonnaise, pepper, and jalapeños until fully coated. Serve cod warm over cabbage slaw on four medium plates.

Per Serving:
calories: 161 | fat: 7g | protein: 19g | carbs: 5g | net carbs: 3g | fiber: 2g

Crab au Gratin

Prep time: 10 minutes | Cook time: 35 minutes | Serves 4

½ cup (1 stick) butter
1 (8-ounce / 227-g) container crab claw meat
2 ounces (57 g) full-fat cream cheese
½ cup heavy (whipping) cream
2 tablespoons freshly squeezed lemon juice
1 tablespoon white wine vinegar
1 teaspoon pink Himalayan sea salt
½ teaspoon freshly ground black pepper
½ teaspoon onion powder
1 cup shredded Cheddar cheese, divided
1 (12-ounce / 340-g) package cauliflower rice, cooked and drained

1. Preheat the oven to 350°F (180°C). 2. In a medium sauté pan or skillet, melt the butter over medium heat. Add the crab and cook until warmed through. 3. Add the cream cheese, cream, lemon juice, vinegar, salt, pepper, and onion powder. Keep stirring until the cream cheese fully melts into the sauce. 4. Add ½ cup of Cheddar cheese and stir it into the sauce. 5. Spread the cauliflower rice on the bottom of an 8-inch square baking dish. 6. Pour the crab and sauce over, then sprinkle with the remaining ½ cup of Cheddar cheese. 7. Bake for 25 to 30 minutes, until the sauce is bubbling. Turn the broiler on to high. 8. Broil for an additional 2 to 3 minutes, until the cheese topping is slightly browned. 9. Allow to cool for 5 to 10 minutes, then serve.

Per Serving:
calories: 555 | fat: 49g | protein: 23g | carbs: 7g | net carbs: 5g | fiber: 2g

Mackerel and Broccoli Casserole

Prep time: 15 minutes | Cook time: 15 minutes | Serves 5

1 cup shredded broccoli
10 ounces (283 g) mackerel, chopped
½ cup shredded Cheddar cheese
1 cup coconut milk
1 teaspoon ground cumin
1 teaspoon salt

1. Sprinkle the chopped mackerel with ground cumin and salt and transfer in the instant pot. 2. Top the fish with shredded broccoli and Cheddar cheese, 3. Then add coconut milk. Close and seal the lid. 4. Cook the casserole on Manual mode (High Pressure) for 15 minutes. 5. Allow the natural pressure release for 10 minutes and open the lid.

Per Serving:
calories: 312 | fat: 25g | protein: 18g | carbs: 4g | net carbs: 2g | fiber: 2g

Sushi Shrimp Rolls

Prep time: 5 minutes | Cook time: 0 minutes | Serves 5

2 cups cooked and chopped shrimp
1 tablespoon sriracha sauce
¼ cucumber, julienned
5 hand roll nori sheets
¼ cup mayonnaise

1. Combine shrimp, mayonnaise, cucumber and sriracha sauce in a bowl. Lay out a single nori sheet on a flat surface and spread about 1/5 of the shrimp mixture. Roll the nori sheet as desired. Repeat with the other ingredients. Serve with sugar-free soy sauce.

Per Serving:
calories: 180 | fat: 12g | protein: 16g | carbs: 2g | net carbs: 1g | fiber: 1g

Steamed Halibut with Lemon

Prep time: 10 minutes | Cook time: 9 minutes | Serves 3

3 halibut fillet
½ lemon, sliced
½ teaspoon white pepper
½ teaspoon ground coriander
1 tablespoon avocado oil
1 cup water, for cooking

1. Pour water and insert the steamer rack in the instant pot. 2. Rub the fish fillets with white pepper, ground coriander, and avocado oil. 3. Place the fillets in the steamer rack. 4. Then top the halibut with sliced lemon. Close and seal the lid. 5. Cook the meal on High Pressure for 9 minutes. Make a quick pressure release.

Per Serving:
calories: 328 | fat: 7g | protein: 60g | carbs: 1g | net carbs: 1g | fiber: 0g

Aromatic Monkfish Stew

Prep time: 5 minutes | Cook time: 6 minutes | Serves 6

Juice of 1 lemon
1 tablespoon fresh basil
1 tablespoon fresh parsley
1 tablespoon olive oil
1 teaspoon garlic, minced
1½ pounds (680 g) monkfish
1 tablespoon butter
1 bell pepper, chopped
1 onion, sliced
½ teaspoon cayenne pepper
½ teaspoon mixed peppercorns
¼ teaspoon turmeric powder
¼ teaspoon ground cumin
Sea salt and ground black pepper, to taste
2 cups fish stock
½ cup water
¼ cup dry white wine
2 bay leaves
1 ripe tomato, crushed

1. Stir together the lemon juice, basil, parsley, olive oil, and garlic in a ceramic dish. Add the monkfish and marinate for 30 minutes. 2. Set your Instant Pot to Sauté. Add and melt the butter. Once hot, cook the bell pepper and onion until fragrant. 3. Stir in the remaining ingredients. 4. Lock the lid. Select the Manual mode and set the cooking time for 6 minutes at High Pressure. 5. When the timer beeps, perform a quick pressure release. Carefully remove the lid. 6. Discard the bay leaves and divide your stew into serving bowls. Serve hot.

Per Serving:
calories: 153 | fat: 6.9g | protein: 18.9g | carbs: 3.8g | net carbs: 3.0g | fiber: 0.8g

Dill Salmon Cakes

Prep time: 15 minutes | Cook time: 10 minutes | Serves 4

1 pound (454 g) salmon fillet, chopped
1 tablespoon chopped dill
2 eggs, beaten
½ cup almond flour
1 tablespoon coconut oil

1. Put the chopped salmon, dill, eggs, and almond flour in the food processor. 2. Blend the mixture until it is smooth. 3. Then make the small balls (cakes) from the salmon mixture. 4. After this, heat up the coconut oil on Sauté mode for 3 minutes. 5. Put the salmon cakes in the instant pot in one layer and cook them on Sauté mode for 2 minutes from each side or until they are light brown.

Per Serving:
calories: 297 | fat: 19g | protein: 28g | carbs: 4g | net carbs: 2g | fiber: 2g

Parchment-Baked Cod and Asparagus with Beurre Blanc

Prep time: 15 minutes | Cook time: 15 minutes | Serves 4

1 pound (454 g) skinless cod, halibut, or other white flaky fish
1 teaspoon salt, divided
½ teaspoon freshly ground black pepper, divided
2 garlic cloves, thinly sliced
1 lemon, thinly sliced
½ pound (227 g) asparagus spears, rough ends trimmed
4 tablespoons extra-virgin olive oil, divided
1 tablespoon finely chopped red onion
¼ cup white wine vinegar
¼ cup heavy cream
½ cup (1 stick) chilled unsalted butter, cut into tablespoon-size pieces

1. Preheat the oven to 375ºF (190ºC). 2. Place 1 large sheet of parchment paper (about twice the size of the fish fillet) on a rimmed baking sheet. Place the fish in the center of the parchment and sprinkle with ½ teaspoon of the salt and ¼ teaspoon of the pepper. 3. Top the fish with the garlic and lemon slices. Top with the asparagus spears and drizzle with 2 tablespoons of olive oil. 4. Top the fish with a second large piece of parchment. Starting on a long side, fold the paper up to about 1 inch from the fish and vegetables. Repeat on the remaining sides, going in a clockwise direction. Fold in each corner once to secure. 5. Bake for 10 to 12 minutes, until the fish is cooked through and flakes easily when poked with a paring knife. 6. Meanwhile, prepare the sauce. Heat the remaining 2 tablespoons of olive oil over medium heat. Add the red onion and sauté until tender, 3 to 4 minutes. Add the vinegar, cream, remaining ½ teaspoon of salt, and ¼ teaspoon of pepper. Bring to a simmer and reduce heat to low. 7. Whisking constantly, add the butter, a couple tablespoons at a time, until melted and creamy. Remove the sauce from the heat and serve warm, poured over the fish and asparagus.

Per Serving:
calories: 472 | fat: 43g | protein: 19g | carbs: 4g | net carbs: 3g | fiber: 1g

Cod with Parsley Pistou

Prep time: 15 minutes | Cook time: 10 minutes |

Serves 4

1 cup packed roughly chopped fresh flat-leaf Italian parsley	½ teaspoon freshly ground black pepper
1 to 2 small garlic cloves, minced	1 cup extra-virgin olive oil, divided
Zest and juice of 1 lemon	1 pound (454 g) cod fillets, cut
1 teaspoon salt	into 4 equal-sized pieces

1. In a food processor, combine the parsley, garlic, lemon zest and juice, salt, and pepper. Pulse to chop well. 2. While the food processor is running, slowly stream in ¾ cup olive oil until well combined. Set aside. 3. In a large skillet, heat the remaining ¼ cup olive oil over medium-high heat. Add the cod fillets, cover, and cook 4 to 5 minutes on each side, or until cooked through. Thicker fillets may require a bit more cooking time. Remove from the heat and keep warm. 4. Add the pistou to the skillet and heat over medium-low heat. Return the cooked fish to the skillet, flipping to coat in the sauce. Serve warm, covered with pistou.

Per Serving:
calories: 580 | fat: 55g | protein: 21g | carbs: 2g | fiber: 1g | sodium: 591mg

Parmesan Mackerel with Coriander

Prep time: 10 minutes | Cook time: 7 minutes | Serves 2

12 ounces (340 g) mackerel fillet	grated
	1 teaspoon ground coriander
2 ounces (57 g) Parmesan,	1 tablespoon olive oil

1. Sprinkle the mackerel fillet with olive oil and put it in the air fryer basket. 2. Top the fish with ground coriander and Parmesan. 3. Cook the fish at 390°F (199°C) for 7 minutes.

Per Serving:
calories: 522 | fat: 39g | protein: 42g | carbs: 1g | fiber: 0g | sodium: 544mg

Roasted Salmon with Avocado Salsa

Prep time: 10 minutes | Cook time: 12 minutes |

Serves 4

FOR THE SALSA	½ teaspoon ground coriander
1 avocado, peeled, pitted, and diced	½ teaspoon onion powder
1 scallion, white and green parts, chopped	¼ teaspoon sea salt
½ cup halved cherry tomatoes	Pinch freshly ground black pepper
Juice of 1 lemon	Pinch cayenne pepper
Zest of 1 lemon	4 (4-ounce) boneless, skinless salmon fillets
FOR THE FISH	2 tablespoons olive oil
1 teaspoon ground cumin	

TO MAKE THE SALSA 1. In a small bowl, stir together the avocado, scallion, tomatoes, lemon juice, and lemon zest until mixed. 2. Set aside. TO MAKE THE FISH 1. Preheat the oven to 400°F. Line a baking sheet with aluminum foil and set aside. 2. In a small bowl, stir together the cumin, coriander, onion powder, salt, black pepper, and cayenne until well mixed. 3. Rub the salmon fillets with the spice mix and place them on the baking sheet. 4. Drizzle the fillets with the olive oil and roast the fish until it is just cooked through, about 15 minutes. 5. Serve the salmon topped with the avocado salsa.

Per Serving:
calories: 320 | fat: 26g | protein: 22g | carbs: 4g | net carbs: 1g | fiber: 3g

Halibut Curry

Prep time: 5 minutes | Cook time: 35 minutes |

Serves 4

1 tablespoon avocado oil	½ tablespoon garlic powder
½ cup finely chopped celery	½ tablespoon ground turmeric
½ cup frozen butternut squash cubes	1 teaspoon ground ginger
1 cup full-fat coconut milk	1 pound (454 g) skinless halibut fillet, cut into chunks
½ cup seafood stock	Cooked cauliflower rice, for serving (optional)
1½ tablespoons curry powder	
1 tablespoon dried cilantro	

1. In a large pot with a lid, heat the avocado oil over medium-high heat. Add the celery and cook for about 3 minutes. Add the squash and cook for 5 minutes more. 2. Pour in the coconut milk and seafood stock and cook, stirring, for another 3 minutes. Stir in the curry powder, cilantro, garlic, turmeric, and ginger. 3. Add the halibut to the pot and stir into the rest of the mixture. Reduce the heat to medium, cover the pot, and cook for 15 to 20 minutes, or until the fish is completely white and flakes easily with a fork. 4. Serve the halibut curry over cauliflower rice if you'd like, or just eat it by itself!

Per Serving:
calories: 362 | fat: 22g | protein: 33g | carbs: 8g | net carbs: 5g | fiber: 3g

Sheet Pan Garlic Butter Shrimp

Prep time: 10 minutes | Cook time: 10 minutes | serves 4

1½ pounds medium shrimp, peeled and deveined	parsley
	2 cloves garlic, minced
½ cup (1 stick) salted butter, melted	Pinch of salt
	Pinch of ground black pepper
¼ cup chopped fresh flat-leaf	1 lemon, sliced

1. Preheat the oven to 400°F. Line a sheet pan with parchment paper. 2. Pat the shrimp dry. Arrange the shrimp in a single layer on the lined pan. 3. In a small bowl, stir together the melted butter, parsley, garlic, salt, and pepper. Pour the butter mixture evenly over the shrimp. Place the lemon slices on top of the shrimp. Bake for 8 to 10 minutes, until the shrimp is pink and opaque. Serve immediately.

Per Serving:
calories: 320 | fat: 24g | protein: 25g | carbs: 1g | net carbs: 1g | fiber: 0g

Chapter 5 Vegetarian Mains

Eggplant and Zucchini Bites

Prep time: 30 minutes | Cook time: 30 minutes | Serves 8

2 teaspoons fresh mint leaves, chopped	1 pound (454 g) eggplant, peeled and cubed
1½ teaspoons red pepper chili flakes	1 pound (454 g) zucchini, peeled and cubed
2 tablespoons melted butter	3 tablespoons olive oil

1. Toss all the above ingredients in a large-sized mixing dish. 2. Roast the eggplant and zucchini bites for 30 minutes at 325°F (163°C) in your air fryer, turning once or twice. 3. Serve with a homemade dipping sauce.

Broccoli Crust Pizza

Prep time: 15 minutes | Cook time: 12 minutes | Serves 4

3 cups riced broccoli, steamed and drained well	3 tablespoons low-carb Alfredo sauce
1 large egg	½ cup shredded Mozzarella cheese
½ cup grated vegetarian Parmesan cheese	

1. In a large bowl, mix broccoli, egg, and Parmesan. 2. Cut a piece of parchment to fit your air fryer basket. Press out the pizza mixture to fit on the parchment, working in two batches if necessary. Place into the air fryer basket. 3. Adjust the temperature to 370°F (188°C) and air fry for 5 minutes. 4. The crust should be firm enough to flip. If not, add 2 additional minutes. Flip crust. 5. Top with Alfredo sauce and Mozzarella. Return to the air fryer basket and cook an additional 7 minutes or until cheese is golden and bubbling. Serve warm.
Per Serving:
calories: 87 | fat: 2g | protein: 11g | carbs: 5g | fiber: 1g | sodium: 253mg

Tangy Asparagus and Broccoli

Prep time: 25 minutes | Cook time: 22 minutes | Serves 4

½ pound (227 g) asparagus, cut into 1½-inch pieces	Salt and white pepper, to taste
½ pound (227 g) broccoli, cut into 1½-inch pieces	½ cup vegetable broth
2 tablespoons olive oil	2 tablespoons apple cider vinegar

1. Place the vegetables in a single layer in the lightly greased air fryer basket. Drizzle the olive oil over the vegetables. 2. Sprinkle with salt and white pepper. 3. Cook at 380°F (193°C) for 15 minutes, shaking the basket halfway through the cooking time. 4.

Add ½ cup of vegetable broth to a saucepan; bring to a rapid boil and add the vinegar. Cook for 5 to 7 minutes or until the sauce has reduced by half. 5. Spoon the sauce over the warm vegetables and serve immediately. Bon appétit!
Per Serving:
calories: 93 | fat: 7g | protein: 3g | carbs: 6g | fiber: 3g | sodium: 89mg

Cheese Stuffed Zucchini

Prep time: 20 minutes | Cook time: 8 minutes | Serves 4

1 large zucchini, cut into four pieces	parsley, roughly chopped
2 tablespoons olive oil	1 heaping tablespoon coriander, minced
1 cup Ricotta cheese, room temperature	2 ounces (57 g) Cheddar cheese, preferably freshly grated
2 tablespoons scallions, chopped	1 teaspoon celery seeds
1 heaping tablespoon fresh	½ teaspoon salt
	½ teaspoon garlic pepper

1. Cook your zucchini in the air fryer basket for approximately 10 minutes at 350°F (177°C). Check for doneness and cook for 2-3 minutes longer if needed. 2. Meanwhile, make the stuffing by mixing the other items. 3. When your zucchini is thoroughly cooked, open them up. Divide the stuffing among all zucchini pieces and bake an additional 5 minutes.
Per Serving:
calories: 242 | fat: 20g | protein: 12g | carbs: 5g | fiber: 1g | sodium: 443mg

Spinach Cheese Casserole

Prep time: 15 minutes | Cook time: 15 minutes | Serves 4

1 tablespoon salted butter, melted	¼ cup chopped pickled jalapeños
¼ cup diced yellow onion	2 cups fresh spinach, chopped
8 ounces (227 g) full-fat cream cheese, softened	2 cups cauliflower florets, chopped
⅓ cup full-fat mayonnaise	1 cup artichoke hearts, chopped
⅓ cup full-fat sour cream	

1. In a large bowl, mix butter, onion, cream cheese, mayonnaise, and sour cream. Fold in jalapeños, spinach, cauliflower, and artichokes. 2. Pour the mixture into a round baking dish. Cover with foil and place into the air fryer basket. 3. Adjust the temperature to 370°F (188°C) and set the timer for 15 minutes. In the last 2 minutes of cooking, remove the foil to brown the top. Serve warm.

Italian Baked Egg and Veggies

Prep time: 10 minutes | Cook time: 10 minutes | Serves 2

2 tablespoons salted butter	1 medium Roma tomato, diced
1 small zucchini, sliced lengthwise and quartered	2 large eggs
½ medium green bell pepper, seeded and diced	¼ teaspoon onion powder
1 cup fresh spinach, chopped	¼ teaspoon garlic powder
	½ teaspoon dried basil
	¼ teaspoon dried oregano

1. Grease two ramekins with 1 tablespoon butter each. 2. In a large bowl, toss zucchini, bell pepper, spinach, and tomatoes. Divide the mixture in two and place half in each ramekin. 3. Crack an egg on top of each ramekin and sprinkle with onion powder, garlic powder, basil, and oregano. Place into the air fryer basket. 4. Adjust the temperature to 330ºF (166ºC) and bake for 10 minutes. 5. Serve immediately.

Zucchini Pasta with Spinach, Olives, and Asiago

Prep time: 10 minutes | Cook time: 10 minutes | Serves 4

3 tablespoons good-quality olive oil	2 tablespoons chopped fresh basil
1 tablespoon grass-fed butter	3 zucchini, spiralized
1½ tablespoons minced garlic	Sea salt, for seasoning
1 cup packed fresh spinach	Freshly ground black pepper, for seasoning
½ cup sliced black olives	½ cup shredded Asiago cheese
½ cup halved cherry tomatoes	

1. Sauté the vegetables. In a large skillet over medium-high heat, warm the olive oil and butter. Add the garlic and sauté until it's tender, about 2 minutes. Stir in the spinach, olives, tomatoes, and basil and sauté until the spinach is wilted, about 4 minutes. Stir in the zucchini noodles, toss to combine them with the sauce, and cook until the zucchini is tender, about 2 minutes. 2. Serve. Season with salt and pepper. Divide the mixture between four bowls and serve topped with the Asiago.

Per Serving:
calories: 199 | fat: 18g | protein: 6g | carbs: 4g | net carbs: 3g | fiber: 1g

Three-Cheese Zucchini Boats

Prep time: 15 minutes | Cook time: 20 minutes | Serves 2

2 medium zucchini	cheese
1 tablespoon avocado oil	¼ teaspoon dried oregano
¼ cup low-carb, no-sugar-added pasta sauce	¼ teaspoon garlic powder
¼ cup full-fat ricotta cheese	½ teaspoon dried parsley
¼ cup shredded Mozzarella	2 tablespoons grated vegetarian Parmesan cheese

1. Cut off 1 inch from the top and bottom of each zucchini. Slice zucchini in half lengthwise and use a spoon to scoop out a bit of the inside, making room for filling. Brush with oil and spoon 2 tablespoons pasta sauce into each shell. 2. In a medium bowl, mix ricotta, Mozzarella, oregano, garlic powder, and parsley. Spoon the mixture into each zucchini shell. Place stuffed zucchini shells into the air fryer basket. 3. Adjust the temperature to 350ºF (177ºC) and air fry for 20 minutes. 4. To remove from the basket, use tongs or a spatula and carefully lift out. Top with Parmesan. Serve immediately.

Per Serving:
calories: 208 | fat: 14g | protein: 12g | carbs: 11g | fiber: 3g | sodium: 247mg

Asparagus and Fennel Frittata

Prep time: 10 minutes | Cook time: 30 minutes | Serves 4

1 teaspoon coconut or regular butter, plus more for greasing	½ cup full-fat regular milk or coconut milk
8 asparagus spears, diced	1 tomato, sliced
½ cup diced fennel	1 teaspoon salt
½ cup mushrooms, sliced (optional)	½ teaspoon freshly ground black pepper
8 eggs	Grated cheese (optional)

1. Preheat the oven to 350ºF (180ºC). Grease a pie dish with butter. 2. Melt 1 teaspoon of butter in a shallow skillet over medium-high heat and sauté the asparagus, fennel, and mushrooms (if using) for about 5 minutes, or until fork-tender. 3. Transfer the vegetables to the prepared pie dish. 4. Crack the eggs into a mixing bowl and pour in the milk. Whisk together until fully combined. 5. Pour the egg mixture over the vegetables in the pie dish, season with salt and pepper, and carefully and lightly mix everything together. Lay the tomato slices on top. 6. Bake the frittata for about 30 minutes. 7. Remove from the oven and let cool for 5 to 10 minutes. Slice into wedges and sprinkle with grated cheese, if desired.

Per Serving:
calories: 188 | fat: 12g | protein: 14g | carbs: 6g | net carbs: 4g | fiber: 2g

Herbed Ricotta–Stuffed Mushrooms

Prep time: 10 minutes | Cook time: 30 minutes | Serves 4

6 tablespoons extra-virgin olive oil, divided	(such as basil, parsley, rosemary, oregano, or thyme)
4 portobello mushroom caps, cleaned and gills removed	2 garlic cloves, finely minced
1 cup whole-milk ricotta cheese	½ teaspoon salt
⅓ cup chopped fresh herbs	¼ teaspoon freshly ground black pepper

1. Preheat the oven to 400ºF (205ºC). 2. Line a baking sheet with parchment or foil and drizzle with 2 tablespoons olive oil, spreading evenly. Place the mushroom caps on the baking sheet, gill-side up. 3. In a medium bowl, mix together the ricotta, herbs, 2 tablespoons olive oil, garlic, salt, and pepper. Stuff each mushroom cap with one-quarter of the cheese mixture, pressing down if needed. Drizzle with remaining 2 tablespoons olive oil and bake until golden brown and the mushrooms are soft, 30 to 35 minutes, depending on the size of the mushrooms.

Per Serving:
calories: 308 | fat: 29g | protein: 9g | carbs: 6g | fiber: 1g | sodium: 351mg

Baked Zucchini

Prep time: 10 minutes | Cook time: 8 minutes | Serves 4

2 tablespoons salted butter	cheese
¼ cup diced white onion	1 cup shredded sharp Cheddar
½ teaspoon minced garlic	cheese
½ cup heavy whipping cream	2 medium zucchini, spiralized
2 ounces (57 g) full-fat cream	

1. In a large saucepan over medium heat, melt butter. Add onion and sauté until it begins to soften, 1 to 3 minutes. Add garlic and sauté for 30 seconds, then pour in cream and add cream cheese. 2. Remove the pan from heat and stir in Cheddar. Add the zucchini and toss in the sauce, then put into a round baking dish. Cover the dish with foil and place into the air fryer basket. 3. Adjust the temperature to 370°F (188°C) and set the timer for 8 minutes. 4. After 6 minutes remove the foil and let the top brown for remaining cooking time. Stir and serve.

Pesto Vegetable Skewers

Prep time: 30 minutes | Cook time: 8 minutes |
Makes 8 skewers

1 medium zucchini, trimmed	squares
and cut into ½-inch slices	16 whole cremini mushrooms
½ medium yellow onion, peeled	⅓ cup basil pesto
and cut into 1-inch squares	½ teaspoon salt
1 medium red bell pepper,	¼ teaspoon ground black
seeded and cut into 1-inch	pepper

1. Divide zucchini slices, onion, and bell pepper into eight even portions. Place on 6-inch skewers for a total of eight kebabs. Add 2 mushrooms to each skewer and brush kebabs generously with pesto. 2. Sprinkle each kebab with salt and black pepper on all sides, then place into ungreased air fryer basket. Adjust the temperature to 375°F (191°C) and air fry for 8 minutes, turning kebabs halfway through cooking. Vegetables will be browned at the edges and tender-crisp when done. Serve warm.

Per Serving:
calories: 75 | fat: 6g | protein: 3g | carbs: 4g | fiber: 1g | sodium: 243mg

Cauliflower Steak with Gremolata

Prep time: 15 minutes | Cook time: 25 minutes | Serves 4

2 tablespoons olive oil	Gremolata:
1 tablespoon Italian seasoning	1 bunch Italian parsley (about 1
1 large head cauliflower, outer	cup packed)
leaves removed and sliced	2 cloves garlic
lengthwise through the core	Zest of 1 small lemon, plus 1 to
into thick "steaks"	2 teaspoons lemon juice
Salt and freshly ground black	½ cup olive oil
pepper, to taste	Salt and pepper, to taste
¼ cup Parmesan cheese	

1. Preheat the air fryer to 400°F (204°C). 2. In a small bowl, combine the olive oil and Italian seasoning. Brush both sides of each cauliflower "steak" generously with the oil. Season to taste with salt and black pepper. 3. Working in batches if necessary, arrange the cauliflower in a single layer in the air fryer basket. Pausing halfway through the cooking time to turn the "steaks," air fry for 15 to 20 minutes until the cauliflower is tender and the edges begin to brown. Sprinkle with the Parmesan and air fry for 5 minutes longer. 4. To make the gremolata: In a food processor fitted with a metal blade, combine the parsley, garlic, and lemon zest and juice. With the motor running, add the olive oil in a steady stream until the mixture forms a bright green sauce. Season to taste with salt and black pepper. Serve the cauliflower steaks with the gremolata spooned over the top.

Per Serving:
calories: 336 | fat: 30g | protein: 7g | carbs: 15g | fiber: 5g | sodium: 340mg

White Cheddar and Mushroom Soufflés

Prep time: 15 minutes | Cook time: 12 minutes | Serves 4

3 large eggs, whites and yolks	¼ teaspoon cream of tartar
separated	¼ teaspoon salt
½ cup sharp white Cheddar	¼ teaspoon ground black
cheese	pepper
3 ounces (85 g) cream cheese,	½ cup cremini mushrooms,
softened	sliced

1. In a large bowl, whip egg whites until stiff peaks form, about 2 minutes. In a separate large bowl, beat Cheddar, egg yolks, cream cheese, cream of tartar, salt, and pepper together until combined. 2. Fold egg whites into cheese mixture, being careful not to stir. Fold in mushrooms, then pour mixture evenly into four ungreased ramekins. Place ramekins into air fryer basket. Adjust the temperature to 350°F (177°C) and bake for 12 minutes. Eggs will be browned on the top and firm in the center when done. Serve warm.

Greek Stuffed Eggplant

Prep time: 15 minutes | Cook time: 20 minutes | Serves 2

1 large eggplant	1 cup fresh spinach
2 tablespoons unsalted butter	2 tablespoons diced red bell
¼ medium yellow onion, diced	pepper
¼ cup chopped artichoke hearts	½ cup crumbled feta

1. Slice eggplant in half lengthwise and scoop out flesh, leaving enough inside for shell to remain intact. Take eggplant that was scooped out, chop it, and set aside. 2. In a medium skillet over medium heat, add butter and onion. Sauté until onions begin to soften, about 3 to 5 minutes. Add chopped eggplant, artichokes, spinach, and bell pepper. Continue cooking 5 minutes until peppers soften and spinach wilts. Remove from the heat and gently fold in the feta. 3. Place filling into each eggplant shell and place into the air fryer basket. 4. Adjust the temperature to 320°F (160°C) and air fry for 20 minutes. 5. Eggplant will be tender when done. Serve warm.

Per Serving:
calories: 259 | fat: 16.32g | protein: 9.81g | carbs: 22.16g | sugars: 12.44g | fiber: 10.1g | sodium: 386mg

Stuffed Eggplant

Prep time: 20 minutes | Cook time: 1 hour | Serves 2 to 4

1 small eggplant, halved lengthwise
3 tablespoons olive, avocado, or macadamia nut oil
1 onion, diced
12 asparagus spears or green beans, diced
1 red bell pepper, diced
1 large tomato, chopped
2 garlic cloves, minced
½ block (8 ounces / 227 g)

extra-firm tofu (optional)
3 tablespoons chopped fresh basil leaves
Salt and freshly ground black pepper, to taste
¼ cup water
2 eggs
Chopped fresh parsley, for garnish (optional)
Shredded cheese, for garnish (optional)

1. Preheat the oven to 350ºF (180ºC). 2. Scoop out the flesh from the halved eggplant and chop it into cubes. Reserve the eggplant skin. 3. In a sauté pan with a lid, heat the oil over medium-high heat. Add the eggplant, onion, asparagus, bell pepper, tomato, garlic, and tofu (if using) and stir. Stir in the basil, season with salt and pepper, and cook for about 5 minutes. 4. Add the water, cover the pan, reduce the heat to medium, and cook for about 15 minutes longer. 5. Put the eggplant "boats" (the reserved skin) on a baking sheet. Scoop some of the cooked eggplant mixture into each boat (you may have some filling left over, which is fine—you can roast it alongside the eggplant). 6. Crack an egg into each eggplant boat, on top of the filling, then bake for about 40 minutes, or until desired doneness. 7. Remove the eggplant from the oven and, if desired, sprinkle parsley and cheese over the top. Let the cheese melt and cool for about 5 minutes, then serve them up!

Per Serving:
calories: 380 | fat: 26g | protein: 12g | carbs: 25g | net carbs: 15g | fiber: 10g

Cauliflower Tikka Masala

Prep time: 10 minutes | Cook time: 20 minutes | Serves 4

FOR THE CAULIFLOWER
1 head cauliflower, cut into small florets
1 tablespoon coconut oil, melted
1 teaspoon ground cumin
½ teaspoon ground coriander
FOR THE SAUCE
2 tablespoons coconut oil
½ onion, chopped

1 tablespoon minced garlic
1 tablespoon grated ginger
2 tablespoons garam masala
1 tablespoon tomato paste
½ teaspoon salt
1 cup crushed tomatoes
1 cup heavy (whipping) cream
1 tablespoon chopped fresh cilantro

TO MAKE THE CAULIFLOWER 1. Preheat the oven. Set the oven temperature to 425ºF. Line a baking sheet with aluminum foil. 2. Prepare the cauliflower. In a large bowl, toss the cauliflower with the coconut oil, cumin, and coriander. Spread the cauliflower on the baking sheet in a single layer and bake it for 20 minutes, until the cauliflower is tender. TO MAKE THE SAUCE 1. Sauté the vegetables. While the cauliflower is baking, in a large skillet over medium-high heat, warm the coconut oil. Add the onion, garlic, and ginger and sauté until they've softened, about 3 minutes. 2. Finish the sauce. Stir in the garam masala, tomato paste, and salt until the vegetables are coated. Stir in the crushed tomatoes and bring to a boil, then reduce the heat to low and simmer the sauce

for 10 minutes, stirring it often. Remove the skillet from the heat and stir in the cream and cilantro. 3. Assemble and serve. Add the cauliflower to the sauce, stirring to combine everything. Divide the mixture between four bowls and serve it hot.

Per Serving:
calories: 372 | fat: 32g | protein: 8g | carbs: 17g | net carbs: 10g | fiber: 7g

Zucchini-Ricotta Tart

Prep time: 15 minutes | Cook time: 60 minutes | Serves 6

½ cup grated Parmesan cheese, divided
1½ cups almond flour
1 tablespoon coconut flour
½ teaspoon garlic powder
¾ teaspoon salt, divided
¼ cup unsalted butter, melted

1 zucchini, thinly sliced (about 2 cups)
1 cup ricotta cheese
3 eggs
2 tablespoons heavy cream
2 cloves garlic, minced
½ teaspoon dried tarragon

1. Preheat the air fryer to 330ºF (166ºC). Coat a round pan with olive oil and set aside. 2. In a large bowl, whisk ¼ cup of the Parmesan with the almond flour, coconut flour, garlic powder, and ¼ teaspoon of the salt. Stir in the melted butter until the dough resembles coarse crumbs. Press the dough firmly into the bottom and up the sides of the prepared pan. Air fry for 12 to 15 minutes until the crust begins to brown. Let cool to room temperature. 3. Meanwhile, place the zucchini in a colander and sprinkle with the remaining ½ teaspoon salt. Toss gently to distribute the salt and let sit for 30 minutes. Use paper towels to pat the zucchini dry. 4. In a large bowl, whisk together the ricotta, eggs, heavy cream, garlic, and tarragon. Gently stir in the zucchini slices. Pour the cheese mixture into the cooled crust and sprinkle with the remaining ¼ cup Parmesan. 5. Increase the air fryer to 350ºF (177ºC). Place the pan in the air fryer basket and air fry for 45 to 50 minutes, or until set and a tester inserted into the center of the tart comes out clean. Serve warm or at room temperature.

Vegetable Burgers

Prep time: 10 minutes | Cook time: 12 minutes | Serves 4

8 ounces (227 g) cremini mushrooms
2 large egg yolks
½ medium zucchini, trimmed and chopped
¼ cup peeled and chopped

yellow onion
1 clove garlic, peeled and finely minced
½ teaspoon salt
¼ teaspoon ground black pepper

1. Place all ingredients into a food processor and pulse twenty times until finely chopped and combined. 2. Separate mixture into four equal sections and press each into a burger shape. Place burgers into ungreased air fryer basket. Adjust the temperature to 375ºF (191ºC) and air fry for 12 minutes, turning burgers halfway through cooking. Burgers will be browned and firm when done. 3. Place burgers on a large plate and let cool 5 minutes before serving.

Per Serving:
calories: 50 | fat: 3g | protein: 3g | carbs: 4g | fiber: 1g | sodium: 299mg

Sweet Pepper Nachos

Prep time: 10 minutes | Cook time: 5 minutes | Serves 2

6 mini sweet peppers, seeded and sliced in half
¾ cup shredded Colby jack cheese
¼ cup sliced pickled jalapeños
½ medium avocado, peeled, pitted, and diced
2 tablespoons sour cream

1. Place peppers into an ungreased round nonstick baking dish. Sprinkle with Colby and top with jalapeños. 2. Place dish into air fryer basket. Adjust the temperature to 350ºF (177ºC) and bake for 5 minutes. Cheese will be melted and bubbly when done. 3. Remove dish from air fryer and top with avocado. Drizzle with sour cream. Serve warm.

Cheesy Garden Veggie Crustless Quiche

Prep time: 5 minutes | Cook time: 25 minutes | Serves 4

1 tablespoon grass-fed butter, divided
6 eggs
¾ cup heavy (whipping) cream
3 ounces goat cheese, divided
½ cup sliced mushrooms,
chopped
1 scallion, white and green parts, chopped
1 cup shredded fresh spinach
10 cherry tomatoes, cut in half

1. Preheat the oven. Set the oven temperature to 350°F. Grease a 9-inch pie plate with ½ teaspoon of the butter and set it aside. 2. Mix the quiche base. In a medium bowl, whisk the eggs, cream, and 2 ounces of the cheese until it's all well blended. Set it aside. 3. Sauté the vegetables. In a small skillet over medium-high heat, melt the remaining butter. Add the mushrooms and scallion and sauté them until they've softened, about 2 minutes. Add the spinach and sauté until it's wilted, about 2 minutes. 4. Assemble and bake. Spread the vegetable mixture in the bottom of the pie plate and pour the egg-and-cream mixture over the vegetables. Scatter the cherry tomatoes and the remaining 1 ounce of goat cheese on top. Bake for 20 to 25 minutes until the quiche is cooked through, puffed, and lightly browned. 5. Serve. Cut the quiche into wedges and divide it between four plates. Serve it warm or cold.

Per Serving:
calories: 355 | fat: 30g | protein: 18g | carbs: 5g | net carbs: 4g | fiber: 1g

Quiche-Stuffed Peppers

Prep time: 5 minutes | Cook time: 15 minutes | Serves 2
2 medium green bell peppers
3 large eggs
¼ cup full-fat ricotta cheese
¼ cup diced yellow onion
½ cup chopped broccoli
½ cup shredded medium Cheddar cheese

1. Cut the tops off of the peppers and remove the seeds and white membranes with a small knife. 2. In a medium bowl, whisk eggs and ricotta. 3. Add onion and broccoli. Pour the egg and vegetable mixture evenly into each pepper. Top with Cheddar. Place peppers into a 4-cup round baking dish and place into the air fryer basket. 4. Adjust the temperature to 350ºF (177ºC) and bake for 15 minutes. 5. Eggs will be mostly firm and peppers tender when fully cooked. Serve immediately.

Zucchini Lasagna

Prep time: 15 minutes | Cook time: 1 hour | Serves 8

½ cup extra-virgin olive oil, divided
4 to 5 medium zucchini squash
1 teaspoon salt
8 ounces (227 g) frozen spinach, thawed and well drained (about 1 cup)
2 cups whole-milk ricotta cheese
¼ cup chopped fresh basil or 2 teaspoons dried basil
1 teaspoon garlic powder
½ teaspoon freshly ground black pepper
2 cups shredded fresh whole-milk mozzarella cheese
1¾ cups shredded Parmesan cheese
½ (24-ounce / 680-g) jar low-sugar marinara sauce (less than 5 grams sugar)

1. Preheat the oven to 425ºF (220ºC). 2. Line two baking sheets with parchment paper or aluminum foil and drizzle each with 2 tablespoons olive oil, spreading evenly. 3. Slice the zucchini lengthwise into ¼-inch-thick long slices and place on the prepared baking sheet in a single layer. Sprinkle with ½ teaspoon salt per sheet. Bake until softened, but not mushy, 15 to 18 minutes. Remove from the oven and allow to cool slightly before assembling the lasagna. 4. Reduce the oven temperature to 375ºF (190ºC). 5. While the zucchini cooks, prep the filling. In a large bowl, combine the spinach, ricotta, basil, garlic powder, and pepper. In a small bowl, mix together the mozzarella and Parmesan cheeses. In a medium bowl, combine the marinara sauce and remaining ¼ cup olive oil and stir to fully incorporate the oil into sauce. 6. To assemble the lasagna, spoon a third of the marinara sauce mixture into the bottom of a 9-by-13-inch glass baking dish and spread evenly. Place 1 layer of softened zucchini slices to fully cover the sauce, then add a third of the ricotta-spinach mixture and spread evenly on top of the zucchini. Sprinkle a third of the mozzarella-Parmesan mixture on top of the ricotta. Repeat with 2 more cycles of these layers: marinara, zucchini, ricotta-spinach, then cheese blend. 7. Bake until the cheese is bubbly and melted, 30 to 35 minutes. Turn the broiler to low and broil until the top is golden brown, about 5 minutes. Remove from the oven and allow to cool slightly before slicing.

Per Serving:
calories: 473 | fat: 36g | protein: 23g | carbs: 17g | fiber: 3g | sodium: 868mg

Loaded Cauliflower Steak

Prep time: 5 minutes | Cook time: 7 minutes | Serves 4

1 medium head cauliflower
¼ cup hot sauce
2 tablespoons salted butter,
melted
¼ cup blue cheese crumbles
¼ cup full-fat ranch dressing

1. Remove cauliflower leaves. Slice the head in ½-inch-thick slices. 2. In a small bowl, mix hot sauce and butter. Brush the mixture over the cauliflower. 3. Place each cauliflower steak into the air fryer, working in batches if necessary. 4. Adjust the temperature to 400ºF (204ºC) and air fry for 7 minutes. 5. When cooked, edges will begin turning dark and caramelized. 6. To serve, sprinkle steaks with crumbled blue cheese. Drizzle with ranch dressing.

Broccoli with Garlic Sauce

Prep time: 19 minutes | Cook time: 15 minutes | Serves 4

2 tablespoons olive oil
Kosher salt and freshly ground
black pepper, to taste
1 pound (454 g) broccoli florets
Dipping Sauce:
2 teaspoons dried rosemary,

crushed
3 garlic cloves, minced
⅓ teaspoon dried marjoram,
crushed
¼ cup sour cream
⅓ cup mayonnaise

1. Lightly grease your broccoli with a thin layer of olive oil. Season with salt and ground black pepper. 2. Arrange the seasoned broccoli in the air fryer basket. Bake at 395°F (202°C) for 15 minutes, shaking once or twice. In the meantime, prepare the dipping sauce by mixing all the sauce ingredients. Serve warm broccoli with the dipping sauce and enjoy!

Crispy Eggplant Rounds

Prep time: 15 minutes | Cook time: 10 minutes | Serves 4

1 large eggplant, ends trimmed,
cut into ½-inch slices
½ teaspoon salt
2 ounces (57 g) Parmesan 100%

cheese crisps, finely ground
½ teaspoon paprika
¼ teaspoon garlic powder
1 large egg

1. Sprinkle eggplant rounds with salt. Place rounds on a kitchen towel for 30 minutes to draw out excess water. Pat rounds dry. 2. In a medium bowl, mix cheese crisps, paprika, and garlic powder. In a separate medium bowl, whisk egg. Dip each eggplant round in egg, then gently press into cheese crisps to coat both sides. 3. Place eggplant rounds into ungreased air fryer basket. Adjust the temperature to 400°F (204°C) and air fry for 10 minutes, turning rounds halfway through cooking. Eggplant will be golden and crispy when done. Serve warm.

Per Serving:
calories: 113 | fat: 5g | protein: 7g | carbs: 10g | fiber: 4g | sodium: 567mg

Almond-Cauliflower Gnocchi

Prep time: 5 minutes | Cook time: 25 to 30 minutes | Serves 4

5 cups cauliflower florets
⅔ cup almond flour
½ teaspoon salt

¼ cup unsalted butter, melted
¼ cup grated Parmesan cheese

1. In a food processor fitted with a metal blade, pulse the cauliflower until finely chopped. Transfer the cauliflower to a large microwave-safe bowl and cover it with a paper towel. Microwave for 5 minutes. Spread the cauliflower on a towel to cool. 2. When cool enough to handle, draw up the sides of the towel and squeeze tightly over a sink to remove the excess moisture. Return the cauliflower to the food processor and whirl until creamy. Sprinkle in the flour and salt and pulse until a sticky dough comes together. 3. Transfer the dough to a workspace lightly floured with almond flour. Shape the dough into a ball and divide into 4 equal sections. Roll each section into a rope 1 inch thick. Slice the dough into

squares with a sharp knife. 4. Preheat the air fryer to 400°F (204°C). 5. Working in batches if necessary, place the gnocchi in a single layer in the basket of the air fryer and spray generously with olive oil. Pausing halfway through the cooking time to turn the gnocchi, air fry for 25 to 30 minutes until golden brown and crispy on the edges. Transfer to a large bowl and toss with the melted butter and Parmesan cheese.

Roasted Veggie Bowl

Prep time: 10 minutes | Cook time: 15 minutes | Serves 2

1 cup broccoli florets
1 cup quartered Brussels
sprouts
½ cup cauliflower florets
¼ medium white onion, peeled
and sliced ¼ inch thick

½ medium green bell pepper,
seeded and sliced ¼ inch thick
1 tablespoon coconut oil
2 teaspoons chili powder
½ teaspoon garlic powder
½ teaspoon cumin

1. Toss all ingredients together in a large bowl until vegetables are fully coated with oil and seasoning. 2. Pour vegetables into the air fryer basket. 3. Adjust the temperature to 360°F (182°C) and roast for 15 minutes. 4. Shake two or three times during cooking. Serve warm.

Per Serving:
calories: 112 | fat: 7.68g | protein: 3.64g | carbs: 10.67g | sugars: 3.08g | fiber: 4.6g | sodium: 106mg

Mediterranean Filling Stuffed Portobello Mushrooms

Prep time: 10 minutes | Cook time: 35 minutes | Serves 4

4 large portobello mushroom
caps
3 tablespoons good-quality
olive oil, divided
1 cup chopped fresh spinach
1 red bell pepper, chopped
1 celery stalk, chopped
½ cup chopped sun-dried
tomato

¼ onion, chopped
2 teaspoons minced garlic
1 teaspoon chopped fresh
oregano
2 cups chopped pecans
¼ cup balsamic vinaigrette
Sea salt, for seasoning
Freshly ground black pepper,
for seasoning

1. Preheat the oven. Set the oven temperature to 350°F. Line a baking sheet with parchment paper. 2. Prepare the mushrooms. Use a spoon to scoop the black gills out of the mushrooms. Massage 2 tablespoons of the olive oil all over the mushroom caps and place the mushrooms on the prepared baking sheet. Set them aside. 3. Prepare the filling. In a large skillet over medium-high heat, warm the remaining 1 tablespoon of olive oil. Add the spinach, red bell pepper, celery, sun-dried tomato, onion, garlic, and oregano and sauté until the vegetables are tender, about 10 minutes. Stir in the pecans and balsamic vinaigrette and season the mixture with salt and pepper. 4. Assemble and bake. Stuff the mushroom caps with the filling and bake for 20 to 25 minutes until they're tender and golden. 5. Serve. Place one stuffed mushroom on each of four plates and serve them hot.

Per Serving:
calories: 595 | fat: 56g | protein: 10g | carbs: 18g | net carbs: 9g | fiber: 9g

Greek Vegetable Briam

Prep time: 10 minutes | Cook time: 30 minutes | Serves 4

⅓ cup good-quality olive oil, divided
1 onion, thinly sliced
1 tablespoon minced garlic
¾ small eggplant, diced
2 zucchini, diced
2 cups chopped cauliflower
1 red bell pepper, diced
2 cups diced tomatoes

2 tablespoons chopped fresh parsley
2 tablespoons chopped fresh oregano
Sea salt, for seasoning
Freshly ground black pepper, for seasoning
1½ cups crumbled feta cheese
¼ cup pumpkin seeds

1. Preheat the oven. Set the oven to broil and lightly grease a 9-by-13-inch casserole dish with olive oil. 2. Sauté the aromatics. In a medium stockpot over medium heat, warm 3 tablespoons of the olive oil. Add the onion and garlic and sauté until they've softened, about 3 minutes. 3. Sauté the vegetables. Stir in the eggplant and cook for 5 minutes, stirring occasionally. Add the zucchini, cauliflower, and red bell pepper and cook for 5 minutes. Stir in the tomatoes, parsley, and oregano and cook, giving it a stir from time to time, until the vegetables are tender, about 10 minutes. Season it with salt and pepper. 4. Broil. Transfer the vegetable mixture to the casserole dish and top with the crumbled feta. Broil for about 4 minutes until the cheese is golden. 5. Serve. Divide the casserole between four plates and top it with the pumpkin seeds. Drizzle with the remaining olive oil.

Per Serving:
calories: 356 | fat: 28g | protein: 11g | carbs: 18g | net carbs: 11g | fiber: 7g

Broccoli-Cheese Fritters

Prep time: 5 minutes | Cook time: 20 to 25 minutes | Serves 4

1 cup broccoli florets
1 cup shredded Mozzarella cheese
¾ cup almond flour
½ cup flaxseed meal, divided
2 teaspoons baking powder

1 teaspoon garlic powder
Salt and freshly ground black pepper, to taste
2 eggs, lightly beaten
½ cup ranch dressing

1. Preheat the air fryer to 400ºF (204ºC). 2. In a food processor fitted with a metal blade, pulse the broccoli until very finely chopped. 3. Transfer the broccoli to a large bowl and add the Mozzarella, almond flour, ¼ cup of the flaxseed meal, baking powder, and garlic powder. Stir until thoroughly combined. Season to taste with salt and black pepper. Add the eggs and stir again to form a sticky dough. Shape the dough into 1¼-inch fritters. 4. Place the remaining ¼ cup flaxseed meal in a shallow bowl and roll the fritters in the meal to form an even coating. 5. Working in batches if necessary, arrange the fritters in a single layer in the basket of the air fryer and spray generously with olive oil. Pausing halfway through the cooking time to shake the basket, air fry for 20 to 25 minutes until the fritters are golden brown and crispy. Serve with the ranch dressing for dipping.

Per Serving:
calories: 388 | fat: 30g | protein: 19g | carbs: 14g | fiber: 7g | sodium: 526mg

Spinach-Artichoke Stuffed Mushrooms

Prep time: 10 minutes | Cook time: 10 to 14 minutes | Serves 4

2 tablespoons olive oil
4 large portobello mushrooms, stems removed and gills scraped out
½ teaspoon salt
¼ teaspoon freshly ground pepper
4 ounces (113 g) goat cheese,

crumbled
½ cup chopped marinated artichoke hearts
1 cup frozen spinach, thawed and squeezed dry
½ cup grated Parmesan cheese
2 tablespoons chopped fresh parsley

1. Preheat the air fryer to 400ºF (204ºC). 2. Rub the olive oil over the portobello mushrooms until thoroughly coated. Sprinkle both sides with the salt and black pepper. Place top-side down on a clean work surface. 3. In a small bowl, combine the goat cheese, artichoke hearts, and spinach. Mash with the back of a fork until thoroughly combined. Divide the cheese mixture among the mushrooms and sprinkle with the Parmesan cheese. 4. Air fry for 10 to 14 minutes until the mushrooms are tender and the cheese has begun to brown. Top with the fresh parsley just before serving.

Per Serving:
calories: 284 | fat: 21g | protein: 16g | carbs: 10g | fiber: 4g | sodium: 686mg

Crispy Tofu

Prep time: 30 minutes | Cook time: 15 to 20 minutes | Serves 4

1 (16-ounce / 454-g) block extra-firm tofu
2 tablespoons coconut aminos
1 tablespoon toasted sesame oil
1 tablespoon olive oil

1 tablespoon chili-garlic sauce
1½ teaspoons black sesame seeds
1 scallion, thinly sliced

1. Press the tofu for at least 15 minutes by wrapping it in paper towels and setting a heavy pan on top so that the moisture drains. 2. Slice the tofu into bite-size cubes and transfer to a bowl. Drizzle with the coconut aminos, sesame oil, olive oil, and chili-garlic sauce. Cover and refrigerate for 1 hour or up to overnight. 3. Preheat the air fryer to 400ºF (204ºC). 4. Arrange the tofu in a single layer in the air fryer basket. Pausing to shake the pan halfway through the cooking time, air fry for 15 to 20 minutes until crisp. Serve with any juices that accumulate in the bottom of the air fryer, sprinkled with the sesame seeds and sliced scallion.

Per Serving:
calories: 173 | fat: 14g | protein: 12g | carbs: 3g | fiber: 1g | sodium: 49mg

Crispy Cabbage Steaks

Prep time: 5 minutes | Cook time: 10 minutes | Serves 4

1 small head green cabbage, cored and cut into ½-inch-thick slices
¼ teaspoon salt
¼ teaspoon ground black pepper
2 tablespoons olive oil

1 clove garlic, peeled and finely minced
½ teaspoon dried thyme
½ teaspoon dried parsley

1. Sprinkle each side of cabbage with salt and pepper, then place into ungreased air fryer basket, working in batches if needed. 2. Drizzle each side of cabbage with olive oil, then sprinkle with remaining ingredients on both sides. Adjust the temperature to 350ºF (177ºC) and air fry for 10 minutes, turning "steaks" halfway through cooking. 3.Cabbage will be browned at the edges and tender when done. Serve warm.

Per Serving:
calories: 63 | fat: 7g | protein: 0g | carbs: 1g | fiber: 0g | sodium: 155mg

Spaghetti Squash Alfredo

Prep time: 10 minutes | Cook time: 15 minutes | Serves 2

½ large cooked spaghetti squash
2 tablespoons salted butter, melted
½ cup low-carb Alfredo sauce
¼ cup grated vegetarian Parmesan cheese

½ teaspoon garlic powder
1 teaspoon dried parsley
¼ teaspoon ground peppercorn
½ cup shredded Italian blend cheese

1. Using a fork, remove the strands of spaghetti squash from the shell. Place into a large bowl with butter and Alfredo sauce. Sprinkle with Parmesan, garlic powder, parsley, and peppercorn. 2. Pour into a 4-cup round baking dish and top with shredded cheese. Place dish into the air fryer basket. 3. Adjust the temperature to 320ºF (160ºC) and bake for 15 minutes. When finished, cheese will be golden and bubbling. Serve immediately.

Chapter 6 Salads

Caprese Salad

Prep time: 10 minutes | Cook time: 0 minutes | Serves 2

¾ cup cherry tomatoes
4 ounces (113 g) fresh mozzarella pearls
2 tablespoons extra-virgin olive

oil
5 to 6 fresh basil leaves
Pink Himalayan sea salt
Freshly ground black pepper

1. In a large bowl, toss to combine the tomatoes, mozzarella, and olive oil. 2. Stack the basil leaves, roll them into a cylinder, and then cut into ribbons (chiffonade). Add the basil to the bowl. 3. Toss the ingredients until everything is coated in the dressing. Season with salt and pepper.

Per Serving:
calories: 300 | fat: 26g | protein: 13g | carbs: 3g | net carbs: 2g | fiber: 1g

Bacon and Spinach Salad

Prep time: 20 minutes | Cook time: 0 minutes | Serves 4

2 large avocados, 1 chopped and 1 sliced
1 spring onion, sliced
4 cooked bacon slices, crumbled
2 cups spinach

2 small lettuce heads, chopped
2hard-boiled eggs, chopped
Vinaigrette:
3tbsp olive oil
1 tsp Dijon mustard
1 tbsp apple cider vinegar

1. Combine the spinach, lettuce, eggs, chopped avocado, and spring onion, in a large bowl. Whisk together the vinaigrette ingredients in another bowl. Pour the dressing over, toss to combine and top with the sliced avocado and bacon.

Per Serving:
Per serving: Kcal 350, Fat: 33g, Net Carbs: 3.4g, Protein: 7g

Special Sauce Cobb Salad

Prep time: 15 minutes | Cook time: 10 minutes | Serves 4

4 bacon slices
¼ cup mayonnaise
½ teaspoon coconut vinegar or apple cider vinegar
¼ teaspoon paprika
¼ teaspoon garlic powder
¼ teaspoon onion powder
¼ teaspoon sea salt

Dash monk fruit or sweetener of choice
8 cherry tomatoes, halved
4 hard-boiled eggs, sliced
1 cup shredded sharp Cheddar cheese
8 cups chopped romaine lettuce or spinach

1. In a large skillet over medium-high heat, cook the bacon until crisp, 5 to 7 minutes. Remove the bacon to a paper towel. 2. While the bacon is cooking, prepare the dressing. In a medium bowl, whisk together the mayonnaise, vinegar, paprika, garlic powder, onion powder, salt, and sweetener. 3. To serve immediately, divide the lettuce among four serving bowls. To each bowl, add 4 tomato halves, 1 sliced egg, ¼ cup Cheddar, 1 crumbled bacon slice, and 1 tablespoon of dressing. Mix well. 4. To assemble and store for future meals, divide and layer the components in four quart-sized, wide-mouth mason jars, adding the ingredients in the following order: 1 tablespoon of dressing, 4 tomato halves, 1 sliced egg, ¼ cup Cheddar, 2 cups of romaine, and top with 1 crumbled bacon slice. Secure the lid tightly and store in the refrigerator. To serve, shake well and empty the jar into a bowl, or you can eat the salad right out of the jar!

Per Serving:
1 bowl: calories: 396 | fat: 34g | protein: 17g | carbs: 5g | net carbs: 3g | fiber: 2g

Bigass Salad

Prep time: 5 minutes | Cook time: 0 minutes | Serves 1

3 to 4 cups lettuce or mixed greens
1 to 2 cups sliced veggies
¼ cup shredded Cheddar cheese (optional)
1 can (5 ounces / 142 g) tuna

packed in water, drained
¼ cup nuts (walnuts, pecans, almonds)
2 tablespoons sunflower or pumpkin seeds
2 tablespoons olive oil

1. In a large, shallow bowl, layer lettuce, veggies, and cheese in that order. Flake the tuna over the top. 2. When you are ready to eat, sprinkle the nuts and seeds over the top, and drizzle with the olive oil.

Per Serving:
calories: 843 | fat: 63g | protein: 54g | carbs: 24g | net carbs: 10g | fiber: 14g

Crispy Bacon Salad with Mozzarella & Tomato

Prep time: 10 minutes | Cook time: 5 minutes | Serves 2

1 large tomato, sliced
4 basil leaves
8 mozzarella cheese slices
2 tsp olive oil

4 bacon slices, chopped
1 tsp balsamic vinegar
Salt, to taste

1. Place the bacon in a skillet over medium heat and cook until crispy, about 5 minutes. Divide the tomato slices between two serving plates. Arrange the mozzarella slices over and top with the basil leaves. Add the crispy bacon on top, drizzle with olive oil and vinegar. Sprinkle with salt and serve.

Per Serving:
Per serving: Kcal 279, Fat: 26g, Net Carbs: 1.5g, Protein: 21g

Tuscan Kale Salad with Anchovies

Prep time: 15 minutes | Cook time: 0 minutes | Serves 4

1 large bunch lacinato or dinosaur kale
¼ cup toasted pine nuts
1 cup shaved or coarsely shredded fresh Parmesan cheese
¼ cup extra-virgin olive oil
8 anchovy fillets, roughly

chopped
2 to 3 tablespoons freshly squeezed lemon juice (from 1 large lemon)
2 teaspoons red pepper flakes (optional)

1. Remove the rough center stems from the kale leaves and roughly tear each leaf into about 4-by-1-inch strips. Place the torn kale in a large bowl and add the pine nuts and cheese. 2. In a small bowl, whisk together the olive oil, anchovies, lemon juice, and red pepper flakes (if using). Drizzle over the salad and toss to coat well. Let sit at room temperature 30 minutes before serving, tossing again just prior to serving.

Per Serving:
calories: 333 | fat: 27g | protein: 16g | carbs: 12g | fiber: 4g | sodium: 676mg

Classic Egg Salad

Prep time: 10 minutes | Cook time: 0 minutes | serves 4

6 hard-boiled eggs, peeled and chopped
¼ cup mayonnaise
1 tablespoon finely chopped onions
1 tablespoon dill relish
1 teaspoon prepared yellow

mustard
¼ teaspoon paprika
¼ teaspoon ground black pepper
⅛ teaspoon salt
Fresh spinach leaves, for serving (optional)

1. In a medium-sized mixing bowl, stir together all the ingredients until well incorporated. Serve over spinach leaves, if desired. Leftovers can be stored in an airtight container in the refrigerator for up to 3 days.

Per Serving:
calories: 213 | fat: 18g | protein: 10g | carbs: 1g | net carbs: 1g | fiber: 0g

Summer Tuna Avocado Salad

Prep time: 10 minutes | Cook time: 0 minutes | Serves 4

3 (5-ounce) cans tuna in water, drained and flaked
1 medium cucumber, sliced
3 medium avocados, peeled, pitted, and sliced
1 medium red onion, peeled and

sliced
¼ cup finely chopped cilantro
2 tablespoons lemon juice
2 tablespoons olive oil
⅛ teaspoon salt
⅛ teaspoon black pepper

1 In a medium mixing bowl, add drained, flaked tuna. 2 Lightly toss cucumber, avocados, onion, cilantro, lemon juice, and olive oil with tuna. Lightly add salt and pepper at end. 3 Serve immediately.
Per Serving:
PER SERVING:
CALORIES: 362 , FAT: 23G , PROTEIN: 23G , SODIUM:403MG , FIBER:8G , CARBOHYDRATE:15G , SUGAR:3G

Taco Salad

Prep time: 10 minutes | Cook time: 10 minutes | Serves 2

1 tablespoon ghee
1 pound ground beef
Pink Himalayan salt
Freshly ground black pepper
2 cups chopped romaine

1 avocado, cubed
½ cup halved grape tomatoes
½ cup shredded cheese (I use Mexican blend)

1. In a large skillet over medium-high heat, heat the ghee. 2. When the ghee is hot, add the ground beef, breaking it up into smaller pieces with a spoon. Stir, cooking until the beef is browned, about 10 minutes. Season with pink Himalayan salt and pepper. 3. Divide the romaine into two bowls. Season with pink Himalayan salt and pepper. 4. Add the avocado and tomatoes, top with the beef and shredded cheese, and serve.

Per Serving:
calories: 659 | fat: 52g | protein: 48g | carbs: 10g | net carbs: 4g | fiber: 6g

Olive Garden Salad

Prep time: 10 minutes | Cook time: 0 minutes | Serves 4

6 cups chopped iceberg lettuce
2 Roma tomatoes, sliced into rounds
¼ cup sliced red onion
1 cup whole pepperoncini
1 cup whole black olives

3 tablespoons olive oil
1 tablespoon red wine vinegar
¼ teaspoon garlic powder
⅛ teaspoon salt
⅛ teaspoon black pepper
⅓ cup grated Parmesan cheese

1 Mix all vegetables and olives in a large salad bowl. 2 In a small bowl, mix oil, vinegar, and spices together. 3 Pour dressing over salad, toss, and top with Parmesan cheese. Serve immediately.
Per Serving:
PER SERVING:
CALORIES: 217 , FAT: 18G , PROTEIN: 4G , SODIUM:948MG , FIBER:2G , CARBOHYDRATE:8G , SUGAR:3G

Broccoli & Raspberry "Bacon" Salad

Prep time: 5 minutes | Cook time: 0 minutes | serves 6

4 tablespoons tahini
Juice of 2 lemons
1 tablespoon apple cider vinegar
1 tablespoon paprika
1 teaspoon cayenne pepper (optional)

Sea salt
Freshly ground black pepper
1 pound broccoli florets
¼ red onion, finely chopped
⅓ cup freeze-dried raspberries, crushed

1. In a medium mixing bowl, whisk together the tahini, lemon juice, vinegar, paprika, and cayenne, and season with salt and pepper. 2. In a large bowl, toss the broccoli with the onion. 3. Top the vegetables with the tahini mixture and toss vigorously to coat. 4. Sprinkle the raspberries on top and toss again. 5. Allow to marinate in the refrigerator for at least 1 hour, and overnight for the best result.

Per Serving:
calories: 99 | fat: 6g | protein: 3g | carbs: 9g | net carbs: 6g | fiber: 3g

Salmon Salad Cups

Prep time: 10 minutes | Cook time: 0 minutes | Serves 4

12 ounces (340 g) canned salmon (no salt added)	salt
3 tablespoons prepared horseradish	½ teaspoon ground black pepper
1 tablespoon chopped fresh dill	12 butter lettuce leaves (from 1 head)
2 teaspoons lemon juice	½ cup (105 g) mayonnaise
½ teaspoon finely ground sea	

1. Place the salmon, horseradish, dill, lemon juice, salt, and pepper in a medium-sized bowl. Stir until the ingredients are fully incorporated. 2. Set the lettuce leaves on a serving plate. Fill each leaf with 2 tablespoons of the salmon salad mixture and top with 2 teaspoons of mayonnaise.

Per Serving:
calories: 314 | fat: 27g | protein: 15g | carbs: 4g | net carbs: 3g | fiber: 1g

Vintage Three Bean Salad

Prep time: 15 minutes | Cook time: 4 minutes | Serves 4

3 cups fresh green beans, trimmed and cut into 2" lengths	1 tablespoon lemon juice
½ cup shelled soybeans (edamame), cooked	1 teaspoon spicy mustard
1 cup black soybeans	1 clove garlic, peeled and minced
3 tablespoons olive oil	2 tablespoons dried basil, or chopped fresh
2 tablespoons apple cider vinegar	⅛ teaspoon salt
	⅛ teaspoon black pepper

1 In a medium microwave-safe bowl, microwave raw green beans 4 minutes with ¼ cup water. Drain water and let cool. 2 In a medium mixing bowl, combine green beans with other two beans. 3 In a small bowl, whisk remaining ingredients to make dressing. 4 Pour dressing over beans and lightly toss. 5 If desired, chill before serving.

Per Serving:

PER SERVING:
CALORIES: 204 , FAT: 14G , PROTEIN: 10G , SODIUM:111MG , FIBER:7G , CARBOHYDRATE:13G , SUGAR:3G

Spinach Turnip Salad with Bacon

Prep time: 10 minutes | Cook time: 30 minutes |
Serves 4

2 turnips, cut into wedges	2 tsp mustard seeds
1 tsp olive oil	1 tsp Dijon mustard
1 cup baby spinach, chopped	1 tbsp red wine vinegar
3 radishes, sliced	Salt and black pepper to taste
3bacon slices	1 tbsp chopped chives
4tbsp sour cream	

1. Preheat the oven to 400ºF. Line a baking sheet with parchment paper, toss the turnips with salt and black pepper, drizzle with the olive oil, and bake for 25 minutes, turning halfway. Let cool. 2.

Spread the baby spinach in the bottom of a salad bowl and top with the radishes. Remove the turnips to the salad bowl. Fry the bacon in a skillet over medium heat until crispy, about 5 minutes. 3. Mix sour cream, mustard seeds, mustard, vinegar, and salt with the bacon. Add a little water to deglaze the bottom of the skillet. Pour the bacon mixture over the vegetables, scatter the chives over it. Serve.

Per Serving:
Per serving: Kcal 193, Fat 18.3g, Net Carbs 3.1g, Protein 9.5g

Kale Salad with Spicy Lime-Tahini Dressing

Prep time: 15 minutes | Cook time: 0 minutes | Serves 4

DRESSING:	¼ teaspoon red pepper flakes
½ cup (120 ml) avocado oil	SALAD:
¼ cup (60 ml) lime juice	6 cups (360 g) destemmed kale leaves, roughly chopped
¼ cup (60 ml) tahini	12 radishes, thinly sliced
2 cloves garlic, minced	1 green bell pepper, sliced
1 jalapeño pepper, seeded and finely diced	1 medium Hass avocado, peeled, pitted, and cubed (about 4 oz/110 g of flesh)
Handful of fresh cilantro leaves, chopped	¼ cup (30 g) hulled pumpkin seeds
½ teaspoon ground cumin	
½ teaspoon finely ground sea salt	

1. Make the dressing: Place the dressing ingredients in a medium-sized bowl and whisk to combine. Set aside. 2. Make the salad: Rinse the kale under hot water for about 30 seconds to soften it and make it easier to digest. Dry the kale well, then place it in a large salad bowl. Add the remaining salad ingredients and toss to combine. 3. Divide the salad evenly among 4 bowls. Drizzle each bowl with ¼ cup (60 ml) of the dressing and serve.

Per Serving:
calories: 517 | fat: 47g | protein: 11g | carbs: 21g | net carbs: 12g | fiber: 9g

Cheeseburger Salad

Prep time: 10 minutes | Cook time: 10 minutes | Serves 2

1 tablespoon ghee	2 cups chopped romaine
1 pound ground beef	½ cup shredded Cheddar cheese
Pink Himalayan salt	2 tablespoons ranch salad dressing (I use Primal Kitchen Ranch)
Freshly ground black pepper	
½ cup finely chopped dill pickles	

1. In a medium skillet over medium-high heat, heat the ghee. 2. When the ghee is hot, add the ground beef, breaking it up into smaller pieces with a spoon. Stir, cooking until the beef is browned, about 10 minutes. Season with pink Himalayan salt and pepper. 3. Put the pickles in a large bowl, and add the romaine and cheese. 4. Using a slotted spoon, transfer the browned beef from the skillet to the bowl. 5. Top the salad with the dressing, and toss to thoroughly coat. 6. Divide into two bowls and serve.

Per Serving:
calories: 662 | fat: 50g | protein: 47g | carbs: 6g | net carbs: 4g | fiber: 2g

Zucchini Pasta Salad

Prep time: 5 minutes | Cook time: 0 minutes | Serves 4

4 medium zucchinis, spiral sliced
12 ounces (340 g) pitted black olives, cut in half lengthwise
1 pint (290 g) cherry tomatoes, cut in half lengthwise

½ cup (75 g) pine nuts
¼ cup plus 2 tablespoons (55 g) sesame seeds
⅔ cup (160 ml) creamy Italian dressing or other creamy salad dressing of choice

1. Place all the ingredients in a large mixing bowl. Toss to coat, then divide evenly between 4 serving plates or bowls.

Per Serving:
calories: 562 | fat: 53g | protein: 9g | carbs: 22g | net carbs: 14g | fiber: 9g

Mixed Green Salad with BLT Deviled Eggs and Bacon Vinaigrette

Prep time: 15 minutes | Cook time: 15 minutes | Serves 6

12 large eggs
4 slices bacon, cut into ¼-inch dice
2 tablespoons diced onions
3 tablespoons plus 2 teaspoons coconut vinegar or red wine vinegar, divided
1 teaspoon Dijon mustard
3 tablespoons MCT oil or extra-virgin olive oil

½ cup mayonnaise, homemade or store-bought
2 teaspoons prepared yellow mustard
½ teaspoon fine sea salt
6 cherry tomatoes, quartered
6 cups mixed greens, plus a few tablespoons finely chopped greens for garnish
Sliced fresh chives, for garnish

1. Place the eggs in a large saucepan and cover with cold water. Bring to a boil, then immediately cover the pan and remove it from the heat. Allow the eggs to cook in the hot water for 11 minutes. 2. Meanwhile, make the bacon vinaigrette: Cook the diced bacon in a skillet over medium heat until crispy, about 5 minutes. Remove the bacon from the pan, leaving the drippings in the skillet. Add the onions, 3 tablespoons of the vinegar, and the Dijon mustard. Cook over medium heat until the onions soften, about 2 minutes. While stirring with a whisk, slowly add the oil to the pan. Whisk well to combine. Set aside. 3. To make the deviled eggs: After the eggs cook for 11 minutes, drain the hot water and rinse the eggs with very cold water for a minute or two to stop the cooking process. Peel the eggs and cut them in half lengthwise. Remove the yolks and place them in a bowl (or food processor). Mash the yolks with a fork (or in a food processor) until they are the texture of very fine crumbles. Add the mayonnaise, remaining 2 teaspoons of vinegar, yellow mustard, and salt. Fill the egg white halves with the yolk mixture. Top each deviled egg with a cherry tomato quarter and sprinkle with the crispy bacon, chopped lettuce, and sliced chives. 4. Dress the rest of the lettuce with the bacon vinaigrette, divide among six plates, and place four deviled eggs on each plate. 5. If not serving immediately, do not dress the lettuce with the vinaigrette until just before serving. Store the vinaigrette in an airtight jar in the fridge for up to 5 days. Keep leftover deviled eggs in an airtight container in the fridge for up to 3 days.

Per Serving:
calories: 418 | fat: 37g | protein: 17g | carbs: 4g | net carbs: 3g | fiber: 1g

German No-Tato Salad

Prep time: 10 minutes | Cook time: 10 minutes | Serves 5

2 medium rutabaga (2 lbs/910 g), peeled
1 teaspoon finely ground sea salt
1 small red onion, finely diced
¼ cup (60 ml) apple cider vinegar
¼ cup (60 ml) avocado oil or olive oil
4 green onions, sliced
1 tablespoon Dijon mustard

1 teaspoon erythritol
¾ teaspoon ground black pepper
FOR SERVING:
1 tablespoon plus 2 teaspoons Dijon mustard
1 tablespoon plus 2 teaspoons mayonnaise
10 ounces (285 g) thinly sliced deli ham or other meat of choice

1. Cut the rutabaga into ½-inch (1.25-cm) cubes, place in a large saucepan, cover completely with water, and add the salt. Cover with the lid, bring to a boil over high heat, then reduce the heat to a simmer and cook for 10 minutes, or until fork-tender. 2. Meanwhile, place the remaining ingredients in a large salad bowl. Once the rutabaga is cooked, drain completely and transfer to the salad bowl. Toss to combine, then divide among 5 plates. 3. In a small bowl, mix together the mustard and mayonnaise. 4. Serve the ham slices alongside the salad with 2 teaspoons of the mustard sauce.

Per Serving:
calories: 296 | fat: 19g | protein: 14g | carbs: 19g | net carbs: 14g | fiber: 5g

Curried Okra Salad

Prep time: 15 minutes | Cook time: 15 minutes | Serves 4

FRIED OKRA:
¼ cup (55 g) plus 2 tablespoons coconut oil, divided
15 ounces (420 g) okra, trimmed and quartered lengthwise
SALAD:
¾ packed cup (60 g) fresh cilantro leaves, chopped
1 large tomato (about 2½ ounces/70 g), diced

½ small red onion, sliced (optional)
DRESSING:
⅓ cup (80 ml) extra-virgin olive oil, unrefined canola oil, or refined avocado oil
2 tablespoons fresh lemon juice
2 teaspoons curry powder
¼ teaspoon finely ground gray sea salt
2 drops liquid stevia

1. Melt ¼ cup (55 g) of the coconut oil in a large frying pan over medium-high heat. Place half of the okra in the pan and fry for 6 to 8 minutes, until the pieces are browned. Transfer the browned okra pieces to a clean plate, add the remaining 2 tablespoons of oil to the pan, and repeat with the remaining okra. 2. Meanwhile, place the ingredients for the salad in a large bowl. After all the okra is browned, transfer it to the bowl with the salad. 3. In a separate small bowl, whisk together the ingredients for the dressing, then drizzle the dressing over the salad and toss to coat. Divide among 4 salad bowls and serve.

Per Serving:
calories: 390 | fat: 38g | protein: 3g | carbs: 9g | net carbs: 5g | fiber: 5g

Chopped Salad in Jars

Prep time: 8 minutes | Cook time: 0 minutes | Serves 4

½ cup ranch dressing
1 cup diced tomatoes
1 cup diced cucumber
1 cup coarsely chopped
radicchio or romaine lettuce

1 cup diced celery
4 hard-boiled eggs, chopped
(omit for egg-free)
4 slices bacon, diced and
cooked until crispy

1. Have on hand four pint-sized mason jars. Place 2 tablespoons of ranch dressing in the bottom of each jar. Top with a quarter of the diced tomatoes. Then add the rest of the salad ingredients to the jars in the order listed, dividing the ingredients equally among the jars.

Per Serving:
calories: 382 | fat: 31g | protein: 18g | carbs: 8g | net carbs: 5g | fiber: 3g

Traditional Greek Salad

Prep time: 10 minutes | Cook time: 0 minutes | Serves 4

2 large English cucumbers
4 Roma tomatoes, quartered
1 green bell pepper, cut into 1-
to 1½-inch chunks
¼ small red onion, thinly sliced
4 ounces (113 g) pitted
Kalamata olives
¼ cup extra-virgin olive oil
2 tablespoons freshly squeezed

lemon juice
1 tablespoon red wine vinegar
1 tablespoon chopped fresh
oregano or 1 teaspoon dried
oregano
¼ teaspoon freshly ground
black pepper
4 ounces (113 g) crumbled
traditional feta cheese

1. Cut the cucumbers in half lengthwise and then into ½-inch-thick half-moons. Place in a large bowl. 2. Add the quartered tomatoes, bell pepper, red onion, and olives. 3. In a small bowl, whisk together the olive oil, lemon juice, vinegar, oregano, and pepper. Drizzle over the vegetables and toss to coat. 4. Divide between salad plates and top each with 1 ounce (28 g) of feta.

Per Serving:
calories: 256 | fat: 22g | protein: 6g | carbs: 11g | fiber: 3g | sodium: 476mg

Caesar Salad with Anchovies and Pancetta

Prep time: 10 minutes | Cook time: 10 minutes | Serves 2

1 egg yolk, at room temperature
2 garlic cloves, chopped
2 teaspoons Dijon mustard
Juice from 1 large lemon, at
room temperature
1 teaspoon kosher salt
½ teaspoon freshly ground
black pepper, plus more as

needed
1 can (2 ounces / 57 g)
anchovies packed in olive oil
1 cup extra-virgin olive oil
1 cup grated Parmesan cheese
1 teaspoon butter
4 ounces (113 g) diced pancetta
4 cups chopped romaine lettuce

1. In a high-powered blender, combine the egg yolk, garlic, Dijon mustard, lemon juice, salt, pepper, half the anchovies, and ¼ cup oil. Blend for 10 seconds. With the blender running, slowly pour in the remaining oil in a thin stream so the dressing emulsifies. Add in ½ cup of the Parmesan cheese and pulse a few times to combine. 2. Melt the butter in a small skillet and sauté the pancetta until crisp. 3. Toss the lettuce with ½ cup of the dressing. Roughly chop the remaining anchovies and place on top. Sprinkle with the crispy pancetta. Top with Parmesan crisps or the remaining grated Parmesan, and additional freshly ground pepper. If desired, drizzle with more dressing.

Per Serving:
calories: 602 | fat: 53g | protein: 28g | carbs: 5g | net carbs: 3g | fiber: 2g

Asian-Style Cucumber Salad

Prep time: 8 minutes | Cook time: 0 minutes | serves 6

2 large cucumbers, chopped
into bite-size cubes
¼ red onion, thinly sliced
½ cup white rice vinegar

1 teaspoon sesame oil
3 or 4 drops liquid stevia
2 tablespoons black sesame
seeds

1. Toss the cucumbers and onion together in a large mixing bowl with the vinegar, sesame oil, and stevia. 2. Cover the bowl with plastic wrap or a lid and place the salad in the refrigerator for about 1 hour to marinate. 3. Top the salad with the sesame seeds and serve.

Per Serving:
calories: 39 | fat: 2g | protein: 1g | carbs: 4g | net carbs: 3g | fiber: 1g

Superfood Salmon Salad Bowl

Prep time: 5 minutes | Cook time: 10 minutes | Serves 2

Salmon:
2 fillets wild salmon
Salt and black pepper, to taste
2 teaspoons extra-virgin
avocado oil
Dressing:
1 tablespoon capers
1 teaspoon Dijon or whole-
grain mustard
1 tablespoon apple cider
vinegar or fresh lemon juice
3 tablespoons extra-virgin olive
oil
1 teaspoon coconut aminos
Salt and black pepper, to taste

Salad:
½ medium cucumber, diced
1 cup sugar snap peas, sliced
into matchsticks
½ small red bell pepper, sliced
⅓ cup pitted Kalamata olives,
halved
2 sun-dried tomatoes, chopped
1 medium avocado, diced
3 tablespoons chopped fresh
herbs, such as dill, chives,
parsley, and/or basil
1 tablespoon pumpkin seeds
1 tablespoon sunflower seeds

1. Make the salmon: Season the salmon with salt and pepper. Heat a pan greased with the avocado oil over medium heat. Add the salmon, skin-side down, and cook for 4 to 5 minutes. Flip and cook for 1 to 2 minutes or until cooked through. Remove from the heat and transfer to a plate to cool. Remove the skin from the salmon and flake into chunks. 2. Make the dressing: Mix all the dressing ingredients together in a small bowl. Set aside. 3. Make the salad: Place the cucumber, sugar snap peas, bell pepper, olives, sun-dried tomatoes, avocado, and herbs in a mixing bowl, and combine well. Add the flaked salmon. Dry-fry the seeds in a pan placed over medium-low heat until lightly golden. Allow to cool, then add to the bowl. Drizzle with the prepared dressing and serve. This salad can be stored in the fridge for up to 1 day.

Per Serving:
calories: 660 | fat: 54g | protein: 31g | carbs: 18g | fiber: 9g | sodium: 509mg

Calamari Salad

Prep time: 10 minutes | Cook time: 7 minutes | Serves 4

12 ounces (340 g) uncooked calamari rings, defrosted
1½ cups (210 g) grape tomatoes, halved
½ cup (60 g) pitted kalamata olives, halved
½ packed cup (35 g) chopped fresh parsley
¼ cup (20 g) sliced green onions
DRESSING:

½ cup (120 ml) extra-virgin olive oil or refined avocado oil
1 tablespoon red wine vinegar
Grated zest of ½ lemon
Juice of ½ lemon
2 small cloves garlic, minced
¼ teaspoon finely ground gray sea salt
¼ teaspoon ground black pepper

1. Place the calamari in a steamer and steam for 7 minutes. Transfer to the freezer to cool for a couple of minutes. 2. Meanwhile, make the dressing: Place the ingredients for the dressing in a small bowl. Whisk to combine and set aside. 3. Once the calamari has cooled, place it in a large bowl along with the grape tomatoes, olives, parsley, and green onions. Add the dressing and toss to coat. 4. Divide among 4 serving plates and enjoy.

Per Serving:
calories: 507 | fat: 30g | protein: 55g | carbs: 4g | net carbs: 3g | fiber: 2g

Chicken and Bacon Salad with Sun-Dried Tomato Dressing

Prep time: 10 minutes | Cook time: 5 minutes | Serves 1

2 slices bacon
3 sun-dried tomatoes (packed in olive oil)
1 tablespoon olive oil
1 teaspoon minced shallots
¼ teaspoon garlic powder
½ teaspoon dried oregano
1 teaspoon nutritional yeast or grated cheese (optional but recommended)
½ teaspoon freshly squeezed lemon juice (optional)

Pinch each salt and freshly ground black pepper
1 cup Bibb or butter lettuce leaves
4 ounces (113 g) cooked chicken breast and/or thigh meat, diced (if you use store-bought, make sure it doesn't contain any added sugar)
¼ cup cherry tomatoes, halved
½ avocado, pitted, peeled, and diced

1. Heat a shallow skillet over medium heat. When warm, cook the bacon to your desired crispness, about 5 minutes. Turn off the heat and let the bacon sit in the skillet. 2. To make the dressing, in a blender, combine the sun-dried tomatoes, olive oil, shallots, garlic powder, oregano, nutritional yeast or cheese (if using), lemon juice (if using), and salt and pepper. Whirl away until smooth. 3. To construct the salad, put the lettuce on a plate. Top with the chicken, cherry tomatoes, and avocado. Lay the bacon on top (alternatively, you can chop up the bacon and sprinkle it on after you've dressed the salad). If you'd like, pour the bacon pan drippings over the salad (trust me, it's amazing). Spoon on about 1 to 2 tablespoons of dressing and dig in!

Per Serving:
calories: 858 | fat: 62g | protein: 52g | carbs: 23g | net carbs: 9g | fiber: 14g

Powerhouse Arugula Salad

Prep time: 10 minutes | Cook time: 0 minutes | Serves 4

4 tablespoons extra-virgin olive oil
Zest and juice of 2 clementines or 1 orange (2 to 3 tablespoons)
1 tablespoon red wine vinegar
½ teaspoon salt

¼ teaspoon freshly ground black pepper
8 cups baby arugula
1 cup coarsely chopped walnuts
1 cup crumbled goat cheese
½ cup pomegranate seeds

1. In a small bowl, whisk together the olive oil, zest and juice, vinegar, salt, and pepper and set aside. 2. To assemble the salad for serving, in a large bowl, combine the arugula, walnuts, goat cheese, and pomegranate seeds. Drizzle with the dressing and toss to coat.

Per Serving:
calories: 448 | fat: 41g | protein: 11g | carbs: 13g | fiber: 4g | sodium: 647mg

Mediterranean Cucumber Salad

Prep time: 10 minutes | Cook time: 0 minutes | Serves 2

1 large cucumber, peeled and finely chopped
½ cup halved grape tomatoes
¼ cup halved black olives (I use Kalamata)
¼ cup crumbled feta cheese

Pink Himalayan salt
Freshly ground black pepper
2 tablespoons vinaigrette salad dressing (I use Primal Kitchen Greek Vinaigrette)

1. In a large bowl, combine the cucumber, tomatoes, olives, and feta cheese. Season with pink Himalayan salt and pepper. Add the dressing and toss to combine. 2. Divide the salad between two bowls and serve.

Per Serving:
calories: 152 | fat: 13g | protein: 4g | carbs: 6g | net carbs: 4g | fiber: 2g

Marinated Cucumber Salad

Prep time: 10 minutes | Cook time: 0 minutes | serves 4

1 large English cucumber
Salt
½ red onion
½ cup apple cider vinegar
2 tablespoons avocado oil

2 tablespoons granular erythritol
½ teaspoon dried ground oregano
Ground black pepper

1. Slice the cucumber crosswise into thin rounds. Place the cucumber slices in a colander over the sink. Sprinkle with salt and allow to sit for 10 minutes. This will cause the excess moisture to drain from the cucumbers. 2. Thinly slice the onion and place in a medium-sized bowl. 3. Use a paper towel to remove any remaining moisture from the cucumber slices, then add the cucumbers to the bowl with the onion slices. Add the vinegar, oil, erythritol, and oregano and gently stir with a spoon. Season to taste with salt and pepper. 4. Place the salad in the refrigerator to chill for at least 2 hours before serving. Leftovers can be stored in an airtight container in the refrigerator for up to 3 days.

Per Serving:
calories: 85 | fat: 7g | protein: 1g | carbs: 4g | net carbs: 4g | fiber: 1g

Berry Avocado Salad

Prep time: 10 minutes | Cook time: 0 minutes | Serves 4

DRESSING:
2 tablespoons extra-virgin olive oil or refined avocado oil
1½ teaspoons fresh lime juice
1½ teaspoons chili powder
1 small clove garlic, minced
2 drops liquid stevia
Finely ground gray sea salt, to taste
SALAD:
2 large Hass avocados, skinned, pitted, and cubed (12 ounces/340 g flesh) 12 strawberries, cut into quarters or eighths (depending on size)
½ packed cup (30 g) fresh parsley, chopped
1 packed tablespoon fresh cilantro leaves, chopped
1 tablespoon finely diced white onion

1. Place the ingredients for the dressing in a large bowl and whisk to combine. Add the salad ingredients and toss gently to coat. 2. Divide the salad among 4 bowls and serve immediately.

Per Serving:
calories: 259 | fat: 22g | protein: 4g | carbs: 13g | net carbs: 3g | fiber: 10g

Avocado Salad with Arugula and Red Onion

Prep time: 10 minutes | Cook time: 0 minutes | Serves 2

2 cups arugula, washed and dried
¼ red onion, thinly sliced
½ cup olive oil
¼ cup balsamic vinegar
1 tablespoon Dijon mustard
Salt and freshly ground black pepper, to taste
1 avocado, peeled, halved, pitted, and diced or sliced

1. In a large bowl, combine the arugula and red onion. 2. In a small bowl, whisk together the olive oil, vinegar, mustard, and some salt and pepper. Pour the dressing over the salad and toss well to combine. 3. Divide the salad between two bowls and top each with half an avocado. Season with a bit more salt and pepper and serve.

Per Serving:
calories: 686 | fat: 70g | protein: 3g | carbs: 11g | net carbs: 3g | fiber: 8g

Avocado Egg Salad Lettuce Cups

Prep time: 15 minutes | Cook time: 15 minutes | Serves 2

FOR THE HARDBOILED EGGS
4 large eggs
FOR THE EGG SALAD
1 avocado, halved
Pink Himalayan salt
Freshly ground black pepper
½ teaspoon freshly squeezed lemon juice
4 butter lettuce cups, washed and patted dry with paper towels or a clean dish towel
2 radishes, thinly sliced

TO MAKE THE HARDBOILED EGGS 1. In a medium saucepan, cover the eggs with water. Place over high heat, and bring the water to a boil. Once it is boiling, turn off the heat, cover, and leave on the burner for 10 to 12 minutes. 2. Remove the eggs with a slotted spoon and run them under cold water for 1 minute or submerge them in an ice bath. 3. Then gently tap the shells and peel. Run cold water over your hands as you remove the shells. TO MAKE THE EGG SALAD 1. In a medium bowl, chop the hardboiled eggs. 2. Add the avocado to the bowl, and mash the flesh with a fork. Season with pink Himalayan salt and pepper, add the lemon juice, and stir to combine. 3. Place the 4 lettuce cups on two plates. Top the lettuce cups with the egg salad and the slices of radish and serve.

Per Serving:
calories: 258 | fat: 20g | protein: 15g | carbs: 8g | net carbs: 3g | fiber: 5g

Taverna-Style Greek Salad

Prep time: 20 minutes | Cook time: 0 minutes | Serves 4

4 to 5 medium tomatoes, roughly chopped
1 large cucumber, peeled and roughly chopped
1 medium green bell pepper, sliced
1 small red onion, sliced
16 pitted Kalamata olives
¼ cup capers, or more olives
1 teaspoon dried oregano or fresh herbs of your choice, such as parsley, cilantro, chives, or basil, divided
½ cup extra-virgin olive oil, divided
1 pack feta cheese
Optional: salt, pepper, and fresh oregano, for garnish

1. Place the vegetables in a large serving bowl. Add the olives, capers, feta, half of the dried oregano and half of the olive oil. Mix to combine. Place the whole piece of feta cheese on top, sprinkle with the remaining dried oregano, and drizzle with the remaining olive oil. Season to taste and serve immediately, or store in the fridge for up to 1 day.

Per Serving:
calories: 320 | fat: 31g | protein: 3g | carbs: 11g | fiber: 4g | sodium: 445mg

Marinated Bok Choy Salad

Prep time: 20 minutes | Cook time: 0 minutes | Serves 6

DRESSING:
⅓ cup (80 ml) extra-virgin olive oil or refined avocado oil
3 tablespoons MCT oil
3 tablespoons apple cider vinegar
2 tablespoons coconut aminos
4 small cloves garlic, minced
1 (2-inch/5-cm) piece fresh ginger root, minced
2 teaspoons prepared yellow mustard
¼ teaspoon finely ground gray sea salt
¼ teaspoon ground black pepper
2 drops liquid stevia
SALAD:
8 cups (900 g) chopped bok choy (about 1 large head)
⅓ cup (40 g) sliced raw almonds, divided

1. Combine the ingredients for the dressing in a large bowl. 2. Add the bok choy and ¼ cup (30 g) of the sliced almonds. Toss to coat. Cover the bowl and place in the fridge for at least 12 hours, but not longer than 3 days. 3. When ready to serve, divide the salad among 6 bowls and sprinkle each salad with the remaining sliced almonds.

Per Serving:
calories: 234 | fat: 21g | protein: 4g | carbs: 7g | net carbs: 5g | fiber: 2g

Chapter 7 Stews and Soups

Brazilian Moqueca (Shrimp Stew)

Prep time: 15 minutes | Cook time: 10 minutes | Serves 6

1cup coconut milk
2tbsp lime juice
¼ cup diced roasted peppers
1 ½ pounds shrimp, peeled and deveined
¼ cup olive oil
1 garlic clove, minced

14 ounces diced tomatoes
2 tbsp sriracha sauce
1 chopped onion
¼ cup chopped cilantro
Fresh dill, chopped to garnish
Salt and black pepper, to taste

1. Heat the olive oil in a pot over medium heat. Add onion and cook for 3 minutes or until translucent. Add the garlic and cook for another minute, until soft. Add tomatoes, shrimp, and cilantro. Cook until the shrimp becomes opaque, about 3-4 minutes. 2. Stir in sriracha sauce and coconut milk, and cook for 2 minutes. Do not bring to a boil. Stir in the lime juice and season with salt and pepper. Spoon the stew in bowls, garnish with fresh dill to serve.

Per Serving:
Per serving: Kcal 324, Fat: 21g, Net Carbs: 5g, Protein: 23.1g

Tomato Bisque

Prep time: 10 minutes | Cook time: 40 minutes | serves 8

Nonstick coconut oil cooking spray
1 pound heirloom cherry tomatoes, coarsely chopped
1 yellow onion, coarsely chopped
2 garlic cloves, coarsely chopped
¼ cup cold-pressed olive oil,

plus more for drizzling
2 thyme sprigs
Sea salt
Freshly ground black pepper
1 lemon, halved
1 cup coconut cream
⅓ cup chopped fresh basil, for garnish

1. Preheat the oven to 400°F. Grease a baking dish with cooking spray and set aside. 2. Combine the tomatoes, onion, and garlic in the baking dish. Drizzle with the olive oil and toss in the thyme. Season with salt and pepper. Top with the lemon halves and roast for 20 minutes or until the tomatoes start to blister. 3. Remove from the oven and transfer the mixture to a large saucepan over low heat. 4. Stir in the coconut cream and bring the soup to a simmer. Cook for 20 minutes to allow the flavors to meld together. 5. Remove and discard the lemon halves. 6. Turn off the heat and blend the soup with an immersion blender until it is silky smooth (adding warm water if necessary to reach desired texture). 7. Finish with cracked black pepper, olive oil drizzle, the basil, and additional salt, if desired.

Per Serving:
calories: 142 | fat: 14g | protein: 1g | carbs: 7g | net carbs: 5g | fiber: 2g

Cabbage Roll Soup

Prep time: 10 minutes | Cook time: 8 minutes | Serves 4

½ pound (227 g) 84% lean ground pork
½ pound (227 g) 85% lean ground beef
½ medium onion, diced
½ medium head cabbage, thinly sliced
2 tablespoons sugar-free tomato

paste
½ cup diced tomatoes
2 cups chicken broth
1 teaspoon salt
½ teaspoon thyme
½ teaspoon garlic powder
¼ teaspoon pepper

1. Press the Sauté button and add beef and pork to Instant Pot. Brown meat until no pink remains. Add onion and continue cooking until onions are fragrant and soft. Press the Cancel button. 2. Add remaining ingredients to Instant Pot. Press the Manual button and adjust time for 8 minutes. 3. When timer beeps, allow a 15-minute natural release and then quick-release the remaining pressure. Serve warm.

Per Serving:
calories: 304 | fat: 16g | protein: 24g | carbs: 12g | net carbs: 8g | fiber: 4g

Broccoli Brie Soup

Prep time: 5 minutes | Cook time: 14 minutes | Serves 6

1 tablespoon coconut oil or unsalted butter
1 cup finely diced onions
1 head broccoli, cut into small florets
2½ cups chicken broth or vegetable broth
8 ounces (227 g) Brie cheese, cut off rind and cut into chunks

1 cup unsweetened almond milk or heavy cream, plus more for drizzling
Fine sea salt and ground black pepper, to taste
Extra-virgin olive oil, for drizzling
Coarse sea salt, for garnish

1. Place the coconut oil in the Instant Pot and press Sauté. Once hot, add the onions and sauté for 4 minutes, or until soft. Press Cancel to stop the Sauté. 2. Add the broccoli and broth. Seal the lid, press Manual, and set the timer for 10 minutes. Once finished, let the pressure release naturally. 3. Remove the lid and add the Brie and almond milk to the pot. Transfer the soup to a food processor or blender and process until smooth, or purée the soup right in the pot with a stick blender. 4. Season with salt and pepper to taste. Ladle the soup into bowls and drizzle with almond milk and olive oil. Garnish with coarse sea salt and freshly ground pepper.

Per Serving:
calories: 210 | fat: 16g | protein: 9g | carbs: 7g | net carbs: 6g | fiber: 1g

Bacon Cheddar Cauliflower Soup

Prep time: 15 minutes | Cook time: 30 minutes | Serves 6

1 large head cauliflower, chopped into florets
¼ cup olive oil
Salt and freshly ground black pepper, to taste
12 ounces (340 g) bacon, chopped
½ onion, roughly chopped
2 garlic cloves, minced

2 cups chicken broth, or vegetable broth, plus more as needed
2 cups heavy (whipping) cream, plus more as needed
½ cup shredded Cheddar cheese, plus more for topping
Sliced scallion, green parts only, or fresh chives, for garnish

1. Preheat the oven to 400°F (205°C). 2. On a large rimmed baking sheet, toss the cauliflower with the olive oil and season with salt and pepper. Bake for 25 to 30 minutes or until slightly browned. 3. While the cauliflower roasts, in a large saucepan over medium heat, cook the bacon for 5 to 7 minutes until crispy. Transfer the bacon to a paper towel-lined plate to drain; leave the bacon fat in the pan. 4. Return the pan to medium heat and add the onion and garlic. Stir well to combine and sauté for 5 to 7 minutes until the onion is softened and translucent. Season with salt and pepper. 5. Remove the cauliflower from the oven and add it to the pan with the onion and garlic. Stir in the broth and bring the liquid to a simmer. Reduce the heat to low. Cook for 5 to 7 minutes. Remove from the heat. With an immersion blender, carefully blend the soup. Alternatively, transfer the soup to a regular blender (working in batches if necessary), blend until smooth, and return the soup to the pan. 6. Stir in the cream. You may need to add a bit more broth or cream, depending on how thick you like your soup. Add the Cheddar and stir until melted and combined. Spoon the soup into bowls and top with bacon and more Cheddar. Garnish with scallion.

Per Serving:
1 cup: calories: 545 | fat: 49g | protein: 15g | carbs: 11g | net carbs: 7g | fiber: 4g

Loaded Fauxtato Soup

Prep time: 5 minutes | Cook time: 20 minutes | serves 4

3 tablespoons salted butter
½ cup chopped white onions
2 cloves garlic, minced
1 (16-ounce) bag frozen cauliflower florets
2 cups vegetable broth

2 cups shredded sharp cheddar cheese, plus extra for garnish
1 cup heavy whipping cream
Salt and ground black pepper
8 slices bacon, cooked and cut into small pieces, for garnish

1. Melt the butter in a stockpot over medium heat. Sauté the onions and garlic in the butter until the onions are tender and translucent. 2. Add the cauliflower and broth to the pot. Bring to a gentle boil over high heat, then reduce the heat to maintain a simmer and continue cooking until the cauliflower is tender, stirring occasionally, about 15 minutes. 3. Turn the heat down to the lowest setting and add the cheese and cream to the pot. Stir until the cheese is melted and well combined with the rest of the soup. 4. Season to taste with salt and pepper. Serve garnished with extra cheese and bacon pieces. Leftovers can be stored in an airtight container in the refrigerator for up to 5 days.

Per Serving:
calories: 560 | fat: 45g | protein: 5g | carbs: 9g | net carbs: 6g | fiber: 3g

Summer Vegetable Soup

Prep time: 10 minutes | Cook time: 6 minutes | Serves 6

3 cups finely sliced leeks
6 cups chopped rainbow chard, stems and leaves separated
1 cup chopped celery
2 tablespoons minced garlic, divided
1 teaspoon dried oregano
1 teaspoon salt
2 teaspoons freshly ground

black pepper
3 cups chicken broth, plus more as needed
2 cups sliced yellow summer squash, ½-inch slices
¼ cup chopped fresh parsley
¾ cup heavy (whipping) cream
4 to 6 tablespoons grated Parmesan cheese

1. Put the leeks, chard, celery, 1 tablespoon of garlic, oregano, salt, pepper, and broth into the inner cooking pot of the Instant Pot. 2. Lock the lid into place. Select Manual and adjust the pressure to High. Cook for 3 minutes. When the cooking is complete, quick-release the pressure. Unlock the lid. 3. Add more broth if needed. 4. Turn the pot to Sauté and adjust the heat to high. Add the yellow squash, parsley, and remaining 1 tablespoon of garlic. 5. Allow the soup to cook for 2 to 3 minutes, or until the squash is softened and cooked through. 6. Stir in the cream and ladle the soup into bowls. Sprinkle with the Parmesan cheese and serve.

Per Serving:
calories: 210 | fat: 14g | protein: 10g | carbs: 12g | net carbs: 8g | fiber: 4g

Mexican Chicken Soup

Prep time: 5 minutes | Cook time: 20 minutes | Serves 4

¼ cup (60 ml) avocado oil
1 small white onion, diced
2 cloves garlic, minced
1 red bell pepper, diced
1 pound (455 g) boneless, skinless chicken breasts, thinly sliced
1 (14½-oz/410-g) can fire-roasted whole tomatoes
1½ cups (355 ml) chicken bone broth
1 cup (240 ml) full-fat coconut milk
1 tablespoon apple cider

vinegar
1 teaspoon ground cumin
1 teaspoon dried oregano leaves
1 teaspoon paprika
¾ teaspoon finely ground sea salt
1 cup (140 g) shredded cheddar cheese (dairy-free or regular) (optional)
2 medium Hass avocados, peeled, pitted, and sliced (about 8 oz/220 g of flesh)
Handful of fresh cilantro leaves

1. Heat the oil in a large saucepan over medium heat. Add the onion, garlic, and bell pepper and sauté until fragrant, about 5 minutes. 2. Add the chicken, tomatoes, broth, coconut milk, vinegar, cumin, oregano, paprika, and salt. Stir to combine, cover, and bring to a light simmer over medium-high heat. Once simmering, reduce the heat and continue to simmer for 15 minutes, until the chicken is cooked through and the bell peppers are soft. 3. When the soup is done, divide evenly among 4 bowls. Top each bowl with ¼ cup (35 g) of the cheese (if using), one-quarter of the avocado slices, and a sprinkle of cilantro.

Per Serving:
calories: 602 | fat: 45g | protein: 31g | carbs: 21g | net carbs: 8g | fiber: 13g

Venison and Tomato Stew

Prep time: 12 minutes | Cook time: 42 minutes | Serves 8

1 tablespoon unsalted butter
1 cup diced onions
2 cups button mushrooms, sliced in half
2 large stalks celery, cut into ¼-inch pieces
Cloves squeezed from 2 heads roasted garlic or 4 cloves garlic, minced
2 pounds (907 g) boneless venison or beef roast, cut into 4 large pieces
5 cups beef broth

1 (14½-ounce / 411-g) can diced tomatoes
1 teaspoon fine sea salt
1 teaspoon ground black pepper
½ teaspoon dried rosemary, or 1 teaspoon fresh rosemary, finely chopped
½ teaspoon dried thyme leaves, or 1 teaspoon fresh thyme leaves, finely chopped
½ head cauliflower, cut into large florets
Fresh thyme leaves, for garnish

1. Place the butter in the Instant Pot and press Sauté. Once melted, add the onions and sauté for 4 minutes, or until soft. 2. Add the mushrooms, celery, and garlic and sauté for another 3 minutes, or until the mushrooms are golden brown. Press Cancel to stop the Sauté. Add the roast, broth, tomatoes, salt, pepper, rosemary, and thyme. 3. Seal the lid, press Manual, and set the timer for 30 minutes. Once finished, turn the valve to venting for a quick release. 4. Add the cauliflower. Seal the lid, press Manual, and set the timer for 5 minutes. Once finished, let the pressure release naturally. 5. Remove the lid and shred the meat with two forks. Taste the liquid and add more salt, if needed. Ladle the stew into bowls. Garnish with thyme leaves.

Per Serving:
calories: 359 | fat: 21g | protein: 32g | carbs: 9g | net carbs: 6g | fiber: 3g

No-Guilt Vegetable Soup

Prep time: 20 minutes | Cook time: 35 minutes | Serves 12

2 tablespoons vegetable oil
1 cup diced celery
1 small carrot, peeled and diced
1 medium head cauliflower, chopped into bite-sized florets
1 small eggplant, diced
2 cups finely cut broccoli florets
2 (64-ounce) cans chicken bone broth

1 cup cut green beans (cut into 1" sections)
2 medium zucchini, diced
1½ teaspoons dried basil
¼ teaspoon dried thyme leaves
1 teaspoon black pepper
¼ teaspoon dried sage
¼ teaspoon garlic salt
4 ounces full-fat cream cheese

1 In a large soup pot over medium heat, add oil and then sauté celery, carrot, cauliflower, eggplant, and broccoli until lightly softened (about 3–5 minutes), stirring regularly. 2 Add bone broth and remaining vegetables and spices. 3 Cover pot and bring to boil. Reduce heat and simmer 30 minutes until vegetables reach desired level of softness. Stir every 5 minutes. 4 Stir in cream cheese until fully blended. 5 Let cool 10 minutes and then serve.
Per Serving:
PER SERVING:
CALORIES: 153 , FAT: 5G , PROTEIN: 16G , SODIUM:348MG , FIBER:4G , CARBOHYDRATE:10G , SUGAR:5G

Cauliflower Soup

Prep time: 10 minutes | Cook time: 6 minutes | Serves 4

2 cups chopped cauliflower
2 tablespoons fresh cilantro
1 cup coconut cream

2 cups beef broth
3 ounces (85 g) Provolone cheese, chopped

1. Put cauliflower, cilantro, coconut cream, beef broth, and cheese in the Instant Pot. Stir to mix well. 2. Select Manual mode and set cooking time for 6 minutes on High Pressure. 3. When timer beeps, allow a natural pressure release for 4 minutes, then release any remaining pressure. Open the lid. 4. Blend the soup and ladle in bowls to serve.

Per Serving:
calories: 244 | fat: 21g | protein: 10g | carbs: 7g | net carbs: 4g | fiber: 3g

Chilled Creamy Cucumber Soup

Prep time: 8 minutes | Cook time: 0 minutes | Serves 6

1 large cucumber, peeled, seeded, and coarsely chopped
1 avocado, peeled, halved, and pitted
2 tablespoons lime juice or lemon juice
¼ cup fresh cilantro leaves
2 tablespoons chopped leeks or green onions
1 cup sour cream

1 cup chicken bone broth, homemade or store-bought (or vegetable broth for vegetarian)
1 teaspoon fine sea salt
For Garnish:
Extra-virgin olive oil, for drizzling
Diced cucumber
Freshly ground black pepper

1. Place all the ingredients in a blender and purée until smooth. Divide the soup among six bowls. Garnish each bowl with a drizzle of extra-virgin olive oil, diced cucumber, and a sprinkle of freshly ground pepper. Store leftover soup in an airtight container in the fridge for up to 3 days.

Per Serving:
calories: 157 | fat: 14g | protein: 3g | carbs: 5g | net carbs: 3g | fiber: 2g

Chicken Creamy Soup

Prep time: 5 minutes | Cook time: 10 minutes | Serves 4

2cups cooked and shredded chicken
3tbsp butter, melted
4cups chicken broth

4 tbsp chopped cilantro
⅓ cup buffalo sauce
½ cup cream cheese
Salt and black pepper, to taste

1. Blend the butter, buffalo sauce, and cream cheese, in a food processor, until smooth. Transfer to a pot, add chicken broth and heat until hot but do not bring to a boil. Stir in chicken, salt, black pepper and cook until heated through. When ready, remove to soup bowls and serve garnished with cilantro.

Per Serving:
calories: 480| fat: 41g | protein: 16g | carbs: 13g | net carbs: 12g | fiber: 1g

Chicken Soup

Prep time: 15 minutes | Cook time: 45 minutes | Serves 4

3 tablespoons olive oil
1 (14-ounce / 397-g) bag frozen peppers and onions
1 pound (454 g) chicken thigh meat, diced
1 tablespoon dried thyme
½ tablespoon garlic powder
1 teaspoon salt

1 teaspoon freshly ground black pepper
1 (32-ounce / 907-g) container chicken or vegetable broth, or bone broth
½ pound (227 g) spinach
1 teaspoon dried basil (optional)

1. Heat the oil in a large pot over medium heat. 2. Add the peppers and onions and cook until no longer frozen, 8 to 10 minutes. 3. Add the chicken and cook, stirring occasionally. 4. Stir in the thyme, garlic powder, salt, and pepper. Add the broth and cook for about 25 minutes. 5. Add the spinach and cook for another 5 minutes. 6. Serve the soup in bowls, sprinkled with the basil (if using).

Per Serving:
calories: 323 | fat: 19g | protein: 28g | carbs: 10g | net carbs: 7g | fiber: 3g

Cream of Cauliflower Gazpacho

Prep time: 15 minutes | Cook time: 25 minutes | Serves 4 to 6

1 cup raw almonds
½ teaspoon salt
½ cup extra-virgin olive oil, plus 1 tablespoon, divided
1 small white onion, minced
1 small head cauliflower, stalk removed and broken into florets (about 3 cups)

2 garlic cloves, finely minced
2 cups chicken or vegetable stock or broth, plus more if needed
1 tablespoon red wine vinegar
¼ teaspoon freshly ground black pepper

1. Bring a small pot of water to a boil. Add the almonds to the water and boil for 1 minute, being careful to not boil longer or the almonds will become soggy. Drain in a colander and run under cold water. Pat dry and, using your fingers, squeeze the meat of each almond out of its skin. Discard the skins. 2. In a food processor or blender, blend together the almonds and salt. With the processor running, drizzle in ½ cup extra-virgin olive oil, scraping down the sides as needed. Set the almond paste aside. 3. In a large stockpot, heat the remaining 1 tablespoon olive oil over medium-high heat. Add the onion and sauté until golden, 3 to 4 minutes. Add the cauliflower florets and sauté for another 3 to 4 minutes. Add the garlic and sauté for 1 minute more. 4. Add 2 cups stock and bring to a boil. Cover, reduce the heat to medium-low, and simmer the vegetables until tender, 8 to 10 minutes. Remove from the heat and allow to cool slightly. 5. Add the vinegar and pepper. Using an immersion blender, blend until smooth. Alternatively, you can blend in a stand blender, but you may need to divide the mixture into two or three batches. With the blender running, add the almond paste and blend until smooth, adding extra stock if the soup is too thick. 6. Serve warm, or chill in refrigerator at least 4 to 6 hours to serve a cold gazpacho.

Per Serving:
calories: 328 | fat: 31g | protein: 8g | carbs: 10g | fiber: 4g | sodium: 232mg

Green Garden Soup

Prep time: 20 minutes | Cook time: 29 minutes | Serves 5

1 tablespoon olive oil
1 garlic clove, diced
½ cup cauliflower florets
1 cup kale, chopped

2 tablespoons chives, chopped
1 teaspoon sea salt
6 cups beef broth

1. Heat the olive oil in the Instant Pot on Sauté mode for 2 minutes and add the garlic. Sauté for 2 minutes or until fragrant. 2. Add cauliflower, kale, chives, sea salt, and beef broth. 3. Close the lid. Select Manual mode and set cooking time for 5 minutes on High Pressure. 4. When timer beeps, use a quick pressure release and open the lid. 5. Ladle the soup into the bowls. Serve warm.

Per Serving:
calories: 80 | fat: 4.5g | protein: 6.5g | carbs: 2.3g | net carbs: 1.8g | fiber: 0.5g

Fennel and Cod Chowder with Fried Mushrooms

Prep time: 20 minutes | Cook time: 35 minutes | Serves 4

1 cup extra-virgin olive oil, divided
1 small head cauliflower, core removed and broken into florets (about 2 cups)
1 small white onion, thinly sliced
1 fennel bulb, white part only, trimmed and thinly sliced
½ cup dry white wine (optional)
2 garlic cloves, minced
1 teaspoon salt
¼ teaspoon freshly ground

black pepper
4 cups fish stock, plus more if needed
1 pound (454 g) thick cod fillet, cut into ¾-inch cubes
4 ounces (113 g) shiitake mushrooms, stems trimmed and thinly sliced (⅛-inch slices)
¼ cup chopped Italian parsley, for garnish (optional)
¼ cup plain whole-milk Greek yogurt, for garnish (optional)

1. In large stockpot, heat ¼ cup olive oil over medium-high heat. Add the cauliflower florets, onion, and fennel and sauté for 10 to 12 minutes, or until almost tender. Add the white wine (if using), garlic, salt, and pepper and sauté for another 1 to 2 minutes. 2. Add 4 cups fish stock and bring to a boil. Cover, reduce the heat to medium-low, and simmer until vegetables are very tender, another 8 to 10 minutes. Remove from the heat and allow to cool slightly. 3. Using an immersion blender, purée the vegetable mixture, slowly drizzling in ½ cup olive oil, until very smooth and silky, adding additional fish stock if the mixture is too thick. 4. Turn the heat back to medium-high and bring the soup to a low simmer. Add the cod pieces and cook, covered, until the fish is cooked through, about 5 minutes. Remove from the heat and keep covered. 5. In a medium skillet, heat the remaining ¼ cup olive oil over medium-high heat. When very hot, add the mushrooms and fry until crispy. Remove with a slotted spoon and transfer to a plate, reserving the frying oil. Toss the mushrooms with a sprinkle of salt. 6. Serve the chowder hot, topped with fried mushrooms and drizzled with 1 tablespoon reserved frying oil. Garnish with chopped fresh parsley and 1 tablespoon of Greek yogurt (if using).

Per Serving:
calories: 663 | fat: 57g | protein: 28g | carbs: 57g | fiber: 4g | sodium: 700mg

Broccoli and Bacon Cheese Soup

Prep time: 6 minutes | Cook time: 10 minutes | Serves 6

3 tablespoons butter
2 stalks celery, diced
½ yellow onion, diced
3 garlic cloves, minced
3½ cups chicken stock
4 cups chopped fresh broccoli florets
3 ounces (85 g) block-style cream cheese, softened and cubed
½ teaspoon ground nutmeg

½ teaspoon sea salt
1 teaspoon ground black pepper
3 cups shredded Cheddar cheese
½ cup shredded Monterey Jack cheese
2 cups heavy cream
4 slices cooked bacon, crumbled
1 tablespoon finely chopped chives

1. Select Sauté mode. Once the Instant Pot is hot, add the butter and heat until the butter is melted. 2. Add the celery, onions, and garlic. Continue sautéing for 5 minutes or until the vegetables are softened. 3. Add the chicken stock and broccoli florets to the pot. Bring the liquid to a boil. 4. Lock the lid,. Select Manual mode and set cooking time for 5 minutes on High Pressure. 5. When cooking is complete, allow the pressure to release naturally for 10 minutes and then release the remaining pressure. 6. Open the lid and add the cream cheese, nutmeg, sea salt, and black pepper. Stir to combine. 7. Select Sauté mode. Bring the soup to a boil and then slowly stir in the Cheddar and Jack cheeses. Once the cheese has melted, stir in the heavy cream. 8. Ladle the soup into serving bowls and top with bacon and chives. Serve hot.

Per Serving:
calories: 681 | fat: 59.0g | protein: 27.4g | carbs: 11.6g | net carbs: 10.3g | fiber: 1.3g

Keto Pho with Shirataki Noodles

Prep time: 20 minutes | Cook time: 10 minutes | Makes 4 bowls

8 ounces (227 g) sirloin, very thinly sliced
3 tablespoons coconut oil (or butter or ghee)
2 garlic cloves, minced
2 tablespoons liquid or coconut aminos
2 tablespoons fish sauce
1 teaspoon freshly grated or

ground ginger
8 cups bone broth
4 (7-ounce / 198-g) packages shirataki noodles, drained and rinsed
1 cup bean sprouts
1 scallion, chopped
1 tablespoon toasted sesame seeds (optional)

1. Put the sirloin in the freezer while you prepare the broth and other ingredients (about 15 to 20 minutes). This makes it easier to slice. 2. In a large pot over medium heat, melt the coconut oil. Add the garlic and cook for 3 minutes. Then add the aminos, fish sauce, ginger, and bone broth. Bring to a boil. 3. Remove the beef from the freezer and slice it very thin. 4. Divide the noodles, beef, and bean sprouts evenly among four serving bowls. Carefully ladle 2 cups of broth into each bowl. Cover the bowls with plates and let sit for 3 to 5 minutes to cook the meat. 5. Serve garnished with the chopped scallion and sesame seeds (if using).

Per Serving:
1 bowl: calories: 385 | fat: 29g | protein: 23g | carbs: 8g | net carbs: 4g | fiber: 4g

Classic Hearty Beef Chili

Prep time: 10 minutes | Cook time: 6 hours 20 minutes | Serves 10

1 tablespoon olive oil
½ large onion (5½ ounces / 156 g), chopped
8 cloves garlic, minced
2½ pounds (1.1 kg) ground beef
2 (14½-ounce / 411-g) cans diced tomatoes, with liquid
1 (6-ounce/ 170-g) can no-sugar-added tomato paste

1 (4-ounce / 113-g) can green chiles, with liquid
¼ cup chili powder
2 tablespoons ground cumin
1 tablespoon dried oregano
2 teaspoons sea salt
1 teaspoon black pepper
1 medium bay leaf (optional)

Slow Cooker Method: 1. In a large skillet, heat the oil over medium-high heat. Add the onion and cook for 5 to 7 minutes, until translucent, or longer if you like it caramelized. Add the garlic and cook for 1 minute or less, until fragrant. 2. Add the ground beef and cook for 8 to 10 minutes, breaking apart with a spatula, until browned. 3. Transfer the ground beef mixture to a slow cooker. Add the remaining ingredients, except the bay leaf, and stir until combined. If desired, place the bay leaf in the middle and push down slightly. 4. Cook on low for 6 to 8 hours or on high for 3 to 4 hours. Remove the bay leaf before serving. Stovetop Method: 1. In a soup pot or Dutch oven, heat the oil over medium-high heat. Add the onion and cook for 5 to 7 minutes, until translucent, or longer if you like it caramelized. Add the garlic and cook for 1 minute or less, until fragrant. 2. Add the ground beef and cook for 8 to 10 minutes, breaking apart with a spatula, until browned. 3. Add the remaining ingredients, except the bay leaf, and stir until combined. If desired, place the bay leaf in the middle and push down slightly. 4. Reduce heat to low. Cover and cook for 1 hour, or until the flavors reach the desired intensity. Remove the bay leaf before serving.

Per Serving:
calories: 427 | fat: 27g | protein: 33g | carbs: 10g | net carbs: 8g | fiber: 2g

Broc Obama Cheese Soup

Prep time: 25 minutes | Cook time: 25 minutes | Serves 8

8 cups chicken broth
2 large heads broccoli, chopped into bite-sized florets
1 clove garlic, peeled and minced

¼ cup heavy whipping cream
¼ cup shredded Cheddar cheese
⅛ teaspoon salt
⅛ teaspoon black pepper

1 In a medium pot over medium heat, add broth and bring to boil (about 5 minutes). Add broccoli and garlic. Reduce heat to low, cover pot, and simmer until vegetables are fully softened, about 15 minutes. 2 Remove from heat and blend using a hand immersion blender to desired consistency while still in pot. Leave some chunks of varying sizes for variety. 3 Return pot to medium heat and add cream and cheese. Stir 3–5 minutes until fully blended. Add salt and pepper. 4 Remove from heat, let cool 10 minutes, and serve.
Per Serving:

PER SERVING:
CALORIES: 106 , FAT: 4G , PROTEIN: 7G , SODIUM:1,035MG , FIBER:4G , CARBOHYDRATE:12G , SUGAR:4G

Bacon, Leek, and Cauliflower Soup

Prep time: 15 minutes | Cook time: 15 minutes | Serves 6

6 slices bacon
1 leek, remove the dark green end and roots, sliced in half lengthwise, rinsed, cut into ½-inch-thick slices crosswise
½ medium yellow onion, sliced
4 cloves garlic, minced
3 cups chicken broth

1 large head cauliflower, roughly chopped into florets
1 cup water
1 teaspoon kosher salt
1 teaspoon ground black pepper
⅔ cup shredded sharp Cheddar cheese, divided
½ cup heavy whipping cream

1. Set the Instant Pot to Sauté mode. When heated, place the bacon on the bottom of the pot and cook for 5 minutes or until crispy. 2. Transfer the bacon slices to a plate. Let stand until cool enough to handle, crumble it with forks. 3. Add the leek and onion to the bacon fat remaining in the pot. Sauté for 5 minutes or until fragrant and the onion begins to caramelize. Add the garlic and sauté for 30 seconds more or until fragrant. 4. Stir in the chicken broth, cauliflower florets, water, salt, pepper, and three-quarters of the crumbled bacon. 5. Secure the lid. Press the Manual button and set cooking time for 3 minutes on High Pressure. 6. When timer beeps, perform a quick pressure release. Open the lid. 7. Stir in ½ cup of the Cheddar and the cream. Use an immersion blender to purée the soup until smooth. 8. Ladle into bowls and garnish with the remaining Cheddar and crumbled bacon. Serve immediately.

Per Serving:
calories: 251 | fat: 18.9g | protein: 10.5g | carbs: 12.0g | net carbs: 8.6g | fiber: 3.4g

Bone Marrow Chili Con Keto

Prep time: 12 minutes | Cook time: 2 hours | Serves 12

4 slices bacon, diced
1 pound (454 g) 80% lean ground beef
1 pound (454 g) Mexican-style fresh (raw) chorizo, removed from casings
1 (26½-ounce / 751-g) box diced tomatoes with juices
1 cup tomato sauce
¼ cup chopped onions
1 red bell pepper, chopped
2 green chiles, chopped
½ cup beef bone broth, homemade or store-bought
2 tablespoons chili powder
2 teaspoons minced garlic
2 teaspoons dried oregano

leaves
1 teaspoon ground cumin
½ teaspoon cayenne pepper
½ teaspoon paprika
½ teaspoon fine sea salt
½ teaspoon freshly ground black pepper
2 bay leaves
Bone Marrow:
8 (2-inch) cross-cut beef or veal marrow bones, split lengthwise
1 teaspoon fine sea salt
½ teaspoon freshly ground black pepper
For Garnish:
Chopped fresh cilantro

1. In a large stockpot over medium-high heat, fry the bacon until crisp, then remove it from the pan and set aside, leaving the fat in the pot. Crumble the ground beef and chorizo into the hot fat and cook over medium-high heat until evenly browned, about 5 minutes. 2. Pour in the diced tomatoes and tomato sauce. Add the onions, bell pepper, chiles, beef broth, and half of the cooked bacon. Season with the chili powder, garlic, oregano, cumin, cayenne, paprika, salt, and pepper. Add the bay leaves and stir to combine. Cover and simmer over low heat for at least 2 hours, stirring occasionally.

3. After 2 hours, taste the chili and add more salt, pepper, or chili powder, if desired. The longer the chili simmers, the better it will taste. Remove the bay leaves before serving. 4. While the chili is simmering, make the bone marrow. Preheat the oven to 450°F (235°C). Rinse and drain the bones and pat dry, then season them with the salt and pepper. 5. Place the bones cut side up in a roasting pan. Roast for 15 to 25 minutes, until the marrow in the center has puffed slightly and is warm. (The exact timing will depend on the diameter of the bones; if they are 2 inches in diameter, it will take closer to 15 minutes.) 6. To test for doneness, insert a metal skewer into the center of the bone. There should be no resistance when it is inserted, and some of the marrow will have started to leak from the bones. Using a small spoon, scoop the marrow out of the bones into each bowl of chili. Garnish with chopped cilantro before serving.

Per Serving:
calories: 366 | fat: 32g | protein: 13g | carbs: 6g | net carbs: 4g | fiber: 2g

Sauerkraut Soup

Prep time: 2 minutes | Cook time: 25 minutes | Serves 4

1 pound (455 g) ground beef
1 small white onion, thinly sliced
1 clove garlic, minced
1¼ teaspoons ground cumin

3 cups (710 ml) beef bone broth
1 cup (235 g) sauerkraut
½ teaspoon finely ground sea salt

1. Place the ground beef, onion, garlic, and cumin in a saucepan. Sauté over medium heat until the onion is translucent, about 10 minutes. 2. Add the broth, sauerkraut, and salt. Cover and cook, still over medium heat, for 15 minutes, until the onion is soft and the soup is fragrant. 3. Divide the soup evenly among 4 bowls and serve.

Per Serving:
calories: 469 | fat: 27g | protein: 49g | carbs: 8g | net carbs: 6g | fiber: 2g

Beef and Eggplant Tagine

**Prep time: 15 minutes | Cook time: 25 minutes |
Serves 6**

1 pound (454 g) beef fillet, chopped
1 eggplant, chopped
6 ounces (170 g) scallions, chopped

4 cups beef broth
1 teaspoon ground allspices
1 teaspoon erythritol
1 teaspoon coconut oil

1. Put all ingredients in the Instant Pot. Stir to mix well. 2. Close the lid. Select Manual mode and set cooking time for 25 minutes on High Pressure. 3. When timer beeps, use a natural pressure release for 15 minutes, then release any remaining pressure. Open the lid. 4. Serve warm.

Per Serving:
calories: 158 | fat: 5.3g | protein: 21.1g | carbs: 8.2g | net carbs: 4.7g | fiber: 3.5g

Coconut, Green Beans & Shrimp Curry Soup

Prep time: 10 minutes | Cook time: 15 minutes | Serves 4

2 tbsp ghee	2 tbsp red curry paste
1lb jumbo shrimp, peeled and deveined	6 oz coconut milk
	Salt and chili pepper to taste
2tsp ginger-garlic puree	1 bunch green beans, halved

1. Melt ghee in a medium saucepan over medium heat. Add the shrimp, season with salt and black pepper, and cook until they are opaque, 2 to 3 minutes. Remove shrimp to a plate. Add the ginger-garlic puree and red curry paste to the ghee and sauté for 2 minutes until fragrant. 2. Stir in the coconut milk; add the shrimp, salt, chili pepper, and green beans. Cook for 4 minutes. Reduce the heat to a simmer and cook an additional 3 minutes, occasionally stirring. Adjust taste with salt, fetch soup into serving bowls, and serve with cauli rice.

Per Serving:
calories: 138| fat: 1g | protein: 28g | carbs: 4g | net carbs: 3g | fiber: 1g

Lamb and Broccoli Soup

Prep time: 10 minutes | Cook time: 25 minutes | Serves 4

7 ounces (198 g) lamb fillet, chopped	¼ daikon, chopped
1 tablespoon avocado oil	2 bell peppers, chopped
½ cup broccoli, roughly chopped	¼ teaspoon ground cumin
	5 cups beef broth

1. Sauté the lamb fillet with avocado oil in the Instant Pot for 5 minutes. 2. Add the broccoli, daikon, bell peppers, ground cumin, and beef broth. 3. Close the lid. Select Manual mode and set cooking time for 20 minutes on High Pressure. 4. When timer beeps, use a natural pressure release for 10 minutes, then release any remaining pressure. Open the lid. 5. Serve warm.

Per Serving:
calories: 169 | fat: 6.0g | protein: 21.0g | carbs: 6.8g | net carbs: 5.5g | fiber: 1.3g

Vegan Pho

Prep time: 10 minutes | Cook time: 20 minutes | serves 8

8 cups vegetable broth	noodles
1-inch knob fresh ginger, peeled and chopped	2 cups shredded cabbage
2 tablespoons tamari	2 cups mung bean sprouts
3 cups shredded fresh spinach	Fresh Thai basil leaves, for garnish
2 cups chopped broccoli	Fresh cilantro leaves, for garnish
1 cup sliced mushrooms	
½ cup chopped carrots	Fresh mint leaves, for garnish
⅓ cup chopped scallions	1 lime, cut into 8 wedges, for garnish
1 (8-ounce) package shirataki	

1. In a large stockpot over medium-high heat, bring the vegetable broth to a simmer with the ginger and tamari. 2. Once the broth is hot, add the spinach, broccoli, mushrooms, carrots, and scallions, and simmer for a few minutes, just until the vegetables start to become tender. 3. Stir in the shirataki noodles, then remove the pot from the heat and divide the soup among serving bowls. 4. Top each bowl with cabbage, sprouts, basil, cilantro, mint, and a lime wedge.

Per Serving:
calories: 47 | fat: 0g | protein: 3g | carbs: 10g | net carbs: 7g | fiber: 3g

Chicken and Kale Soup

Prep time: 5 minutes | Cook time: 5 minutes | Serves 4

2 cups chopped cooked chicken breast	½ teaspoon ground cinnamon
	Pinch ground cloves
12 ounces (340 g) frozen kale	2 teaspoons minced garlic
1 onion, chopped	1 teaspoon freshly ground black pepper
2 cups water	
1 tablespoon powdered chicken broth base	1 teaspoon salt
	2 cups full-fat coconut milk

1. Put the chicken, kale, onion, water, chicken broth base, cinnamon, cloves, garlic, pepper, and salt in the inner cooking pot of the Instant Pot. 2. Lock the lid into place. Select Manual and adjust the pressure to High. Cook for 5 minutes. When the cooking is complete, let the pressure release naturally for 10 minutes, then quick-release any remaining pressure. Unlock the lid. 3. Stir in the coconut milk. Taste and adjust any seasonings as needed before serving.

Per Serving:
calories: 387 | fat: 27g | protein: 26g | carbs: 10g | net carbs: 8g | fiber: 2g

Cabbage Soup

Prep time: 20 minutes | Cook time: 30 minutes | Serves 6

1 tablespoon olive oil	2 tablespoons tomato paste
3 garlic cloves, minced	2 (32-ounce / 907-g) cartons chicken broth
1 onion, diced	
3 carrots, diced	1 large head cabbage, chopped
1 celery stalk, diced	1 teaspoon dried oregano
½ green bell pepper, diced	1 teaspoon dried thyme
Salt and freshly ground black pepper, to taste	Grated Parmesan cheese, for topping
1 cup chopped kale	

1. In a large saucepan over medium heat, heat the olive oil. 2. Add the garlic and onion. Sauté for 5 minutes. 3. Add the carrots and celery. Cook for 5 to 7 minutes until softened. 4. Add the bell pepper and stir well to combine. Cook for 5 to 7 minutes more. Season with salt and pepper and add the kale. 5. Stir in the tomato paste until well combined. 6. Pour in the chicken broth and bring the soup to a gentle boil. 7. Add the cabbage, oregano, and thyme. Season with more salt and pepper. Reduce the heat to low, cover the pan, and simmer for 15 minutes (a little longer if you have the time). Ladle into bowls and top with Parmesan before serving.

Per Serving:
calories: 156 | fat: 5g | protein: 10g | carbs: 23g | net carbs: 16g | fiber: 7g

Cream of Mushroom Soup

Prep time: 10 minutes | Cook time: 10 minutes | Serves 4

1 pound (454 g) sliced button mushrooms	2 cups chicken broth
3 tablespoons butter	½ teaspoon salt
2 tablespoons diced onion	¼ teaspoon pepper
2 cloves garlic, minced	½ cup heavy cream
	¼ teaspoon xanthan gum

1. Press the Sauté button and then press the Adjust button to set heat to Less. Add mushrooms, butter, and onion to pot. Sauté for 5 to 8 minutes or until onions and mushrooms begin to brown. Add garlic and sauté until fragrant. Press the Cancel button. 2. Add broth, salt, and pepper. Click lid closed. Press the Manual button and adjust time for 3 minutes. When timer beeps, quick-release the pressure. Stir in heavy cream and xanthan gum. Allow a few minutes to thicken and serve warm.

Per Serving:
calories: 220 | fat: 19g | protein: 5g | carbs: 6g | net carbs: 5g | fiber: 1g

Broccoli Cheddar Soup

Prep time: 5 minutes | Cook time: 10 minutes | Serves 4

2 tablespoons butter	1 cup chopped broccoli
⅛ cup onion, diced	1 tablespoon cream cheese, softened
½ teaspoon garlic powder	¼ cup heavy cream
½ teaspoon salt	1 cup shredded Cheddar cheese
¼ teaspoon pepper	
2 cups chicken broth	

1. Press the Sauté button and add butter to Instant Pot. Add onion and sauté until translucent. Press the Cancel button and add garlic powder, salt, pepper, broth, and broccoli to pot. 2. Click lid closed. Press the Soup button and set time for 5 minutes. When timer beeps, stir in heavy cream, cream cheese, and Cheddar.

Per Serving:
calories: 250 | fat: 20g | protein: 9g | carbs: 4g | net carbs: 3g | fiber: 1g

Chicken Zucchini Soup

Prep time: 8 minutes | Cook time: 14 minutes | Serves 6

¼ cup coconut oil or unsalted butter	6 cups chicken broth
1 cup chopped celery	1 tablespoon dried parsley
¼ cup chopped onions	1 teaspoon fine sea salt
2 cloves garlic, minced	½ teaspoon dried marjoram
1 pound (454 g) boneless, skinless chicken breasts, cut into 1-inch cubes	½ teaspoon ground black pepper
	1 bay leaf
	2 cups zucchini noodles

1. Place the coconut oil in the Instant Pot and press Sauté. Once melted, add the celery, onions, and garlic and cook, stirring occasionally, for 4 minutes, or until the onions are soft. Press Cancel to stop the Sauté. 2. Add the cubed chicken, broth, parsley, salt, marjoram, pepper, and bay leaf. Seal the lid, press Manual, and set the timer for 10 minutes. Once finished, let the pressure release

naturally. 3. Remove the lid and stir well. Place the noodles in bowls, using ⅓ cup per bowl. Ladle the soup over the noodles and serve immediately; if it sits too long, the noodles will get too soft.

Per Serving:
calories: 253 | fat: 15g | protein: 21g | carbs: 11g | net carbs: 10g | fiber: 1g

Green Minestrone Soup

Prep time: 10 minutes | Cook time: 20 minutes | Serves 4

2tbsp ghee	5 cups vegetable broth
2 tbsp onion-garlic puree	1cup baby spinach
2 heads broccoli, cut in florets	Salt and black pepper to taste
2 stalks celery, chopped	2tbsp Gruyere cheese, grated

1. Melt the ghee in a saucepan over medium heat and sauté the onion-garlic puree for 3 minutes until softened. Mix in the broccoli and celery, and cook for 4 minutes until slightly tender. Pour in the broth, bring to a boil, then reduce the heat to medium-low and simmer covered for about 5 minutes. 2. Drop in the spinach to wilt, adjust the seasonings, and cook for 4 minutes. Ladle soup into serving bowls. Serve with a sprinkle of grated Gruyere cheese.

Per Serving:
Per serving: Kcal 227, Fat 20.3g, Net Carbs 2g, Protein 8g

Spicy Sausage and Chicken Stew

Prep time: 10 minutes | Cook time: 25 minutes | Serves 10

1 tablespoon coconut oil	1 tablespoon ground cumin
2 pounds (907 g) bulk Italian sausage	1 tablespoon dried oregano leaves
2 boneless, skinless chicken thighs, cut into ½-inch pieces	2 teaspoons fine sea salt
½ cup chopped onions	1 teaspoon cayenne pepper
1 (28-ounce / 794-g) can whole peeled tomatoes, drained	1 cup chicken broth
1 cup sugar-free tomato sauce	1 ounce (28 g) unsweetened baking chocolate, chopped
1 (4½-ounce / 128-g) can green chilies	¼ cup lime juice
3 tablespoons minced garlic	Chopped fresh cilantro leaves, for garnish
2 tablespoons smoked paprika	Red pepper flakes, for garnish

1. Place the coconut oil in the Instant Pot and press Sauté. Once melted, add the sausage, chicken, and onions and cook, stirring to break up the sausage, until the sausage is starting to cook through and the onions are soft, about 5 minutes. 2. Meanwhile, make the tomato purée: Place the tomatoes, tomato sauce, and chilies in a food processor and process until smooth. 3. Add the garlic, paprika, cumin, oregano, salt, and cayenne pepper to the Instant Pot and stir to combine. Then add the tomato purée, broth, and chocolate and stir well. Press Cancel to stop the Sauté. 4. Seal the lid, press Manual, and set the timer for 20 minutes. Once finished, let the pressure release naturally. 5. Just before serving, stir in the lime juice. Ladle the stew into bowls and garnish with cilantro and red pepper flakes.

Per Serving:
calories: 341 | fat: 23g | protein: 21g | carbs: 10g | net carbs: 8g | fiber: 2g

Chapter 8 Snacks and Appetizers

Caponata Dip

Prep time: 15 minutes | Cook time: 35 minutes |
Makes about 2 cups

1 large eggplant (about 1¼ pounds / 567 g), cut into ½-inch pieces
1 large yellow onion, cut into ½-inch pieces
4 large cloves garlic, peeled and smashed with the side of a knife
4 tablespoons extra-virgin olive oil, divided, plus extra for garnish
½ teaspoon sea salt
¼ teaspoon ground black pepper
¼ teaspoon ground cumin

1 medium tomato, chopped into 1-inch chunks
Juice of 1 lemon
2 tablespoons chopped fresh cilantro leaves
For Garnish:
Extra-virgin olive oil
Fresh cilantro leaves
Pinch of paprika (optional)
Pine nuts (optional)
For Serving (Optional):
Low-carb flax crackers
Sliced vegetables

1. Preheat the oven to 375ºF (190ºC). 2. Place the eggplant, onion, garlic, 2 tablespoons of the olive oil, salt, pepper, and cumin in a large bowl and toss to combine. 3. Spread the mixture out on a rimmed baking sheet and bake for 30 to 35 minutes, until the eggplant is softened and browned, tossing halfway through. 4. Remove the eggplant mixture from the oven and transfer it to a food processor. Add the tomato, lemon juice, cilantro, and remaining 2 tablespoons of olive oil. Pulse until the mixture is just slightly chunky. Add salt and pepper to taste. 5. Scoop the dip into a serving dish and garnish with additional olive oil, cilantro, paprika (if desired), and pine nuts (optional). Serve with low-carb crackers and sliced vegetables, if desired.

Per Serving:
calories: 90 | fat: 7g | protein: 1g | carbs: 7g | net carbs: 4g | fiber: 3g

Savory Mackerel & Goat'S Cheese "Paradox" Balls

Prep time: 10 minutes | Cook time: 0 minutes |
Makes 10 fat bombs

2 smoked or cooked mackerel fillets, boneless, skin removed
4.4 ounces (125 g) soft goat's cheese
1 tablespoon fresh lemon juice
1 teaspoon Dijon or yellow

mustard
1 small red onion, finely diced
2 tablespoons chopped fresh chives or herbs of choice
¾ cup pecans, crushed
10 leaves baby gem lettuce

1. In a food processor, combine the mackerel, goat's cheese, lemon juice, and mustard. Pulse until smooth. Transfer to a bowl, add the onion and herbs, and mix with a spoon. Refrigerate for 20 to 30 minutes, or until set. 2. Using a large spoon or an ice cream scoop,

divide the mixture into 10 balls, about 40 g/1.4 ounces each. Roll each ball in the crushed pecans. Place each ball on a small lettuce leaf and serve. Keep the fat bombs refrigerated in a sealed container for up to 5 days.

Per Serving:
1 fat bomb: calories: 165 | fat: 12g | protein: 12g | carbs: 2g | fiber: 1g | sodium: 102mg

Garlic Meatballs

Prep time: 20 minutes | Cook time: 15 minutes | Serves 6

7 ounces (198 g) ground beef
7 ounces (198 g) ground pork
1 teaspoon minced garlic
3 tablespoons water

1 teaspoon chili flakes
1 teaspoon dried parsley
1 tablespoon coconut oil
¼ cup beef broth

1. In the mixing bowl, mix up ground beef, ground pork, minced garlic, water, chili flakes, and dried parsley. 2. Make the medium size meatballs from the mixture. 3. After this, heat up coconut oil in the instant pot on Sauté mode. 4. Put the meatballs in the hot coconut oil in one layer and cook them for 2 minutes from each side. 5. Then add beef broth and close the lid. 6. Cook the meatballs for 10 minutes on Manual mode (High Pressure). 7. Then make a quick pressure release and transfer the meatballs on the plate.

Per Serving:
calories: 131 | fat: 6g | protein: 19g | carbs: 0g | net carbs: 0g | fiber: 0g

Sausage Balls

Prep time: 5 minutes | Cook time: 25 minutes |
Makes 2 dozen

1 pound (454 g) bulk Italian sausage (not sweet)
1 cup almond flour
1½ cups finely shredded Cheddar cheese
1 large egg

2 teaspoons baking powder
1 teaspoon onion powder
1 teaspoon fennel seed (optional)
½ teaspoon cayenne pepper (optional)

1. Preheat the oven to 350ºF (180ºC) and line a rimmed baking sheet with aluminum foil. 2. In a large bowl, combine all the ingredients. Use a fork to mix until well blended. 3. Form the sausage mixture into 1½-inch balls and place 1 inch apart on the prepared baking sheet. 4. Bake for 20 to 25 minutes, or until browned and cooked through.

Per Serving:
calories: 241 | fat: 21g | protein: 11g | carbs: 3g | net carbs: 2g | fiber: 1g

Creamed Onion Spinach

Prep time: 3 minutes | Cook time: 5 minutes | Serves 6

4 tablespoons butter	spinach
¼ cup diced onion	½ cup chicken broth
8 ounces (227 g) cream cheese	1 cup shredded whole-milk
1 (12-ounce / 340-g) bag frozen	Mozzarella cheese

1. Press the Sauté button and add butter. Once butter is melted, add onion to Instant Pot and sauté for 2 minutes or until onion begins to turn translucent. 2. Break cream cheese into pieces and add to Instant Pot. Press the Cancel button. Add frozen spinach and broth. Click lid closed. Press the Manual button and adjust time for 5 minutes. When timer beeps, quick-release the pressure and stir in shredded Mozzarella. If mixture is too watery, press the Sauté button and reduce for additional 5 minutes, stirring constantly.

Per Serving:
calories: 273 | fat: 24g | protein: 9g | carbs: 5g | net carbs: 3g | fiber: 2g

Southern Pimento Cheese Dip

Prep time: 5 minutes | Cook time: 0 minutes | Serves 10

8 ounces (227 g) cream cheese, at room temperature	pimentos, diced
1 cup shredded sharp Cheddar cheese	1 teaspoon garlic powder
1 cup shredded Pepper Jack cheese	1 teaspoon onion powder
⅓ cup mayonnaise	¼ teaspoon cayenne pepper
1 (4-ounce / 113-g) jar	Pinch sea salt
	Pinch freshly ground black pepper

1. In a large bowl, combine the cream cheese, Cheddar, Pepper Jack, mayonnaise, pimentos, garlic powder, onion powder, and cayenne. Beat together using an electric mixer. Season with salt and pepper and beat again until well combined. 2. Chill in the refrigerator for a few hours (or overnight) to let the flavors set.

Per Serving:
⅓ cup: calories: 225 | fat: 21g | protein: 7g | carbs: 2g | net carbs: 2g | fiber: 0g

Thyme Sautéed Radishes

Prep time: 5 minutes | Cook time: 15 minutes | Serves 4

1 pound (454 g) radishes, quartered (remove leaves and ends)	¼ teaspoon minced garlic
	⅛ teaspoon salt
2 tablespoons butter	⅛ teaspoon garlic powder
¼ teaspoon dried thyme	⅛ teaspoon dried rosemary

1. Press the Sauté button and then press the Adjust button to lower heat to Less. 2. Place radishes into Instant Pot with butter and seasoning. 3. Sauté, stirring occasionally until tender, about 10 to 15 minutes. Add a couple of teaspoons of water if radishes begin to stick.

Per Serving:
calories: 62 | fat: 5g | protein: 1g | carbs: 3g | net carbs: 2g | fiber: 1g

Cheese Chips and Guacamole

Prep time: 10 minutes | Cook time: 10 minutes | Serves 2

FOR THE CHEESE CHIPS	1 teaspoon diced jalapeño
1 cup shredded cheese (I use Mexican blend)	2 tablespoons chopped fresh cilantro leaves
FOR THE GUACAMOLE	Pink Himalayan salt
1 avocado, mashed	Freshly ground black pepper
Juice of ½ lime	

TO MAKE THE CHEESE CHIPS 1. Preheat the oven to 350°F. Line a baking sheet with parchment paper or a silicone baking mat. 2. Add ¼-cup mounds of shredded cheese to the pan, leaving plenty of space between them, and bake until the edges are brown and the middles have fully melted, about 7 minutes. 3. Set the pan on a cooling rack, and let the cheese chips cool for 5 minutes. The chips will be floppy when they first come out of the oven but will crisp as they cool. TO MAKE THE GUACAMOLE 1. In a medium bowl, mix together the avocado, lime juice, jalapeño, and cilantro, and season with pink Himalayan salt and pepper. 2. Top the cheese chips with the guacamole, and serve.

Per Serving:
calories: 323 | fat: 27g | protein: 15g | carbs: 8g | net carbs: 3g | fiber: 5g

Olive Pâté

Prep time: 10 minutes | Cook time: 0 minutes | serves 6

1 cup pitted green olives	1 teaspoon freshly ground black pepper
1 cup pitted black olives	
¼ cup cold-pressed olive oil	2 thyme sprigs

1. In a food processor, combine all the ingredients and pulse until the mixture is thick and chunky. 2. Transfer the pâté to a small serving bowl and serve with crackers.

Per Serving:
calories: 171 | fat: 17g | protein: 0g | carbs: 4g | net carbs: 4g | fiber: 1g

Hangover Bacon-Wrapped Pickles

Prep time: 5 minutes | Cook time: 20 minutes | Serves 4

3 large pickles
6 strips uncooked no-sugar-added bacon, cut in half lengthwise
¼ cup ranch dressing

1. Preheat oven to 425°F. Line a baking sheet with foil. 2. Quarter each pickle lengthwise (yielding twelve spears). 3. Wrap each spear with a half strip bacon. Place on baking sheet. 4. Bake 20 minutes or until crispy, flipping at the midpoint. 5. Serve your crispy bacon-wrapped pickles while still hot with a side of the ranch dipping sauce.

Per Serving:
calories: 96| fat: 6g | protein: 6g | carbs: 3g | net carbs: 2g | fiber: 1g

Goat'S Cheese & Hazelnut Dip

Prep time: 10 minutes | Cook time: 0 minutes | Serves 8

2 heads yellow chicory or endive
Enough ice water to cover the leaves
Pinch of salt
Dip:
12 ounces (340 g) soft goat's cheese
3 tablespoons extra-virgin olive oil
1 tablespoon fresh lemon juice
1 teaspoon lemon zest (about ½ lemon)

1 clove garlic, minced
Freshly ground black pepper, to taste
Salt, if needed, to taste
Topping:
2 tablespoons chopped fresh chives
¼ cup crushed hazelnuts, pecans, or walnuts
1 tablespoon extra-virgin olive oil
Chile flakes or black pepper, to taste

1. Cut off the bottom of the chicory and trim the leaves to get rid of any that are limp or brown. Place the leaves in salted ice water for 10 minutes. This will help the chicory leaves to become crisp. Drain and leave in the strainer. 2. To make the dip: Place the dip ingredients in a bowl and use a fork or spatula to mix until smooth and creamy. 3. Stir in the chives. Transfer to a serving bowl and top with the crushed hazelnuts, olive oil, and chile flakes. Serve with the crisp chicory leaves. Store in a sealed jar in the fridge for up to 5 days.

Per Serving:
calories: 219 | fat: 18g | protein: 10g | carbs: 5g | fiber: 4g | sodium: 224mg

Liver Bites

Prep time: 5 minutes | Cook time: 28 minutes | Makes 24 bites

8 ounces (225 g) chicken livers
1 tablespoon apple cider vinegar
4 strips bacon (about 4½ oz/130 g)
1 pound (455 g) ground beef
1 cup (75 g) crushed pork rinds

12 cloves garlic, minced
1 tablespoon plus 1 teaspoon onion powder
1 teaspoon ground black pepper
1 teaspoon dried thyme leaves
½ teaspoon finely ground sea salt

1. Place the chicken livers in a medium-sized bowl and cover with water. Add the vinegar. Cover and place in the fridge for 24 to 48 hours. Rinse and drain the livers. 2. Preheat the oven to 375°F (190°C). Line a rimmed baking sheet with parchment paper or a silicone baking mat. 3. Place the livers and bacon in a high-powered blender and pulse until smooth. If using a regular blender or food processor, roughly chop the bacon beforehand. 4. Transfer the liver mixture to a medium-sized bowl and add the remaining ingredients. Mix with your hands until fully incorporated. 5. Pinch a tablespoon of the mixture, roll it into a ball between your hands, and place on the lined baking sheet. Repeat with the remaining liver mixture, making a total of 24 balls. 6. Bake the liver balls for 25 to 28 minutes, until the internal temperature reaches 165°F (74°C).

Per Serving:
calories: 116 | fat: 7g | protein: 11g | carbs: 1g | net carbs: 1g | fiber: 0g

English Cucumber Tea Sandwiches

Prep time: 10 minutes | Cook time: 0 minutes | Makes 12 snacks

1 large cucumber, peeled (approximately 10 ounces / 283 g)
4 ounces (113 g) cream cheese, softened

2 tablespoons finely chopped fresh dill
Freshly ground black pepper, to taste

1. Slice the cucumbers into 24 rounds approximately ¼ inch (6 mm) thick. Place in a single layer between two kitchen towels. Put a cutting board on top. Allow to sit about 5 minutes. 2. Mix the cream cheese and dill. 3. Spread 2 teaspoons cream cheese on half the cucumber slices. Grind black pepper over the cheese. Place another slice of cucumber on top of each and secure with a toothpick, if desired.

Per Serving:
calories: 96 | fat: 8g | protein: 3g | carbs: 3g | net carbs: 1g | fiber: 2g

BLT Dip

Prep time: 10 minutes | Cook time: 15 minutes | Serves 10

8 strips bacon (about 8 oz/225 g)
Blt Dip:
Warm bacon grease, reserved from cooking bacon (above)
1½ cups raw cashews, soaked in water for 12 hours, drained, and rinsed
⅓ cup mayonnaise
¼ cup collagen peptides or protein powder (optional)
2 tablespoons apple cider vinegar
2 tablespoons lemon juice
2 teaspoons paprika or smoked paprika

2 tablespoons diced yellow onions
1 clove garlic
½ teaspoon finely ground sea salt
¼ teaspoon ground black pepper
Toppinhs:
1 cup sliced iceberg lettuce
1 small tomato, diced
Crumbled bacon (from above)
2 green onions, sliced
1 English cucumber (about 12 in/30.5 cm long), sliced crosswise into coins, for serving

1. Cook the bacon in a large frying pan over medium heat until crispy, about 15 minutes, then remove from the pan. When the bacon has cooled, crumble it. 2. Make the dip: Pour the warm bacon grease into a food processor or high-powered blender. Add the soaked cashews, mayonnaise, collagen (if using), vinegar, lemon juice, paprika, onions, garlic, salt, and pepper. Pulse until smooth, about 2 minutes. 3. Transfer the mixture to a 9-inch (23-cm) pie plate. Top with the lettuce, tomato, bacon, and green onions. Serve with the cucumber coins.

Per Serving:
calories: 378 | fat: 28g | protein: 20g | carbs: 13g | net carbs: 11g | fiber: 2g

Bacon-Studded Pimento Cheese

Prep time: 10 minutes | Cook time: 5 minutes | Serves 6

2 ounces (57 g) bacon (about 4 thick slices)	¼ teaspoon cayenne pepper (optional)
4 ounces (113 g) cream cheese, room temperature	1 cup thick-shredded extra-sharp Cheddar cheese
¼ cup mayonnaise	2 ounces (57 g) jarred diced pimentos, drained
¼ teaspoon onion powder	

1. Chop the raw bacon into ½-inch-thick pieces. Cook in a small skillet over medium heat until crispy, 3 to 4 minutes. Use a slotted spoon to transfer the bacon onto a layer of paper towels. Reserve the rendered fat. 2. In a large bowl, combine the cream cheese, mayonnaise, onion powder, and cayenne (if using), and beat with an electric mixer or by hand until smooth and creamy. 3. Add the rendered bacon fat, Cheddar cheese, and pimentos and mix until well combined. 4. Refrigerate for at least 30 minutes before serving to allow flavors to blend. Serve cold with raw veggies.

Per Serving:
calories: 216 | fat: 20g | protein: 8g | carbs: 2g | net carbs: 0g | fiber: 2

Paleo Egg Rolls

Prep time: 20 minutes | Cook time: 10 minutes | Makes 10 egg rolls

1 cup coconut oil, duck fat, or avocado oil, for frying	½ teaspoon fine sea salt
20 slices prosciutto	Sweet 'n' Sour Sauce:
Sliced radishes, for serving (optional)	½ cup Swerve confectioners'-style sweetener or equivalent amount of liquid or powdered sweetener
Filling:	½ cup coconut vinegar
1 pound (454 g) ground pork	2 tablespoons coconut aminos
2 cups shredded cabbage	1 tablespoon tomato paste
1 green onion, chopped	½ teaspoon minced garlic
3 tablespoons coconut aminos	1 teaspoon grated fresh ginger
1 clove garlic, minced	¼ teaspoon guar gum (optional)
1 teaspoon grated fresh ginger	
½ teaspoon five-spice powder	

1. Heat the oil to 350ºF (180ºC) in a deep-fryer or a 4-inch-deep (or deeper) cast-iron skillet over medium heat. The oil should be at least 3 inches deep; add more oil if needed. 2. While the oil is heating up, make the filling: In a large skillet over medium heat, brown the ground pork with the cabbage, green onion, coconut aminos, garlic, ginger, five-spice, and salt, stirring to break up the meat. Cook until the meat is cooked through and cabbage is tender, about 5 minutes. Remove the filling from pan and set aside until cool enough to handle. 3. Make the sauce: Heat the sauce ingredients, except the guar gum, in a small saucepan until simmering. Whisk until smooth. If you want a thicker sauce, sift the guar gum into the sauce; it will thicken in a few minutes. 4. To assemble the egg rolls: Lay one slice of prosciutto on a sushi mat or a sheet of parchment paper, with a short end facing you. Lay another slice of prosciutto on top of it, across the center at a right angle, forming a cross. Spoon 3 to 4 tablespoons of the filling into the center of the cross. 5. Fold the sides of the bottom slice up and over the filling to form the ends of the roll. Tightly roll up the long piece of prosciutto, starting at the edge closest to you, into a tight egg roll shape so that it overlaps by an inch or so. Note: If the prosciutto rips, it's okay. It will seal when you fry it. Repeat until all the prosciutto and filling are used. 6. Working in batches, fry the egg rolls by placing the tightly wrapped roll seam side down in the hot oil for about 2 minutes, until crisp on the outside. Remove from the oil and serve. Serve with sliced radishes, if desired. 7. Store extras in an airtight container for up to 3 days. To reheat, place in a skillet over medium heat and sauté for 3 minutes on all sides, or until warmed.

Per Serving:
calories: 190 | fat: 13g | protein: 15g | carbs: 3g | net carbs: 1g | fiber: 2g

Almond and Chocolate Chia Pudding

Prep time: 10 minutes | Cook time: 0 minutes | Serves 4

1 (14-ounce / 397-g) can full-fat coconut milk	2 to 3 teaspoons granulated sugar-free sweetener of choice (optional)
⅓ cup chia seeds	½ teaspoon vanilla extract
1 tablespoon unsweetened cocoa powder	½ teaspoon almond extract (optional)
2 tablespoons unsweetened almond butter	

1. Combine all the ingredients in a small bowl, whisking well to fully incorporate the almond butter. 2. Divide the mixture between four ramekins or small glass jars. 3. Cover and refrigerate for at least 6 hours, preferably overnight. Serve cold.

Per Serving:
calories: 335 | fat: 31g | protein: 7g | carbs: 13g | net carbs: 6g | fiber: 7g

Low-Carb Granola Bars

Prep time: 10 minutes | Cook time: 15 to 20 minutes | Makes about 12 bars

1 cup almonds	¼ cup unsweetened peanut butter
1 cup hazelnuts	½ cup dark chocolate chips
1 cup unsweetened coconut flakes	1 tablespoon vanilla extract
1 egg	1 tablespoon ground cinnamon
¼ cup coconut oil, melted	Pinch salt

1. Preheat the oven to 350ºF (180ºC). 2. In a food processor, pulse together the almonds and macadamia nuts for 1 to 2 minutes until roughly chopped. (You want them pretty fine but not turning into nut butter.) Transfer them to a large bowl. 3. Stir in the coconut, egg, coconut oil, peanut butter, chocolate chips, vanilla, cinnamon, and salt. Transfer the mixture to an 8- or 9-inch square baking dish and gently press into an even layer. Bake for 15 to 20 minutes or until golden brown. Cool and cut into 12 bars. Refrigerate in an airtight container for up to 2 weeks.

Per Serving:
1 bar: calories: 588 | fat: 58g | protein: 11g | carbs: 6g | net carbs: 5g | fiber: 1g

Strawberry Shortcake Coconut Ice

Prep time: 5 minutes | Cook time: 0 minutes | Serves 5

9 hulled strawberries (fresh or frozen and defrosted)
⅓ cup (85 g) coconut cream
1 tablespoon apple cider

vinegar
2 drops liquid stevia, or 2 teaspoons erythritol
3 cups (420 g) ice cubes

1. Place the strawberries, coconut cream, vinegar, and sweetener in a blender or food processor. Blend until smooth. 2. Add the ice and pulse until crushed. 3. Divide among four ¾-cup (180-ml) or larger bowls and serve immediately.

Per Serving:
calories: 61 | fat: 5g | protein: 0g | carbs: 3g | net carbs: 2g | fiber: 1g

Parmesan Chicken Balls with Chives

Prep time: 10 minutes | Cook time: 15 minutes | Serves 4

1 teaspoon coconut oil, softened
1 cup ground chicken
¼ cup chicken broth
1 tablespoon chopped chives

1 teaspoon cayenne pepper
3 ounces (85 g) Parmesan cheese, grated

1. Set your Instant Pot to Sauté and heat the coconut oil. 2. Add the remaining ingredients except the cheese to the Instant Pot and stir to mix well. 3. Secure the lid. Select the Manual mode and set the cooking time for 15 minutes at High Pressure. 4. Once cooking is complete, do a quick pressure release. Carefully open the lid. 5. Add the grated cheese and stir until combined. Form the balls from the cooked chicken mixture and allow to cool for 10 minutes, then serve.

Per Serving:
calories: 154 | fat: 8.7g | protein: 17.5g | carbs: 1.0g | net carbs: 0.9g | fiber: 0.1g

Grandma's Meringues

Prep time: 10 minutes | Cook time: 1 hour | Makes 12 meringues

2 large egg whites, room temperature
¼ teaspoon cream of tartar
Pinch of finely ground sea salt
½ cup (80 g) confectioners'-style erythritol

½ teaspoon vanilla extract
FOR SERVING:
24 fresh strawberries, sliced
¾ cup (190 g) coconut cream
12 fresh mint leaves

1. Preheat the oven to 225°F (108°C). Line a rimmed baking sheet with parchment paper or a silicone baking mat. 2. Place the egg whites, cream of tartar, and salt in a very clean large bowl. Make sure that the bowl does not have any oil residue in it. Using a handheld electric mixer or stand mixer, mix on low speed until the mixture becomes foamy. 3. Once foamy, increase the speed to high. Slowly add the erythritol, 1 tablespoon at a time, mixing all the while. Add a tablespoon about every 20 seconds. 4. Keep beating until the mixture is shiny and thick and peaks have formed; it should be nearly doubled in volume. (The peaks won't be as stiff as in a traditional meringue.) Fold in the vanilla. 5. Using a large spoon, dollop the meringue mixture onto the lined baking sheet, making a total of 12 meringues. 6. Bake for 1 hour without opening the oven door. After 1 hour, turn off the oven and keep the meringues in the cooling oven for another hour, then remove. 7. To serve, place 2 meringues on each plate. Top each serving with 4 sliced strawberries, 2 tablespoons of coconut cream, and 2 mint leaves.

Per Serving:
calories: 100 | fat: 8g | protein: 2g | carbs: 6g | net carbs: 4g | fiber: 2g

Dairy-Free Queso

Prep time: 10 minutes | Cook time: 10 minutes | Serves 5

1 cup (130 g) raw cashews
½ cup (120 ml) nondairy milk
¼ cup (17 g) nutritional yeast
½ teaspoon finely ground sea salt
¼ cup (60 ml) avocado oil
1 medium yellow onion, sliced
2 cloves garlic, roughly chopped
1 tablespoon chili powder

1 teaspoon ground cumin
¾ teaspoon garlic powder
¼ teaspoon onion powder
½ teaspoon dried oregano leaves
⅛ teaspoon paprika
⅛ teaspoon cayenne pepper
3½ ounces (100 g) pork rinds, or 2 medium zucchinis, cut into sticks, for serving (optional)

1. Place the cashews in a 12-ounce (350-ml) or larger sealable container. Cover with water. Seal and place in the fridge to soak for 12 hours. 2. After 12 hours, drain and rinse the cashews, then place them in a food processor or blender along with the milk, nutritional yeast, and salt. Set aside. 3. Heat the oil in a medium-sized frying pan over medium-low heat until shimmering. Add the onion, garlic, and spices and toss to coat the onion with the seasonings. Stir the mixture every couple of minutes until the onion begins to soften, about 10 minutes. 4. Transfer the onion mixture to the food processor or blender. Cover and blend until smooth. 5. Enjoy the queso with pork rinds or zucchini sticks, if desired.

Per Serving:
calories: 300 | fat: 24g | protein: 7g | carbs: 14g | net carbs: 11g | fiber: 3g

Curried Broccoli Skewers

Prep time: 15 minutes | Cook time: 1 minute | Serves 2

1 cup broccoli florets
½ teaspoon curry paste

2 tablespoons coconut cream
1 cup water, for cooking

1. In the shallow bowl mix up curry paste and coconut cream. 2. Then sprinkle the broccoli florets with curry paste mixture and string on the skewers. 3. Pour water and insert the steamer rack in the instant pot. 4. Place the broccoli skewers on the rack. Close and seal the lid. 5. Cook the meal on Manual mode (High Pressure) for 1 minute. 6. Make a quick pressure release.

Per Serving:
calories: 58 | fat: 4g | protein: 2g | carbs: 4g | net carbs: 2g | fiber: 2g

Bone Broth Fat Bombs

Prep time: 5 minutes | Cook time: 0 minutes | Makes 12 fat bombs

1 tablespoon grass-fed powdered gelatin
2 cups homemade bone broth, any type, warmed

Special Equipment:
Silicone mold with 12 (1⅛-ounce / 53-g) cavities

1. Sprinkle the gelatin over the broth and whisk to combine. 2. Place the silicone mold on a rimmed sheet pan (for easy transport). Pour the broth into the mold. Place in the fridge or freezer until the gelatin is fully set, about 2 hours. To release the fat bombs from the mold, gently push on the mold to pop them out. 3. Store in an airtight container in the fridge for up to 5 days or in the freezer for several months.

Per Serving:
calories: 27 | fat: 5g | protein: 2g | carbs: 2g | net carbs: 2g | fiber: 0g

Parmesan Crisps

Prep time: 5 minutes | Cook time: 5 minutes | Makes about 25 crisps

2 cups grated Parmesan cheese

1. Heat the oven to 400°F (205°C). Line a baking sheet with a silicone mat or parchment paper. Scoop a generous tablespoon of the cheese onto the sheet and flatten it slightly. Repeat with the rest of the cheese, leaving about 1 inch (2.5 cm) space in between them. 2. Bake for 3 to 5 minutes, until crisp.

Per Serving:
calories: 169 | fat: 11g | protein: 11g | carbs: 6g | net carbs: 6g | fiber: 0g

Avocado Feta Dip

Prep time: 15 minutes | Cook time: 0 minutes | Serves 8

2 avocados, diced
2 Roma tomatoes, chopped
¼ medium red onion, finely chopped (about ½ cup)
2 garlic cloves, minced
2 tablespoons chopped fresh parsley (or cilantro)
2 tablespoons olive oil or avocado oil

2 tablespoons red wine vinegar
1 tablespoon freshly squeezed lemon or lime juice
½ teaspoon sea salt
¼ teaspoon freshly ground black pepper
8 ounces (227 g) feta cheese, crumbled

1. In a large bowl, gently stir together the avocados, tomatoes, onion, garlic, and parsley. 2. In a small bowl, whisk together the oil, vinegar, lemon juice, salt, and pepper. Pour the mixture over the avocado mixture. Fold in the cheese. 3. Cover and let chill in the refrigerator for 1 to 2 hours before serving.

Per Serving:
½ cup: calories: 190 | fat: 16g | protein: 6g | carbs: 6g | net carbs: 3g | fiber: 3g

Jelly Cups

Prep time: 10 minutes | Cook time: 10 minutes | Makes 16 jelly cups

BUTTER BASE:
⅔ cup (170 g) coconut butter or smooth unsweetened nut or seed butter
⅔ cup (145 g) coconut oil, ghee, or cacao butter, melted
2 teaspoons vanilla extract
7 drops liquid stevia, or 2 teaspoons confectioners'-style erythritol

JELLY FILLING:
½ cup (70 g) fresh raspberries
¼ cup (60 ml) water
3 drops liquid stevia, or 1 teaspoon confectioners'-style erythritol
1½ teaspoons unflavored gelatin
SPECIAL EQUIPMENT:
16 mini muffin cup liners, or 1 silicone mini muffin pan

1. Set 16 mini muffin cup liners on a tray or have on hand a silicone mini muffin pan. 2. Make the base: Place the coconut butter, melted oil, vanilla, and sweetener in a medium-sized bowl and stir to combine. 3. Take half of the base mixture and divide it equally among the 16 mini muffin cup liners or 16 wells of the mini muffin pan, filling each about one-quarter full. Place the muffin cup liners (or muffin pan) in the fridge. Set the remaining half of the base mixture aside. 4. Make the jelly filling: Place the raspberries, water, and sweetener in a small saucepan and bring to a simmer over medium heat. Simmer for 5 minutes, then sprinkle with the gelatin and mash with a fork. Transfer to the fridge to set for 15 minutes. 5. Pull the muffin cup liners and jelly filling out of the fridge. Using a ½-teaspoon measuring spoon, scoop out a portion of the jelly and roll it into a ball between your palms, then flatten it into a disc about 1 inch (2.5 cm) in diameter (or in a diameter to fit the size of the liners you're using). Press into a chilled butter base cup. Repeat with the remaining jelly filling and cups. Then spoon the remaining butter base mixture over the tops. 6. Place in the fridge for another 15 minutes before serving.

Per Serving:
calories: 151 | fat: 15g | protein: 1g | carbs: 3g | net carbs: 1g | fiber: 2g

Macadamia Nut Cream Cheese Log

Prep time: 10 minutes | Cook time: 0 minutes | Serves 8

1 (8-ounce / 227-g) brick cream cheese, cold
1 cup finely chopped macadamia nuts

1. Place the cream cheese on a piece of parchment paper or wax paper. 2. Roll the paper around the cream cheese, then roll the wrapped cream cheese with the palm of your hands lengthwise on the cream cheese, using the paper to help you roll the cream cheese into an 8-inch log. 3. Open the paper and sprinkle the macadamia nuts all over the top and sides of the cream cheese until the log is entirely covered in nuts. 4. Chill in the refrigerator for 30 minutes before serving. 5. Serve on a small plate, cut into 8 even slices.

Per Serving:
⅛ roll: calories: 285 | fat: 29g | protein: 4g | carbs: 4g | net carbs: 3g | fiber: 1g

Everything Bagel Cream Cheese Dip

Prep time: 10 minutes | Cook time: 0 minutes | Serves 4

1 (8-ounce / 227-g) package cream cheese, at room temperature
½ cup sour cream
1 tablespoon garlic powder

1 tablespoon dried onion, or onion powder
1 tablespoon sesame seeds
1 tablespoon kosher salt

1. In a small bowl, combine the cream cheese, sour cream, garlic powder, dried onion, sesame seeds, and salt. Stir well to incorporate everything together. Serve immediately or cover and refrigerate for up to 6 days.

Per Serving:
calories: 291 | fat: 27g | protein: 6g | carbs: 6g | net carbs: 5g | fiber: 1g

Stuffed Jalapeños with Bacon

Prep time: 10 minutes | Cook time: 6 minutes | Serves 2

1 ounce (28 g) bacon, chopped, fried
2 ounces (57 g) Cheddar cheese, shredded
1 tablespoon coconut cream

1 teaspoon chopped green onions
2 jalapeños, trimmed and seeded

1. Mix together the chopped bacon, cheese, coconut cream, and green onions in a mixing bowl and stir until well incorporated. 2. Stuff the jalapeños evenly with the bacon mixture. 3. Press the Sauté button to heat your Instant Pot. 4. Place the stuffed jalapeños in the Instant Pot and cook each side for 3 minutes until softened. 5. Transfer to a paper towel-lined plate and serve.

Per Serving:
calories: 216 | fat: 17.5g | protein: 12.9g | carbs: 1.7g | net carbs: 1.1g | fiber: 0.6g

Edana's Macadamia Crack Bars

Prep time: 15 minutes | Cook time: 35 minutes | Makes 12 bars

BASE:
1¼ cups (140 g) blanched almond flour
⅓ cup (65 g) erythritol
⅓ cup (70 g) coconut oil, ghee, or cacao butter, melted
1 teaspoon vanilla extract
¼ teaspoon finely ground sea salt
COCONUT CREAM LAYER:
½ cup (95 g) erythritol

½ cup (125 g) coconut cream
¼ cup (55 g) coconut oil, ghee, or cacao butter, melted
2 large egg yolks
1 teaspoon vanilla extract
TOPPINGS:
1 cup (160 g) raw macadamia nuts, roughly chopped
1 cup (100 g) unsweetened shredded coconut

1. Preheat the oven to 350°F (177°C). Line an 8-inch (20-cm) square baking pan with parchment paper, draping it over two opposite sides of the pan for easy lifting. 2. Place the base ingredients in a large mixing bowl and stir to combine. Press into the prepared pan and par-bake for 10 to 12 minutes, until the top is only lightly browned. Remove from the oven and lower the oven temperature to 300°F (150°C). 3. Meanwhile, make the coconut cream layer: Place the erythritol, coconut cream, melted oil, egg yolks, and vanilla in a large mixing bowl. Whisk until smooth. 4. Pour the coconut cream mixture over the par-baked base. Top with the macadamia nuts, then the shredded coconut. 5. Return the pan to the oven and bake for 25 minutes, or until the edges are lightly browned. 6. Let cool in the pan on the counter for 1 hour before transferring to the fridge to chill for another hour. Once chilled, cut into 2-inch (5-cm) squares.

Per Serving:
calories: 303 | fat: 31g | protein: 2g | carbs: 6g | net carbs: 2g | fiber: 3g

Queso Dip

Prep time: 5 minutes | Cook time: 10 minutes | Serves 6

½ cup coconut milk
½ jalapeño pepper, seeded and diced
1 teaspoon minced garlic
½ teaspoon onion powder

2 ounces goat cheese
6 ounces sharp Cheddar cheese, shredded
¼ teaspoon cayenne pepper

1. Place a medium pot over medium heat and add the coconut milk, jalapeño, garlic, and onion powder. 2. Bring the liquid to a simmer and then whisk in the goat cheese until smooth. 3. Add the Cheddar cheese and cayenne and whisk until the dip is thick, 30 seconds to 1 minute. 4. Pour into a serving dish and serve with keto crackers or low-carb vegetables.

Per Serving:
calories: 213 | fat: 19g | protein: 10g | carbs: 2g | net carbs: 2g | fiber: 0g

Buffalo Bill's Chicken Dip

Prep time: 15 minutes | Cook time: 30 minutes | Serves 10

2 (4.2-ounce) chicken breasts from cooked rotisserie chicken
1 (8-ounce) package full-fat cream cheese, softened
2 cups shredded whole milk mozzarella cheese
1 cup shredded Cheddar cheese
1 (1-ounce) package ranch powder seasoning mix

1 cup full-fat mayonnaise
1 cup full-fat sour cream
½ cup finely chopped green onion
¼ cup buffalo wing sauce
1 teaspoon garlic powder
½ pound no-sugar-added bacon, cooked and crumbled

1. Preheat oven to 350°F. Grease a 2-quart (8" × 8") baking dish. 2. In a small bowl, finely shred chicken. 3. Combine chicken with remaining ingredients, except bacon, in baking dish, stirring to mix well. 4. Bake 25–30 minutes; stop when bubbling and browned on top. 5. Take out of the oven and stir again to mix all the melted ingredients. Top with the crumbled bacon. Serve immediately.

Per Serving:
calories: 539| fat: 43g | protein: 25g | carbs: 5g | net carbs: 5g | fiber: 0g

Blueberry Crumble with Cream Topping

Prep time: 5 minutes | Cook time: 25 minutes | Serves 6

18 ounces (510 g) fresh or frozen blueberries
1 cup (110 g) blanched almond flour
⅓ cup (70 g) coconut oil or ghee, room temperature

⅓ cup (65 g) erythritol
2 tablespoons coconut flour
1 teaspoon ground cinnamon
1 cup (250 g) coconut cream, or 1 cup (240 ml) full-fat coconut milk, for serving

1. Preheat the oven to 350°F (177°C). 2. Place the blueberries in an 8-inch (20-cm) square baking pan. 3. Place the almond flour, oil, erythritol, coconut flour, and cinnamon in a medium-sized bowl and mix with a fork until crumbly. Crumble over the top of the blueberries. 4. Bake for 22 to 25 minutes, until the top is golden. 5. Remove from the oven and let sit for 10 minutes before dividing among 6 serving bowls. Top each bowl with 2 to 3 tablespoons of coconut cream.

Per Serving:
calories: 388 | fat: 33g | protein: 5g | carbs: 17g | net carbs: 13g | fiber: 4g

Oregano Sausage Balls

Prep time: 10 minutes | Cook time: 16 minutes | Serves 10

15 ounces (425 g) ground pork sausage
1 teaspoon dried oregano
4 ounces (113 g) Mozzarella,

shredded
1 cup coconut flour
1 garlic clove, grated
1 teaspoon coconut oil, melted

1. In the bowl mix up ground pork sausages, dried oregano, shredded Mozzarella, coconut flour, and garlic clove. 2. When the mixture is homogenous, make the balls. 3. After this, pour coconut oil in the instant pot. 4. Arrange the balls in the instant pot and cook them on Sauté mode for 8 minutes from each side.

Per Serving:
calories: 310 | fat: 23g | protein: 17g | carbs: 10g | net carbs: 5g | fiber: 5g

Rosemary Chicken Wings

Prep time: 10 minutes | Cook time: 16 minutes | Serves 4

4 boneless chicken wings
1 tablespoon olive oil
1 teaspoon dried rosemary

½ teaspoon garlic powder
¼ teaspoon salt

1. In the mixing bowl, mix up olive oil, dried rosemary, garlic powder, and salt. 2. Then rub the chicken wings with the rosemary mixture and leave for 10 minutes to marinate. 3. After this, put the chicken wings in the instant pot, add the remaining rosemary marinade and cook them on Sauté mode for 8 minutes from each side.

Per Serving:
calories: 222 | fat: 11g | protein: 27g | carbs: 2g | net carbs: 2g | fiber: 0g

Bacon Ranch Dip

Prep time: 10 minutes | Cook time: 10 minutes | Serves 10

1 (8-ounce / 227-g) package full-fat cream cheese, at room temperature
1 cup full-fat sour cream
8 bacon slices, cooked and crumbled
1½ teaspoons dried chives
1 teaspoon dry mustard

½ teaspoon dried dill
½ teaspoon celery seed
½ teaspoon garlic powder
½ teaspoon onion powder
Salt and freshly ground black pepper, to taste
¼ cup sliced scallion, or fresh chives, for garnish

1. In a medium bowl, stir the cream cheese until it becomes fluffy and smooth. Add the sour cream and gently fold to combine. 2. Add the bacon, chives, mustard, dill, celery seed, garlic powder, and onion powder. Season with salt and pepper and stir to combine. Top with the scallion and serve immediately, or refrigerate in an airtight container for up to 1 week.

Per Serving:
calories: 211 | fat: 19g | protein: 8g | carbs: 2g | net carbs: 2g | fiber: 0g

Mac Fatties

Prep time: 10 minutes | Cook time: 0 minutes | Makes 20 fat cups

1¾ cups (280 g) roasted and salted macadamia nuts
⅓ cup (70 g) coconut oil
ROSEMARY LEMON FLAVOR:
1 teaspoon finely chopped fresh rosemary
¼ teaspoon lemon juice
SPICY CUMIN FLAVOR:
½ teaspoon ground cumin

¼ teaspoon cayenne pepper
TURMERIC FLAVOR:
½ teaspoon turmeric powder
¼ teaspoon ginger powder
GARLIC HERB FLAVOR:
1¼ teaspoons dried oregano leaves
½ teaspoon paprika
½ teaspoon garlic powder

1. Place the macadamia nuts and oil in a blender or food processor. Blend until smooth, or as close to smooth as you can get it with the equipment you're using. 2. Divide the mixture among 4 small bowls, placing ¼ cup (87 g) in each bowl. 3. To the first bowl, add the rosemary and lemon juice and stir to combine. 4. To the second bowl, add the cumin and cayenne and stir to combine. 5. To the third bowl, add the turmeric and ginger and stir to combine. 6. To the fourth bowl, add the oregano, paprika, and garlic powder and stir to combine. 7. Set a 24-well silicone or metal mini muffin pan on the counter. If using a metal pan, line 20 of the wells with mini foil liners. (Do not use paper; it would soak up all the fat.) Spoon the mixtures into the wells, using about 1 tablespoon per well. 8. Place in the freezer for 1 hour, or until firm. Enjoy directly from the freezer.

Per Serving:
calories: 139 | fat: 14g | protein: 1g | carbs: 2g | net carbs: 1g | fiber: 1g

Classy Crudités and Dip

Prep time: 15 minutes | Cook time: 0 minutes | Serves 8

Vegetables
1 cup whole cherry tomatoes
1 cup green beans, trimmed
2 cups broccoli florets
2 cups cauliflower florets
1 bunch asparagus, trimmed
1 large green bell pepper, seeded and chopped

Sour Cream Dip
2 cups full-fat sour cream
3 tablespoons dry chives
1 tablespoon lemon juice
½ cup dried parsley
½ teaspoon garlic powder
⅛ teaspoon salt
⅛ teaspoon black pepper

1. Cut vegetables into bite-sized uniform pieces. Arrange in like groups around outside edge of a large serving platter, leaving room in middle for dip. 2. Make dip by combining dip ingredients in a medium-sized decorative bowl and mixing well. 3. Place dip bowl in the center of platter and serve.

Per Serving:
calories: 146| fat: 10g | protein: 4g | carbs: 9g | net carbs: 6g | fiber: 3g

Crab Salad–Stuffed Avocado

Prep time: 20 minutes | Cook time: 0 minutes | Serves 2

1 avocado, peeled, halved lengthwise, and pitted
½ teaspoon freshly squeezed lemon juice
4½ ounces Dungeness crabmeat
½ cup cream cheese
¼ cup chopped red bell pepper

¼ cup chopped, peeled English cucumber
½ scallion, chopped
1 teaspoon chopped cilantro
Pinch sea salt
Freshly ground black pepper

1. Brush the cut edges of the avocado with the lemon juice and set the halves aside on a plate. 2. In a medium bowl, stir together the crabmeat, cream cheese, red pepper, cucumber, scallion, cilantro, salt, and pepper until well mixed. 3. Divide the crab mixture between the avocado halves and store them, covered with plastic wrap, in the refrigerator until you want to serve them, up to 2 days.

Per Serving:
calories: 389 | fat: 31g | protein: 19g | carbs: 10g | net carbs: 5g | fiber: 5g

Salami Chips with Buffalo Chicken Dip

Prep time: 10 minutes | Cook time: 10 minutes | Serves 6

8 ounces (227 g) salami, cut crosswise into 24 slices
Buffalo Chicken Dip:
1 cup full-fat coconut milk
¾ cup shredded cooked chicken
⅓ cup nutritional yeast
1 tablespoon coconut aminos
1 tablespoon hot sauce
2 teaspoons onion powder

1½ teaspoons garlic powder
1 teaspoon turmeric powder
½ teaspoon finely ground sea salt
¼ teaspoon ground black pepper
¼ cup roughly chopped fresh parsley

1. Preheat the oven to 400ºF (205ºC). Line 2 rimmed baking sheets with parchment paper or silicone baking mats. 2. Set the salami slices on the lined baking sheets. Bake for 8 to 10 minutes, until the centers look crisp and the edges are just slightly turned up. Meanwhile, make the dip: 1. Place the dip ingredients in a small saucepan. Bring to a simmer over medium-high heat, then reduce the heat to medium-low and cook, uncovered, for 6 minutes, or until thickened, stirring often. 2. Transfer the salami chips to a serving plate and the dip to a serving bowl. Stir the parsley into the dip and dig in! Storage: Store in an airtight container in the fridge for up to 3 days or in the freezer for up to 3 months.

Per Serving:
calories: 294 | fat: 21g | protein: 20g | carbs: 7g | net carbs: 5g | fiber: 2g

Fried Cabbage Wedges

Prep time: 5 minutes | Cook time: 15 minutes | Serves 6

1 large head green or red cabbage (about 2½ lbs/1.2 kg)
2 tablespoons coconut oil or avocado oil
2 teaspoons garlic powder
½ teaspoon finely ground sea

salt
¾ cup (180 ml) green goddess dressing
SPECIAL EQUIPMENT:
12 (4-in/10-cm) bamboo skewers

1. Cut the cabbage in half through the core, from top to bottom. Working with each half separately, remove the core by cutting a triangle around it and pulling it out. Then lay the half cut side down and cut into 6 wedges. Press a bamboo skewer into each wedge to secure the leaves. Repeat with the other half. 2. Heat the oil in a large frying pan over medium-low heat. 3. Place the cabbage wedges in the frying pan and sprinkle with the garlic powder and salt. Cook for 10 minutes on one side, or until lightly browned, then cook for 5 minutes on the other side. Serve with the dressing on the side.

Per Serving:
calories: 252 | fat: 20g | protein: 3g | carbs: 12g | net carbs: 7g | fiber: 5g

Goat Cheese–Mackerel Pâté

Prep time: 10 minutes | Cook time: 0 minutes | Serves 4

4 ounces (113 g) olive oil-packed wild-caught mackerel
2 ounces (57 g) goat cheese
Zest and juice of 1 lemon
2 tablespoons chopped fresh parsley
2 tablespoons chopped fresh arugula

1 tablespoon extra-virgin olive oil
2 teaspoons chopped capers
1 to 2 teaspoons fresh horseradish (optional)
Crackers, cucumber rounds, endive spears, or celery, for serving (optional)

1. In a food processor, blender, or large bowl with immersion blender, combine the mackerel, goat cheese, lemon zest and juice, parsley, arugula, olive oil, capers, and horseradish (if using). Process or blend until smooth and creamy. 2. Serve with crackers, cucumber rounds, endive spears, or celery. 3. Store covered in the refrigerator for up to 1 week.

Per Serving:
calories: 142 | fat: 10g | protein: 11g | carbs: 1g | fiber: 0g | sodium: 203mg

3-Ingredient Almond Flour Crackers

Prep time: 5 minutes | Cook time: 12 minutes | Serves 6

2 cups (8 ounces / 227 g) blanched almond flour

½ teaspoon sea salt
1 large egg, beaten

1. Preheat the oven to 350°F (180°C). Line a large baking sheet with parchment paper. 2. In a large bowl, mix together the almond flour and sea salt. Add the egg and mix well, until a dense, crumbly dough forms. (You can also mix in a food processor if you prefer.) 3. Place the dough between two large pieces of parchment paper. Use a rolling pin to roll out to a very thin rectangle, about 1/16 inch thick. (It will tend to roll into an oval shape, so just rip off pieces of dough and re-attach to form a more rectangular shape.) 4. Cut the cracker dough into rectangles. Place on the lined baking sheet. Prick with a fork a few times. Bake for 8 to 12 minutes, until golden.

Per Serving:
calories: 226 | fat: 19g | protein: 9g | carbs: 8g | net carbs: 4g | fiber: 4g

Parmesan Zucchini Fries

Prep time: 15 minutes | Cook time: 5 minutes | Serves 4

1 zucchini
1 ounce (28 g) Parmesan, grated
1 tablespoon almond flour

½ teaspoon Italian seasoning
1 tablespoon coconut oil

1. Trim the zucchini and cut it into the French fries. 2. Then sprinkle them with grated Parmesan, almond flour, and Italian seasoning. 3. Put coconut oil in the instant pot and melt it on Sauté mode. 4. Put the zucchini in the hot oil in one layer and cook for 2 minutes from each side or until they are golden brown. 5. Dry the zucchini fries with paper towels.

Per Serving:
calories: 102 | fat: 9g | protein: 4g | carbs: 3g | net carbs: 2g | fiber: 1g

Keto Antipasto

Prep time: 20 minutes | Cook time: 0 minutes | Serves 12

8 ounces (227 g) soppressata salami, diced
5 ounces (142 g) Calabrese salami, diced
4 ounces (113 g) sharp provolone or white Cheddar cheese, diced
4 ounces (113 g) Mozzarella, diced
4 celery stalks, diced
¼ medium red onion, finely chopped (about ½ cup)

24 large green olives (or 35 medium), pitted and chopped
10 pepperoncini peppers, diced
¼ cup fresh basil, chopped
1 tablespoon Italian seasoning
2 tablespoons olive oil
2 tablespoons red wine vinegar
1 teaspoon balsamic vinegar
1 teaspoon Dijon mustard
Sea salt and freshly ground black pepper, to taste

1. In a large bowl, combine the soppressata, Calabrese, provolone, Mozzarella, celery, onion, olives, peppers, basil, and Italian seasoning. Mix until well combined. 2. In a small bowl, whisk together the olive oil, red wine vinegar, balsamic vinegar, and mustard. Add salt and pepper. 3. Pour the dressing over the meat and cheese mixture and stir well. 4. Serve immediately or transfer to an airtight container and store in the refrigerator for up to 1 week or in the freezer for up to 3 months.

Per Serving:
⅓ cup: calories: 206 | fat: 16g | protein: 12g | carbs: 3g | net carbs: 3g | fiber: 0g

Charlie's Energy Balls

Prep time: 10 minutes | Cook time: 20 minutes | Makes 20 balls

½ cup natural almond butter, room temperature
¼ cup coconut oil, melted
1 large egg
½ cup coconut flour

2 tablespoons unflavored beef gelatin powder
1 scoop chocolate-flavored whey protein powder

1. Preheat the oven to 350°F and grease a rimmed baking sheet with coconut oil spray. 2. In a large mixing bowl, mix together the almond butter, coconut oil, and egg using a fork. In a small bowl, whisk together the coconut flour, gelatin, and protein powder. 3. Pour the dry ingredients into the wet mixture and mash with a fork until you have a cohesive dough. It should not be too sticky. Note: If the dough doesn't come together well or is very sticky, add a little coconut flour until it combines well. 4. Using your hands, form the dough into 20 even-sized balls, about 1½ inches in diameter, and put them on the prepared baking sheet. 5. Bake for 20 minutes, until slightly browned and hardened. Allow to cool on the baking sheet for 10 minutes prior to serving. 6. Store in a zip-top plastic bag in the refrigerator for up to a week.

Per Serving:
calories: 91 | fat: 7g | protein: 4g | carbs: 3g | net carbs: 2g | fiber: 1g

Deviled Eggs with Tuna

Prep time: 10 minutes | Cook time: 8 minutes | Serves 3

1 cup water
6 eggs
1 (5-ounce / 142-g) can tuna, drained
4 tablespoons mayonnaise
1 teaspoon lemon juice

1 celery stalk, diced finely
¼ teaspoon Dijon mustard
¼ teaspoon chopped fresh dill
¼ teaspoon salt
⅛ teaspoon garlic powder

1. Add water to Instant Pot. Place steam rack or steamer basket inside pot. Carefully put eggs into steamer basket. Click lid closed. Press the Manual button and adjust time for 8 minutes. 2. Add remaining ingredients to medium bowl and mix. 3. When timer beeps, quick-release the steam and remove eggs. Place in bowl of cool water for 10 minutes, then remove shells. 4. Cut eggs in half and remove hard-boiled yolks, setting whites aside. Place yolks in food processor and pulse until smooth, or mash with fork. Add yolks to bowl with tuna and mayo, mixing until smooth. 5. Spoon mixture into egg-white halves. Serve chilled.

Per Serving:
calories: 303 | fat: 22g | protein: 20g | carbs: 2g | net carbs: 2g | fiber: 0g

Cheese Stuffed Mushrooms

Prep time: 15 minutes | Cook time: 8 minutes | Serves 4

1 cup cremini mushroom caps
1 tablespoon chopped scallions
1 tablespoon chopped chives
1 teaspoon cream cheese
1 teaspoon sour cream

1 ounce (28 g) Monterey Jack cheese, shredded
1 teaspoon butter, softened
½ teaspoon smoked paprika
1 cup water, for cooking

1. Trim the mushroom caps if needed and wash them well. 2. After this, in the mixing bowl, mix up scallions, chives, cream cheese, sour cream, butter, and smoked paprika. 3. Then fill the mushroom caps with the cream cheese mixture and top with shredded Monterey Jack cheese. 4. Pour water and insert the trivet in the instant pot. 5. Arrange the stuffed mushrooms caps on the trivet and close the lid. 6. Cook the meal on Manual (High Pressure) for 8 minutes. 7. Then make a quick pressure release.

Per Serving:
calories: 45 | fat: 4g | protein: 3g | carbs: 1g | net carbs: 1g | fiber: 0g

Cauliflower Cheesy Garlic Bread

Prep time: 10 minutes | Cook time: 30 minutes | Serves 6

Butter, or olive oil, for the baking sheet
1 head cauliflower, roughly chopped into florets
3 cups shredded Mozzarella cheese, divided
½ cup grated Parmesan cheese
¼ cup cream cheese, at room temperature
3 teaspoons garlic powder, plus

more for sprinkling
1 teaspoon onion powder
½ teaspoon red pepper flakes
1 tablespoon salt, plus more for seasoning
Freshly ground black pepper, to taste
2 eggs, whisked
Sugar-free marinara sauce, warmed, for dipping

1. Preheat the oven to 400ºF (205ºC). 2. Grease a baking sheet with butter. Set aside. Alternatively, use a pizza stone. 3. In a food processor, pulse the cauliflower until fine. Transfer to a microwave-safe bowl and microwave on high power, uncovered, for 2 minutes. Cool slightly. Place the cauliflower in a thin cloth or piece of cheesecloth and twist to remove any water (not a lot will come out but the little that's there needs to be removed). Transfer to a large bowl. 4. Add 2 cups of Mozzarella, the Parmesan, cream cheese, garlic powder, onion powder, red pepper flakes, and salt. Season generously with black pepper. Stir well to combine. 5. Add the eggs and use your hands to mix, ensuring everything is coated with egg. Transfer to the prepared baking sheet. Spread the mixture out into a large rectangle, about 1 inch thick. Sprinkle with more salt, pepper, and garlic powder. Bake for 20 minutes or until the bread starts to turn golden brown. 6. Remove from the oven, top with the remaining 1 cup of Mozzarella, and bake for about 10 minutes more or until the cheese melts. Cool slightly and cut into breadsticks. Serve with the marinara sauce for dipping. Refrigerate leftovers in an airtight container for up to 4 days.

Per Serving:
calories: 296 | fat: 20g | protein: 21g | carbs: 10g | net carbs: 7g | fiber: 3g

Cauliflower Patties

Prep time: 10 minutes | Cook time: 10 minutes |
Makes 10 patties

1 medium head cauliflower (about 1½ lbs/680 g), or 3 cups (375 g) pre-riced cauliflower
2 large eggs
⅔ cup (75 g) blanched almond flour
¼ cup (17 g) nutritional yeast
1 tablespoon dried chives

1 teaspoon finely ground sea salt
1 teaspoon garlic powder
½ teaspoon turmeric powder
¼ teaspoon ground black pepper
3 tablespoons coconut oil or ghee, for the pan

1. If you're using pre-riced cauliflower, skip ahead to Step 2. Otherwise, cut the base off the head of cauliflower and remove the florets. Transfer the florets to a food processor or blender and pulse 3 or 4 times to break them up into small (¼-inch/6-mm) pieces. 2. Transfer the riced cauliflower to a medium-sized saucepan and add enough water to the pan to completely cover the cauliflower. Cover with the lid and bring to a boil over medium heat. Boil, covered, for 3½ minutes. 3. Meanwhile, place a fine-mesh strainer over a bowl. 4. Pour the hot cauliflower into the strainer, allowing the bowl to catch the boiling water. With a spoon, press down on the cauliflower to remove as much water as possible. 5. Discard the cooking water and place the cauliflower in the bowl, then add the eggs, almond flour, nutritional yeast, chives, salt, and spices. Stir until everything is incorporated. 6. Heat a large frying pan over medium-low heat. Add the oil and allow to melt completely. 7. Using a ¼-cup (60-ml) scoop, scoop up a portion of the mixture and roll between your hands to form a ball about 1¾ inches (4.5 cm) in diameter. Place in the hot oil and flatten the ball with the back of a fork until it is a patty about ½ inch (1.25 cm) thick. Repeat with the remaining cauliflower mixture, making a total of 10 patties. 8. Cook the patties for 5 minutes per side, or until golden brown. Transfer to a serving plate and enjoy!

Per Serving:
calories: 164 | fat: 12g | protein: 7g | carbs: 7g | net carbs: 3g | fiber: 4g

BLT Salad

Prep time: 15 minutes | Cook time: 0 minutes | Serves 4

2 tablespoons melted bacon fat
2 tablespoons red wine vinegar
Freshly ground black pepper
4 cups shredded lettuce
1 tomato, chopped
6 bacon slices, cooked and chopped

2 hardboiled eggs, chopped
1 tablespoon roasted unsalted sunflower seeds
1 teaspoon toasted sesame seeds
1 cooked chicken breast, sliced (optional)

1. In a medium bowl, whisk together the bacon fat and vinegar until emulsified. Season with black pepper. 2. Add the lettuce and tomato to the bowl and toss the vegetables with the dressing. 3. Divide the salad between 4 plates and top each with equal amounts of bacon, egg, sunflower seeds, sesame seeds, and chicken (if using). Serve.

Per Serving:
calories: 228 | fat: 18g | protein: 1g | carbs: 4 | net carbs: 2g | fiber: 2g

Devilish Eggs

Prep time: 10 minutes | Cook time: 9 minutes | Serves 6

6 large eggs
3 tablespoons full-fat mayonnaise
1 teaspoon plain white vinegar
1 teaspoon spicy mustard

⅛ teaspoon salt
⅛ teaspoon black pepper
⅛ teaspoon ground cayenne
⅛ teaspoon paprika

1. Preferred Method: Hard-boil eggs using a steamer basket in the Instant Pot® on high pressure for 9 minutes. Release pressure and remove eggs. 2. Alternate Method: Place eggs in a large pot. Cover with water by 1". Cover with a lid and place the pot over high heat until it reaches a boil. Turn off heat, leave covered, and let it sit for 13 minutes. Then, remove the eggs from the pan, place them in an ice water bath, and let them cool 5 minutes. 3. When cooled, peel eggs and slice in half lengthwise. Place yolks in a medium bowl. 4. Mash and mix yolks with mayonnaise, vinegar, mustard, salt, and black pepper. 5. Scrape mixture into a sandwich-sized plastic bag and snip off one corner, making a hole about the width of a pencil. Use makeshift pastry bag to fill egg white halves with yolk mixture. 6. Garnish Devilish Eggs with cayenne and paprika (mostly for color) and serve.

Per Serving:
calories: 125| fat: 9g | protein: 6g | carbs: 1g | net carbs: 1g | fiber: 0g

Superpower Fat Bombs

Prep time: 10 minutes | Cook time: 0 minutes | Makes 8 bombs

⅔ cup (145 g) coconut oil, cacao butter, or ghee, melted
¼ cup (40 g) collagen peptides or protein powder
¼ cup (25 g) unflavored MCT oil powder
2 tablespoons cocoa powder
2 tablespoons roughly ground flax seeds
1 tablespoon cacao nibs

1 teaspoon instant coffee granules
4 drops liquid stevia, or 1 tablespoon plus 1 teaspoon confectioners'-style erythritol
Pinch of finely ground sea salt
SPECIAL EQUIPMENT (optional):
Silicone mold with eight 2-tablespoon or larger cavities

1. Have on hand your favorite silicone mold. I like to use a large silicone ice cube tray and spoon 2 tablespoons of the mixture into each well, which Prep time: 5 minutes | Cook time: 0 minutes | Makes 4 MAKES 8 cubes total. If you do not have a silicone mold, making this into a bark works well, too. Simply use an 8-inch (20-cm) square silicone or metal baking pan; if using a metal pan, line it with parchment paper, draping some over the sides for easy removal. 2. Place all the ingredients in a medium-sized bowl and stir until well mixed and smooth. 3. Divide the mixture evenly among 8 cavities in the silicone mold or pour into the baking pan. Transfer to the fridge and allow to set for 15 minutes if using cacao butter or 30 minutes if using ghee or coconut oil. If using a baking pan, break the bark into 8 pieces for serving.

Per Serving:
calories: 136 | fat: 12g | protein: 6g | carbs: 3g | net carbs: 1g | fiber: 2g

Sesame Mushrooms

Prep time: 2 minutes | Cook time: 10 minutes | Serves 6

3 tablespoons sesame oil
¾ pound (340 g) small button mushrooms
1 teaspoon minced garlic

½ teaspoon smoked paprika
½ teaspoon cayenne pepper
Salt and ground black pepper, to taste

1. Set your Instant Pot to Sauté and heat the sesame oil. 2. Add the mushrooms and sauté for 4 minutes until just tender, stirring occasionally. 3. Add the remaining ingredients to the Instant Pot and stir to mix well. 4. Lock the lid. Select the Manual mode and set the cooking time for 5 minutes at High Pressure. 5. When the timer beeps, perform a quick pressure release. Carefully remove the lid. 6. Serve warm.

Per Serving:
calories: 77 | fat: 7.6g | protein: 1.9g | carbs: 1.8g | net carbs: 1.0g | fiber: 0.8g

Spinach-Artichoke-Jalapeño Dip

Prep time: 5 minutes | Cook time: 15 minutes | Serves 4

¼ cup cooked fresh spinach or thawed frozen
½ cup grated Parmesan cheese
3 ounces (85 g) full-fat cream cheese
⅓ cup canned artichoke hearts
2 tablespoons sour cream
2 tablespoons mayonnaise

1 jalapeño pepper, seeded and finely chopped
1 garlic clove, minced
½ teaspoon pink Himalayan sea salt
½ teaspoon freshly ground black pepper

1. Preheat the oven to 350ºF (180ºC). 2. In a medium bowl, combine the spinach, Parmesan, cream cheese, artichoke hearts, sour cream, mayonnaise, jalapeño, garlic, salt, and pepper and mix to combine. 3. Transfer the mixture to a ramekin or other small baking dish. Bake for 15 minutes, then serve.

Per Serving:
calories: 196 | fat: 17g | protein: 6g | carbs: 5g | net carbs: 3g | fiber: 2g

Creamy Mashed Cauliflower

Prep time: 3 minutes | Cook time: 1 minute | Serves 4

1 head cauliflower, chopped into florets
1 cup water
1 clove garlic, finely minced

3 tablespoons butter
2 tablespoons sour cream
½ teaspoon salt
¼ teaspoon pepper

1. Place cauliflower on steamer rack. Add water and steamer rack to Instant Pot. Press the Steam button and adjust time to 1 minute. When timer beeps, quick-release the pressure. 2. Place cooked cauliflower into food processor and add remaining ingredients. Blend until smooth and creamy. Serve warm.

Per Serving:
calories: 125 | fat: 9g | protein: 3g | carbs: 8g | net carbs: 5g | fiber: 3g

Jumbo Pickle Cuban Sandwich

Prep time: 5 minutes | Cook time: 5 minutes | Serves 2

2 deli ham slices
2 deli pork tenderloin slices
4 Swiss cheese slices

2 jumbo dill pickles, halved
lengthwise
1 tablespoon yellow mustard

1. In a small sauté pan or skillet, heat the ham and tenderloin slices over medium heat until warm. 2. Using a spatula, roll the deli meats into loose rolls. Top with the Swiss cheese slices and allow the cheese to begin to melt. 3. Transfer the rolls to 2 pickle halves. 4. Top the cheese with some mustard, then close the sandwiches by topping them with the matching pickle halves. 5. Secure with toothpicks and slice in half crosswise, then serve.

Per Serving:
calories: 256 | fat: 16g | protein: 23g | carbs: 5g | net carbs: 1g | fiber: 4g

Cubed Tofu Fries

Prep time: 25 minutes | Cook time: 20 minutes | Serves 4

1 (12-ounce) package extra-firm tofu
2 tablespoons sesame oil
⅛ teaspoon salt, divided

⅛ teaspoon black pepper, divided
⅛ teaspoon creole seasoning, divided

1 Remove tofu from packaging and wrap in paper towel. Set on a clean plate. Place a second plate on top and put a 3- to 5-pound weight on top. Let sit 20 minutes. Drain excess water. 2 Unwrap tofu and slice into small cubes no larger than ½" square (a little larger than sugar cubes). 3 In a large skillet over medium heat, heat oil. 4 Combine salt, pepper, and creole seasoning in a small bowl. Sprinkle one-third of spice mixture evenly into skillet and add tofu evenly. 5 Sprinkle one-third of spices on top and let fry 5 minutes on each side, flipping three times (for the four sides), browning all four sides. 6 Dust tofu with remaining spice mixture. 7 Remove from heat. Enjoy while hot!
Per Serving:
PER SERVING:
CALORIES: 119 , FAT: 10G , PROTEIN: 7G , SODIUM:126MG , FIBER:1G , CARBOHYDRATE:1G , SUGAR:1G

Goat Cheese-Stuffed Jalapeño Poppers

Prep time: 15 minutes | Cook time: 20 minutes | Serves 8

1 (5-ounce / 142-g) package goat cheese, at room temperature
¼ cup shredded white Cheddar cheese
1 teaspoon paprika
½ teaspoon garlic powder

½ teaspoon onion powder
½ teaspoon sea salt
½ teaspoon freshly ground black pepper
8 jalapeño peppers
8 bacon slices

1. Preheat the oven to 400ºF (205ºC) and line a baking sheet with aluminum foil. Put a baking rack on the sheet. 2. In a medium bowl, mix together the goat cheese, Cheddar, paprika, garlic powder, onion powder, salt, and pepper. 3. Cut the jalapeños in half lengthwise and scoop out the seeds. Fill each half generously

with the cheese mixture. 4. Cut the bacon slices in half to make 16 individual pieces. Wrap each jalapeño half with one piece of bacon and place on the baking rack. 5. Cook for 15 to 20 minutes until the bacon begins to crisp. 6. Broil for an additional 2 to 3 minutes until the cheese is bubbly and slightly browned.

Per Serving:
2 poppers: calories: 121 | fat: 9g | protein: 8g | carbs: 2g | net carbs: 1g | fiber: 1g

Lime Brussels Chips

Prep time: 15 minutes | Cook time: 10 minutes |

Serves 2

3 cups Brussels sprouts leaves (from 1½ to 2 pounds fresh Brussels sprouts) Juice of ½ lime

2½ tablespoons avocado oil or melted coconut oil
Pink Himalayan salt

1 Preheat the oven to 400°F. Line a rimmed baking sheet with parchment paper. 2 Trim off the flat stem ends of the Brussels sprouts and separate the leaves. You should end up with 2 to 3 cups of leaves. 3 Place the separated leaves in a large bowl and add the lime juice. 4 Add the oil and season with salt to taste. Toss until the leaves are evenly coated. 5 Spread the leaves evenly on the prepared baking sheet and bake for 7 to 10 minutes, until lightly golden brown. tip: Trimming a little higher up than usual on the stem end of the Brussels sprouts helps the leaves come off easier.

Per Serving:
calories: 173 | fat: 18g | protein: 2g | carbs: 4g | net carbs: 2g | fiber: 2g

Hushpuppies

Prep time: 10 minutes | Cook time: 15 minutes |

Makes 10 hushpuppies

High-quality oil, for frying
1 cup finely ground blanched almond flour
1 tablespoon coconut flour
1 teaspoon baking powder

½ teaspoon salt
¼ cup finely chopped onions
¼ cup heavy whipping cream
1 large egg, beaten

1. Attach a candy thermometer to a Dutch oven or other large heavy pot, then pour in 3 inches of oil and set over medium-high heat. Heat the oil to 375°F. 2. In a medium-sized bowl, stir together the almond flour, coconut flour, baking powder, and salt. Stir in the rest of the ingredients and mix until blended. Do not overmix. 3. Use a tablespoon-sized cookie scoop to gently drop the batter into the hot oil. Don't overcrowd the hushpuppies; cook them in two batches. Fry for 3 minutes, then use a mesh skimmer or slotted spoon to turn and fry them for 3 more minutes or until golden brown on all sides. 4. Use the skimmer or slotted spoon to remove the hushpuppies from the oil and place on a paper towel–lined plate to drain. They are best served immediately.

Per Serving:
calories: 172 | fat: 14g | protein: 6g | carbs: 5g | net carbs: 3g | fiber: 3g

Cheese Almond Crackers

Prep time: 10 minutes | Cook time: 20 minutes | Serves 4

Olive oil cooking spray
1 cup almond flour
½ cup finely shredded Cheddar cheese
1 tablespoon nutritional yeast
¼ teaspoon baking soda
¼ teaspoon garlic powder
¼ teaspoon sea salt
1 egg
2 teaspoons good-quality olive oil

1. Preheat the oven. Set the oven temperature to 350°F. Line a baking sheet with parchment paper and set it aside. Lightly grease two sheets of parchment paper with olive oil cooking spray and set them aside. 2. Mix the dry ingredients. In a large bowl, stir together the almond flour, Cheddar, nutritional yeast, baking soda, garlic powder, and salt until everything is well blended. 3. Mix the wet ingredients. In a small bowl, whisk together the egg and olive oil. Using a wooden spoon, mix the wet ingredients into the dry until the dough sticks together to form a ball. Gather the ball together using your hands, and knead it firmly a few times. 4. Roll out the dough. Place the ball on one of the lightly greased parchment paper pieces and press it down to form a disk. Place the other piece of greased parchment paper on top and use a rolling pin to roll the dough into a 9-by-12-inch rectangle about ⅛ inch thick. 5. Cut the dough. Use a pizza cutter and a ruler to cut the edges of the dough into an even rectangle and cut the dough into 1½-by-1½-inch columns and rows. Transfer the crackers to the baking sheet. 6. Bake. Bake the crackers for 15 to 20 minutes until they're crisp. Transfer them to a wire rack and let them cool completely. 7. Serve. Eat the crackers immediately or store them in an airtight container in the refrigerator for up to one week.

Per Serving:
calories: 146 | fat: 12g | protein: 7g | carbs: 1g | net carbs: 0g | fiber: 1g

Antipasto Skewers

Prep time: 10 minutes | Cook time: 0 minutes | Makes 8 skewers

8 ounces (227 g) fresh whole Mozzarella
16 fresh basil leaves
16 slices salami (4 ounces / 113 g)
16 slices coppa or other cured meat like prosciutto (4 ounces / 113 g)
8 artichoke hearts, packed in water (8 ounces / 227 g)
¼ cup vinaigrette made with olive oil or avocado oil and apple cider vinegar
Flaky salt and freshly ground black pepper, to taste

1. Cut the Mozzarella into 16 small chunks. 2. Skewer 2 pieces each of the Mozzarella, basil leaves, salami slices, and coppa slices, along with one artichoke heart, on each skewer. You'll probably want to fold the basil leaves in half and the salami and coppa in fourths (or more depending on size) before skewering. 3. Place the skewers in a small shallow dish and drizzle with the dressing, turning to coat. If possible, let them marinate for 30 minutes or more. Sprinkle lightly with flaky salt and the pepper before serving.

Per Serving:
calories: 200 | fat: 15g | protein: 11g | carbs: 4g | net carbs: 4g | fiber: 0g

Keto Trail Mix

Prep time: 5 minutes | Cook time: 0 minutes | Serves 4

¼ cup pumpkin seeds
¼ cup salted almonds
¼ cup salted macadamia nuts
¼ cup salted walnuts
1 cup crunchy cheese snack
¼ cup sugar-free chocolate chips

1. In a resealable 1-quart plastic bag, combine the pumpkin seeds, almonds, macadamia nuts, walnuts, cheese snack, and chocolate chips. Seal the bag and shake to mix.

Per Serving:
calories: 253 | fat: 23g | protein: 7g | carbs: 5g | net carbs: 2g | fiber: 3g

Hot Chard Artichoke Dip

Prep time: 10 minutes | Cook time: 20 minutes | Serves 4

4 ounces cream cheese, at room temperature
½ cup coconut milk
½ cup grated Asiago cheese
½ cup shredded Cheddar cheese
1 teaspoon minced garlic
Dash hot sauce (optional)
2 cups chopped Swiss chard
½ cup roughly chopped artichoke hearts (packed in brine, not oil)

1. Preheat the oven. Set the oven temperature to 450°F. 2. Mix the ingredients. In a large bowl, stir together the cream cheese, coconut milk, Asiago, Cheddar, garlic, and hot sauce (if using), until everything is well mixed. Stir in the chard and the artichoke hearts and mix until they're well incorporated. Note: You've got to use artichokes packed in brine rather than oil because the extra oil will come out of the dip when you heat it, which will mess up the texture. 3. Bake. Spoon the mixture into a 1-quart baking dish, and bake it for 15 to 20 minutes until it's bubbly and lightly golden. 4. Serve. Cut up low-carb veggies to serve with this creamy, rich dip.

Per Serving:
calories: 280 | fat: 25g | protein: 11g | carbs: 5g | net carbs: 4g | fiber: 1g

Chicken and Cabbage Salad

Prep time: 15 minutes | Cook time: 10 minutes | Serves 4

12 ounces (340 g) chicken fillet, chopped
1 teaspoon Cajun seasoning
1 tablespoon coconut oil
1 cup chopped Chinese cabbage
1 tablespoon avocado oil
1 teaspoon sesame seeds

1. Sprinkle the chopped chicken with the Cajun seasoning. 2. Set your Instant Pot to Sauté and heat the coconut oil. Add the chicken and cook for 10 minutes, stirring occasionally. 3. When the chicken is cooked, transfer to a salad bowl. Add the cabbage, avocado oil, and sesame seeds and gently toss to combine. Serve immediately.

Per Serving:
calories: 207 | fat: 10.8g | protein: 25.3g | carbs: 0.6g | net carbs: 0.2g | fiber: 0.4g

Pancetta Pizza Dip

Prep time: 10 minutes | Cook time: 4 minutes | Serves 10

10 ounces (283 g) Pepper Jack cheese	1 cup green olives, pitted and halved
10 ounces (283 g) cream cheese	1 teaspoon dried oregano
10 ounces (283 g) pancetta, chopped	½ teaspoon garlic powder
1 pound (454 g) tomatoes, puréed	1 cup chicken broth
	4 ounces (113 g) Mozzarella cheese, thinly sliced

1. Mix together the Pepper Jack cheese, cream cheese, pancetta, tomatoes, olives, oregano, and garlic powder in the Instant Pot. Pour in the chicken broth. 2. Lock the lid. Select the Manual mode and set the cooking time for 4 minutes at High Pressure. 3. When the timer beeps, perform a quick pressure release. Carefully remove the lid. 4. Scatter the Mozzarella cheese on top. Cover and allow to sit in the residual heat. Serve warm.

Per Serving:
calories: 287 | fat: 20.8g | protein: 20.8g | carbs: 3.4g | net carbs: 2.0g | fiber: 1.4g

Avocado Salsa

Prep time: 10 minutes | Cook time: 0 minutes | Serves 4

2 or 3 avocados, peeled, pitted, and diced	Juice of 1 lime
¼ red onion, diced	¼ cup olive oil
1 garlic clove, minced	Salt and freshly ground black pepper, to taste
Zest of ½ lime	¼ cup chopped fresh cilantro

1. In a large bowl, gently toss together the diced avocados, onion, garlic, lime zest and juice, and olive oil. Season with salt and pepper. Cover and refrigerate in an airtight container for up to 4 days. Top with the cilantro before serving.

Per Serving:
calories: 450 | fat: 42g | protein: 3g | carbs: 15g | net carbs: 5g | fiber: 10g

Breaded Mushroom Nuggets

Prep time: 15 minutes | Cook time: 50 minutes | Serves 4

24 cremini mushrooms (about 1 lb/455 g)	salt
2 large eggs	2 tablespoons avocado oil
½ cup (55 g) blanched almond flour	½ cup (120 ml) honey mustard dressing, for serving (optional)
1 teaspoon garlic powder	SPECIAL EQUIPMENT (optional):
1 teaspoon paprika	Toothpicks
½ teaspoon finely ground sea	

1. Preheat the oven to 350°F (177°C). Line a rimmed baking sheet with parchment paper or a silicone baking mat. 2. Break the stems off the mushrooms or cut them short so that the stems are level with the caps. 3. Crack the eggs into a small bowl and whisk. 4. Place the almond flour, garlic powder, paprika, and salt in a medium-sized bowl and whisk to combine. 5. Dip one mushroom at a time into the eggs, then use the same hand to drop it into the flour mixture,

being careful not to get the flour mixture on that hand. Rotate the mushroom in the flour mixture with a fork to coat on all sides, then transfer it to the lined baking sheet. Repeat with the remaining mushrooms. 6. Drizzle the coated mushrooms with the oil. Bake for 50 minutes, or until the tops begin to turn golden. 7. Remove from the oven and serve with the dressing, if using. If serving to friends and family, provide toothpicks.

Per Serving:
calories: 332 | fat: 29g | protein: 8g | carbs: 9g | net carbs: 7g | fiber: 2g

Finger Tacos

Prep time: 15 minutes | Cook time: 0 minutes | serves 4

2 avocados, peeled and pitted	½ cup kale chiffonade
1 lime	½ cup cabbage chiffonade
1 tablespoon tamari	10 fresh mint leaves chiffonade
1 teaspoon sesame oil	⅓ cup cauliflower rice
1 teaspoon ginger powder	1 (0.18-ounce) package nori
1 teaspoon togarashi (optional)	squares or seaweed snack sheets

1. Put the avocados into a large mixing bowl, and squeeze the lime over them. 2. Roughly mash the avocados with a fork, leaving the mixture fairly chunky. 3. Gently stir in the tamari, sesame oil, ginger powder, and togarashi (if using). 4. Gently fold in the kale, cabbage, mint, and cauliflower rice. 5. Arrange some nori squares on a plate. 6. Use a nori or seaweed sheet to pick up a portion of the avocado mixture and pop it into your mouth.

Per Serving:
calories: 180 | fat: 15g | protein: 4g | carbs: 13g | net carbs: 5g | fiber: 8g

Almond Sesame Crackers

Prep time: 15 minutes | Cook time: 15 minutes |
Makes about 36 (1-inch-square) crackers

1½ cups almond flour	divided
1 egg	Salt and freshly ground black pepper, to taste
3 tablespoons sesame seeds,	

1. Preheat the oven to 350ºF (180ºC). 2. Line a baking sheet with parchment paper. 3. In a large bowl, mix together the almond flour, egg, and 1½ tablespoons of sesame seeds. Transfer the dough to a sheet of parchment and pat it out flat with your clean hands. Cover with another piece of parchment paper and roll it into a large square, at least 10 inches wide. 4. Remove the top piece of parchment and use a pizza cutter or sharp knife to cut the dough into small squares, about 1 inch wide. Season with salt and pepper and sprinkle with the remaining 1½ tablespoons of sesame seeds. 5. Remove the crackers from the parchment and place them on the prepared baking sheet. Bake for about 15 minutes or until the crackers begin to brown. Cool before serving, and store any leftovers in an airtight bag or container on your counter for up to 2 weeks.

Per Serving:
10 crackers: calories: 108 | fat: 9g | protein: 5g | carbs: 3g | net carbs: 1g | fiber: 2g

Keto Asian Dumplings

Prep time: 20 minutes | Cook time: 20 minutes | Serves 4

Dipping Sauce:
¼ cup gluten-free soy sauce
2 tablespoons sesame oil
1 tablespoon rice vinegar
1 teaspoon chili garlic sauce
Filling:
1 tablespoon sesame oil
2 garlic cloves
1 teaspoon grated fresh ginger
1 celery stalk, minced
½ onion, minced
1 carrot, minced
8 ounces (227 g) ground pork

8 ounces (227 g) shrimp, peeled, deveined, and finely chopped
2 tablespoons gluten-free soy sauce
½ teaspoon fish sauce
Salt and freshly ground black pepper, to taste
3 scallions, green parts only, chopped
1 head napa cabbage, rinsed, leaves separated (about 12 leaves)

Make the Dipping Sauce 1. In a small bowl, whisk together the soy sauce, sesame oil, vinegar, and chili garlic sauce. Set aside. Make the Filling 2. In a large skillet over medium heat, heat the sesame oil. 3. Add the garlic, ginger, celery, onion, and carrot. Sauté for 5 to 7 minutes until softened. 4. Add the pork. Cook for 5 to 6 minutes, breaking it up with a spoon, until it starts to brown. 5. Add the shrimp and stir everything together well. 6. Stir in the soy sauce and fish sauce. Season with a little salt and pepper. Give it a stir and add the scallions. Keep it warm over low heat until ready to fill the dumplings. 7. Steam the cabbage leaves: Place the leaves in a large saucepan with just 1 to 2 inches of boiling water. Cook for about 5 minutes or until the leaves become tender. Remove from the water and set aside to drain. 8. Lay each leaf out flat. Put about 2 tablespoons of filling in the center of one leaf. Wrap the leaf over itself, tucking the sides in so the whole thing is tightly wrapped. Secure with a toothpick. Continue with the remaining leaves and filling. Serve with the dipping sauce. Refrigerate leftovers in an airtight container for up to 3 days.

Per Serving:
3 dumplings: calories: 305 | fat: 17g | protein: 27g | carbs: 11g | net carbs: 8g | fiber: 3g

Quick Salsa

Prep time: 5 minutes | Cook time: 0 minutes | Makes about 3 cups

¼ cup fresh cilantro, stems and leaves, finely chopped
1 small red onion, finely chopped
8 roma tomatoes or other small to medium tomatoes, finely chopped

1 small jalapeño pepper, minced, seeded if desired for less heat (optional)
Juice of 1 to 2 limes
Sea salt and ground black pepper, to taste

1. Toss together all the ingredients in a large mixing bowl. Alternatively, place all the ingredients in a food processor and pulse until the desired consistency is reached. 2. Season with salt and pepper to taste. 3. Store in an airtight container in the refrigerator for up to 5 days.

Per Serving:
calories: 12 | fat: 3g | protein: 1g | carbs: 3g | net carbs: 2g | fiber 1g

Cream Cheese and Berries

Prep time: 5 minutes | Cook time: 0 minutes | Serves 1

2 ounces (57 g) cream cheese
2 large strawberries, cut into thin slices or chunks

5 blueberries
⅛ cup chopped pecans

1. Place the cream cheese on a small plate or in a bowl. 2. Pour the berries and chopped pecans on top. Enjoy!

Per Serving:
calories: 330 | fat: 31g | protein: 6g | carbs: 7g | net carbs: 5g | fiber: 2g

Red Wine Mushrooms

Prep time: 5 minutes | Cook time: 15 minutes | Serves 2

8 ounces (227 g) sliced mushrooms
¼ cup dry red wine
2 tablespoons beef broth
½ teaspoon garlic powder

¼ teaspoon Worcestershire sauce
Pinch of salt
Pinch of black pepper
¼ teaspoon xanthan gum

1. Add the mushrooms, wine, broth, garlic powder, Worcestershire sauce, salt, and pepper to the pot. 2. Close the lid and seal the vent. Cook on High Pressure for 13 minutes. Quick release the steam. Press Cancel. 3. Turn the pot to Sauté mode. Add the xanthan gum and whisk until the juices have thickened, 1 to 2 minutes.

Per Serving:
calories: 94 | fat: 1g | protein: 4g | carbs: 8g | net carbs: 6g | fiber: 2g

Herbed Shrimp

Prep time: 5 minutes | Cook time: 5 minutes | Serves 4

2 tablespoons olive oil
¾ pound (340 g) shrimp, peeled and deveined
1 teaspoon paprika
1 teaspoon garlic powder
1 teaspoon onion powder
1 teaspoon dried parsley flakes
½ teaspoon dried oregano

½ teaspoon dried thyme
½ teaspoon dried basil
½ teaspoon dried rosemary
¼ teaspoon red pepper flakes
Coarse sea salt and ground black pepper, to taste
1 cup chicken broth

1. Set your Instant Pot to Sauté and heat the olive oil. 2. Add the shrimp and sauté for 2 to 3 minutes. 3. Add the remaining ingredients to the Instant Pot and stir to combine. 4. Secure the lid. Select the Manual mode and set the cooking time for 2 minutes at Low Pressure. 5. When the timer beeps, perform a quick pressure release. Carefully remove the lid. 6. Transfer the shrimp to a plate and serve.

Per Serving:
calories: 146 | fat: 7.7g | protein: 18.5g | carbs: 3.0g | net carbs: 2.3g | fiber: 0.7g

Cheese and Charcuterie Board

Prep time: 15 minutes | Cook time: 0 minutes | Serves 7

4 ounces prosciutto, sliced
4 ounces Calabrese salami, sliced
4 ounces capicola, sliced
7 ounces Parrano Gouda cheese
7 ounces aged Manchego cheese

7 ounces Brie cheese
½ cup roasted almonds
½ cup mixed olives
12 cornichons (small, tart pickles)

1 sprig fresh rosemary or other herbs of choice, for garnish Arrange the meats, cheeses, and almonds on a large wooden cutting board. Place the olives and pickles in separate bowls and set them on or alongside the cutting board. Garnish with a spring of rosemary or other fresh herbs of your choice.

Per Serving:
calories: 445 | fat: 35g | protein: 31g | carbs: 3g | net carbs: 2g | fiber: 1g

Pizza Bites

Prep time: 5 minutes | Cook time: 10 minutes | Makes 12 pizza bites

12 large pepperoni slices
2 tablespoons tomato paste

12 mini Mozzarella balls (approximately 8 ounces / 227 g)
12 fresh basil leaves (optional)

1. Preheat the oven to 400°F (205°C). 2. Line each of 12 cups of a mini muffin pan with one pepperoni slice. To make them sit better, use kitchen shears to make three or four small cuts toward the center of the slice, but do not cut too far in—leave the center intact. 3. Bake 5 minutes, remove from the oven, and allow to cool in the pan for 5 to 10 minutes, until somewhat crisp. Keep the oven turned on. 4. Spoon ½ teaspoon of tomato paste into each pepperoni cup and gently spread to coat the bottom. Place a Mozzarella ball and a basil leaf, if using, in each cup. Return muffin pan to the oven and cook another 3 to 5 minutes, until the cheese is melting. 5. Remove pan from the oven and allow the bites to cool for 5 to 10 minutes before serving.

Per Serving:
calories: 193 | fat: 15g | protein: 11g | carbs: 2g | net carbs: 2g | fiber: 0g

Bacon-Wrapped Jalapeños

Prep time: 10 minutes | Cook time: 20 minutes | Serves 4

10 jalapeños
8 ounces cream cheese, at room temperature
1 pound bacon (you will use about half a slice per popper)

1. Preheat the oven to 450°F. Line a baking sheet with aluminum foil or a silicone baking mat. 2. Halve the jalapeños lengthwise, and remove the seeds and membranes (if you like the extra heat, leave them in). Place them on the prepared pan cut-side up. 3. Spread some of the cream cheese inside each jalapeño half. 4. Wrap a jalapeño half with a slice of bacon (depending on the size of the jalapeño, use a whole slice of bacon, or half). 5. Secure the bacon around each jalapeño with 1 to 2 toothpicks so it stays put while baking. 6. Bake for 20 minutes, until the bacon is done and crispy. 7. Serve hot or at room temperature. Either way, they are delicious!

Per Serving:
calories: 164 | fat: 13g | protein: 9g | carbs: 1g | net carbs: 1g | fiber: 0g

Appendix 1: Measurement Conversion Chart

MEASUREMENT CONVERSION CHART

VOLUME EQUIVALENTS(DRY)

US STANDARD	METRIC (APPROXIMATE)
1/8 teaspoon	0.5 mL
1/4 teaspoon	1 mL
1/2 teaspoon	2 mL
3/4 teaspoon	4 mL
1 teaspoon	5 mL
1 tablespoon	15 mL
1/4 cup	59 mL
1/2 cup	118 mL
3/4 cup	177 mL
1 cup	235 mL
2 cups	475 mL
3 cups	700 mL
4 cups	1 L

VOLUME EQUIVALENTS(LIQUID)

US STANDARD	US STANDARD (OUNCES)	METRIC (APPROXIMATE)
2 tablespoons	1 fl.oz.	30 mL
1/4 cup	2 fl.oz.	60 mL
1/2 cup	4 fl.oz.	120 mL
1 cup	8 fl.oz.	240 mL
1 1/2 cup	12 fl.oz.	355 mL
2 cups or 1 pint	16 fl.oz.	475 mL
4 cups or 1 quart	32 fl.oz.	1 L
1 gallon	128 fl.oz.	4 L

TEMPERATURES EQUIVALENTS

FAHRENHEIT(F)	CELSIUS(C) (APPROXIMATE)
225 °F	107 °C
250 °F	120 °C
275 °F	135 °C
300 °F	150 °C
325 °F	160 °C
350 °F	180 °C
375 °F	190 °C
400 °F	205 °C
425 °F	220 °C
450 °F	235 °C
475 °F	245 °C
500 °F	260 °C

WEIGHT EQUIVALENTS

US STANDARD	METRIC (APPROXIMATE)
1 ounce	28 g
2 ounces	57 g
5 ounces	142 g
10 ounces	284 g
15 ounces	425 g
16 ounces (1 pound)	455 g
1.5 pounds	680 g
2 pounds	907 g

Appendix 2: The Dirty Dozen and Clean Fifteen

The Dirty Dozen and Clean Fifteen

The Environmental Working Group (EWG) is a nonprofit, nonpartisan organization dedicated to protecting human health and the environment Its mission is to empower people to live healthier lives in a healthier environment. This organization publishes an annual list of the twelve kinds of produce, in sequence, that have the highest amount of pesticide residue-the Dirty Dozen-as well as a list of the fifteen kinds ofproduce that have the least amount of pesticide residue-the Clean Fifteen.

THE DIRTY DOZEN	THE CLEAN FIFTEEN
• The 2016 Dirty Dozen includes the following produce. These are considered among the year's most important produce to buy organic:	• The least critical to buy organically are the Clean Fifteen list. The following are on the 2016 list:

Strawberries	Spinach	Avocados	Papayas
Apples	Tomatoes	Corn	Kiw
Nectarines	Bell peppers	Pineapples	Eggplant
Peaches	Cherry tomatoes	Cabbage	Honeydew
Celery	Cucumbers	Sweet peas	Grapefruit
Grapes	Kale/collard greens	Onions	Cantaloupe
Cherries	Hot peppers	Asparagus	Cauliflower
		Mangos	

• *The Dirty Dozen list contains two additional itemskale/collard greens and hot peppers-because they tend to contain trace levels of highly hazardous pesticides.*	• *Some of the sweet corn sold in the United States are made from genetically engineered (GE) seedstock. Buy organic varieties of these crops to avoid GE produce.*

Made in the USA
Las Vegas, NV
07 December 2023

82308625R00050